DRAGON ASCENDING

VIETNAM AND THE VIETNAMESE

HENRY KAMM

ARCADE PUBLISHING • NEW YORK

FIRST EDITION

Library of Congress Cataloging-in-Publication Data
Kamm, Henry.
    Dragon ascending : Vietnam and the Vietnamese / by Henry Kamm. —1st ed.
        p.   cm.
    Includes index.
    ISBN 1-55970-306-7
      1. Vietnam—Description and travel.   I. Title.
    DS556.39.K36   1996
    959.7—dc20
                                                    95-17861

Published in the United States by Arcade Publishing, Inc.

Distributed by Little, Brown and Company

10 9 8 7 6 5 4 3 2 1

Designed by API

BP

PRINTED IN THE UNITED STATES OF AMERICA

For
Lan Huong
and
Bao Son

Contents

Maps appear on pages 20, 30, 56, and 70.
Photographs appear after page 144.

Preface

A book about Vietnam may not be amiss at a time when this Southeast Asian nation of seventy-three million people is leaving behind a long period of virtual isolation and entering the world at large as a united and independent country, after too long an absence. This is a book about Vietnam today, and although written by an American, its subject is Vietnam, not the American intrusion upon the life of Vietnam or the pain that America inflicted upon itself by its willful interference. And although the writer is an American journalist, whose lasting interest in Vietnam was awakened by many wartime working visits and sustained by many subsequent stays, the book is in no way a personal memoir. It is a reporter's book, not a history, a book reporting on an interesting country at a particularly important period in its history.

It is written from a belief that too many people, particularly in the United States, think and speak of Vietnam with assured conviction, although I believe their assurance is justified only by the firmness of their convictions about what their countries, particularly the United States, did in Vietnam. General knowledge of Vietnam itself, its people, their lives, thoughts, and feelings, is, I believe, not deep enough to warrant much assurance. Great sympathy for the Vietnamese people was expressed throughout the world, particularly in America, while they were suffering atrociously from war, a war that was so cruelly and uselessly intensified by the United States.

Compassion for the Vietnamese was expressed on both sides of the great cleft that split America during its war. There were those who asserted that the war was justified to save the Vietnamese people, or at least those who lived in the south, from oppression. There were others who said that their condemnation of America's brutal interference was founded on revulsion at the grievous wounds inflicted on the Vietnamese people and their country by America's frightful firepower, by the burns from its napalm and white phosphorus and the scarring of the landscape by its toxins.

Yet both sides' compassion for the Vietnamese people appeared largely to fade when American troops left in 1973, or at the latest when the war ended in 1975. The voices that over many years expressed the deepest concern over the agony of the Vietnamese were strangely silent during the next period of their suffering, when hundreds of thousands felt that their best choice was to entrust their lives and those of their children to tiny, unseaworthy boats on the treacherous South China Sea, to escape toward shores that they knew to be hostile. We will never know how many never reached shore. It is hard to avoid a suspicion that either a commitment in an ideological global struggle against what was believed to be a monolithic Communist bloc striving for world conquest or passionate opposition to the actions and persons of Lyndon Johnson and particularly Richard Nixon were more compelling motives for those who took sides than compassion with Vietnamese suffering. If American sympathy for the people of Vietnam were of great moment, would the American people have allowed their governments, for more than twenty years after the end of the war, to deny them the reconciliation and help in healing of their wounds for which Germans and Japanese did not need to wait after a much greater war?

I believe that Vietnam and its extraordinarily courageous and resilient people are worthy of interest and sympathy in themselves. The late Bernard B. Fall, to whose books and articles everyone interested in Vietnam is indebted, prefaced his *The Two Viet-Nams* with this remark: "This is a book in praise of no one." I have tried to live up to that evenhanded motto insofar as all governments, Vietnamese and foreign, and men of power of all countries that involved themselves and their might in Vietnam are concerned. But this is a book in praise of the Vietnamese people, north, center, and south.

Thanks are in order. I am deeply grateful to a succession of publishers and editors of the *New York Times*, who for so long have provided unstinting encouragement and support and much freedom of movement to allow me to learn about Vietnam (and many other countries). It is evident that I owe most to my many friends in Vietnam, and Vietnamese now abroad, to those who permitted me to name them and those who, in prudence, I chose to cover with anonymity. But not only friends. Many in Vietnam who will no doubt disagree with my interpretations and conclusions, and knew they would, have nonetheless given sincerely of their views and generously and patiently of their time to help me to understand their country. My ideas about Vietnam owe some of their shape to years of hammering out in discussion, often heated and always warm, with my much-missed friend, too soon departed, Jean-Christophe Öberg, who was Sweden's first ambassador in Hanoi. For the summary chapters on Vietnamese history, I am grateful to the historians whom I have named in the text.

My deep gratitude goes to my late parents, Paula and Rudolf Kamm, who from their own harsh experience taught me to be wary of those who wield power, and to listen with sympathy and respect to those upon whom it is wielded. It has always been with that in mind that I have tried to understand Vietnam. My dear friend Elie Wiesel had more to do with my writing this book than he suspects. And last but not least, I thank my children, Alison, Thomas, and Nicholas, for importuning me for all these years with reminders that perhaps I have, on a few subjects, more to say than fits into a newspaper article.

H. K.
Lagnes, France
January 1996

Chronology

Around 2000 B.C. — Founding of Kingdom of Au Lac, the Vietnam of legend.

208 B.C. — A Chinese renegade general conquers Au Lac and proclaims himself emperor of "Nam Viet."

First century B.C. — The Han dynasty incorporates Nam Viet as a Chinese province.

40 A.D. — The two Trung sisters lead rebellion that establishes short-lived independence.

938 — Ngo Quyen defeats Chinese and establishes independent state, Dai Viet, recognized by China in 967.

1282 — Tran Hung Dao repels Mongol invasion.

1407 — Ming dynasty conquers Dai Viet, incorporates it as Chinese province.

1428 — Emperor Le Loi reestablishes independence, ending Chinese domination.

Seventeenth and eighteenth centuries — Divisive internecine warfare, opening the way for foreign interference through missionaries, mercenaries, and merchants.

1788 — Nguyen Anh drives out a renewed Chinese invasion.

1789 — First fleet of French mercenaries, chartered by a Catholic bishop, lands in southern Vietnam and allies itself with Nguyen Anh.

1802 — Taking title of Emperor Gia Long, Nguyen Anh founds Nguyen dynasty, Vietnam's last, and establishes capital in Hue.

1847 — First official French military intervention, at Da Nang.

1862 — Emperor Tu Duc cedes Saigon and surrounding region to France.

1867 — All southern Vietnam submits to France.

1883 — Central and northern Vietnam submit.

1930 — Ho Chi Minh founds Indochinese Communist party.

1940 — Japan occupies Vietnam.

1941 — Japan declares Vietnam independent from France. Viet

Minh starts general uprising. Last emperor, Bao Dai, abdicates. Ho declares independence. France begins reconquest. Last colonial war breaks out.

1954 — France, defeated at Dien Bien Phu, surrenders. Geneva accords divide Vietnam. United States replaces France as main support of anti-Communist South Vietnam, ruled by Ngo Dinh Diem.

1960 — Hanoi forms National Liberation Front in south; civil war gains pace.

1962 — United States Military Assistance Command formed, and "advisers" begin active role in war.

1963 — Diem overthrown and murdered.

1964 — United States begins air war against north. Tonkin Gulf Resolution gives President Johnson effective war-making powers.

1965 — First American combat units arrive. Methodical bombing of North Vietnam begins, and America takes over conduct of war.

1968 — Communist Tet Offensive is defeated but intensifies American desire to withdraw "with honor." Paris peace conference opens.

1969 — United States begins bombing of Vietnamese Communist bases in Cambodia.

1970 — All of Cambodia engulfed in war.

1973 — Paris peace agreement signed, and American troops withdraw.

1975 — North Vietnam conquers Saigon; war ends.

1976 — Vietnam reunified.

1978 — Vietnam invades Cambodia following Cambodian border raids.

1979 — Vietnam conquers Cambodia, overthrows Pol Pot regime. China mounts brief punitive invasion into northern Vietnam.

1986 — In reaction to Soviet perestroika, Vietnam begins liberal economic reform.

1991 — Collapse of Soviet Union leads to intensified economic liberalization.

1995 — United States, twenty years after end of war, normalizes diplomatic relations with Vietnam.

DRAGON ASCENDING

1

A Village Remembers

By HENRY KAMM
Special to The New York Times

TRUONG AN, South Vietnam, Nov. 16 — A group of South Vietnamese villagers reported today that a small American infantry unit killed 567 unarmed men, women and children as it swept through their hamlet on March 16, 1968.

They survived, they said, because they had been buried under the bodies of their neighbors.

The villagers told their story in the presence of American officers at their new settlement, which lies in contested territory less than a mile from the ruins of their former home.

(New York Times, November 17, 1969)

Heat hangs moist and heavy, making outlines tremble and shimmer. Clothes cling, and movements are gentle, gliding more than treading. Peasants in black pajamas lead their buffalo across fields of rice stubble. Women in conical hats mother their youngest while tending their vegetable patches, now and then shooing intruding hens. Older children, many with a smaller brother or sister astraddle on a hip, flock round a visitor, their number growing as they follow his every step. "Hello!" they chant cheerfully, or "bye-bye!" mindless of the opposite meanings of the greetings they offer to all foreigners.

They see more foreigners in My Lai, now rebuilt on its original site, than is customary in the villages of a country that is only hesitantly removing political and bureaucratic obstacles to travel.

The children's curiosity is exuberant and trusting, which pains deeply when one remembers how atrociously such trust

vas once betrayed. The adults' welcome is courteous, their
miles unforced. The visitor who identifies himself as American
eceives as friendly a welcome as any other. Is this just any
illage in central Vietnam? No.

And yet, even in a place where Americans did their worst
nd where everything is done officially to keep alive the memo-
ies of the war the United States waged, the Vietnamese seem to
ave put those years, which continue to haunt Americans, be-
ind them. They can never lay to rest the personal anguish most
uffered. Yet they retain no discernible hatred of Americans,
/hose country escalated a civil war among the poor to mass
illing on a superpower scale and then left the losing side — My
ai belonged to it, at least during daytime — to the fate that the
oreign intervention did no more than delay. And they are aware
t what cost in lives lost or shattered America bought the delay.

Normal life — that is, life at subsistence level — has re-
irned to My Lai. Even to the tombs of war.

On a large mound in the middle of a rice field, covered by a
oncrete slab, round, flat wicker trays of peanuts and ears of corn
e set out to dry. The sign alongside the mound reads, "Greve
ard of 75 Villagers Killed by G.I. on March 16, 1968." There
e four mass graves, the official guide explained, each containing
om twenty to seventy-five bodies, and many, many smaller
ombs sheltering three to eight victims. All are inconspicuous;
hat counts most at My Lai is the present. It has two faces.

One is the village of rice-farming families, downtrodden
it rich in children as are all villages in the densely populated
ntral region of a country that stretches for more than twelve
indred miles from its northernmost point on the Chinese bor-
r to the tip of the Ca Mau Peninsula on the Gulf of Siam. In
e center, the green mountains of the interior edge close to the
lt flats along the South China Sea and leave only a narrow
ip of farming land, subject to typhoons and the destructive
ects of seawater. Throughout modern history endemic pov-
ty has made the people of this region the most ready to listen
those who preach rebellion. And most of the preachers were
rn in Vietnam's hardscrabble center.

The other face of My Lai is represented by the memorial where grief over an unspeakable atrocity left shamefully unpunished in the land of the perpetrators is officially expressed and converted to political use, following a custom not unknown elsewhere. As in the Communist years Poland or the late German Democratic Republic perverted memory at the sites of Nazi concentration camps to make them anachronistic propaganda showcases for their side in the postwar ideological conflict, the government has made of My Lai a place not only of remembrance but also of justification of its system. But not only Communist countries have made hay where no sun shone.

"To Remember Forever the Crimes Committed by the American Aggressors" reads the sign over the simple building erected to receive visitors. To judge by the guest book, these visitors are mainly Westerners. Earlier, those who stopped here were largely "fraternal" delegations from other Communist countries, dutifully doing their rounds. Since their nations abandoned the creed that still governs Vietnam, their people no longer feel brotherly enough to visit. The guest book is a depository of sincere sentiments on the good of peace and the evil of war; only groups of ultraradical West German ideologues have been tactless enough to inscribe fiery manifestos of hatred, calling on humanity to rise in struggle against ever-present American imperialism. One might have thought that Germans, of all people, might have some second thoughts before condemning other nations with such a sense of moral superiority.

Yet even at the memorial, the mercantile pragmatism to which the government in Hanoi now subscribes, conjointly and contradictorily with its continuing bows of obeisance to the teachings of Marx and Lenin, has made inroads. Under a large banner proclaiming the most ubiquitous of the inescapable sayings of Ho Chi Minh that adorn Vietnam from north to south — "Nothing Is More Precious Than Independence and Liberty" — Pham Thanh Cong, the chief attendant at the memorial, considered a request for interviews with survivors. "There are five here," he said, "How many do you want? Of course you have to pay them something. They have to take time off from their work." Two was agreed on as a suitable number, traded as though survivors were the memorial's merchandise.

Outside, boys were playing soccer around the base of a large Soviet-inspired monument that transforms into a grandiose act of heroic defiance the martyrdom of the unarmed, helpless women, children, and old men massacred by First Lieutenant William Laws Calley Jr. and his platoon, as well as others from C Company of the Eleventh Brigade of the Americal Division on the morning of March 16, 1968. A woman larger than life, a babe in her arms, raises an accusing hand heavenward as she confronts her murderers. Four other victims face the killers in less stylized poses. The true memorial, one that calls forth genuine feelings, is a plaque to the right of the monument. Eight long columns are made up of the names of 504 victims — 182 women, of whom 17 were pregnant, and 173 children, of whom 56 were of infant age. Sixty of the men were over sixty years old. And to the left and right, where the old village stood, small stone markers at ground level recall to the mind's eye the houses that once occupied the same spot. The inscriptions tell all that needs to be told: "Mr. Le Dien's House Destroyed by G.I. on March 16, 1968."

In fact, what the American soldiers destroyed between dawn and noon on that day was the people, much more than their house. The artillery barrage that preceded the landing of Charlie Company by helicopter in a village rice field and the unprovoked carnage that ensued did not wipe out the village. That act of needless warfare was committed almost a year later, when American bulldozers leveled My Lai to deny the use of its humble huts to the Communist forces, and American and South Vietnamese troops herded the population of all the surrounding hamlets into a barren stretch a few minutes' walk from their old homes. They could till their fields but had to return to place themselves under guard after dark.

"Generating refugees," this practice of making of the rural people of Vietnam, as well as Cambodia and Laos, the ruthlessly uprooted flotsam of war was called in the language of the military. Until its destruction My Lai was one of the thousands of villages that were under South Vietnamese and American control during daylight but contested between dusk and dawn, when Communist forces went into action. "The people here were not engaged on either side," said Cong, the memorial's caretaker, asked why there were so few men present at the time of the massacre. "The village was under Saigon's control. Some men had joined the Viet Cong and had to leave the village. Others were drafted into the Saigon army, and others ran away to avoid being drafted. I would say that most ran away from the draft. They left their families here because they couldn't take care of them elsewhere. They went to Da Nang or Saigon to find work. I can assure you there were no revolutionary forces stationed here. I think the majority of the people were neutral. They were wishing only for peace to be restored and not to be threatened by death in that war."

In his simple candor Cong may have unknowingly violated his propagandist duties, which would have required him to say that the entire Vietnamese people, except those few "puppets" in the cities suborned by American riches, supported the Communist liberation struggle. Instead he affirmed a fundamental truth about the war: it was imposed upon the people of Vietnam by the intractable leaders of both sides and the foreign powers that made a distant agrarian nation bleed in sacrifice to their larger purposes.

Cong was eleven years old when American soldiers killed his parents, his two sisters, and his brother. "They turned it into a 'white' place," he said in melancholy reminiscence. "It was a beautiful place. Even mandarins in the old days used to come to admire it."

He needed to be urged to recall the day. "My family was an ordinary family. We were having breakfast, before my parents would go to the field and we to school. Then the artillery began to fire, and we took shelter." Some underground shelters — each house had one — are all that remains today of the original village. "My house was hit and set afire. At eight o'clock three American soldiers came. When we saw them we were happy, because it meant the shelling was over. We came out of the shelter, but when they saw us, they pushed us back down with their rifle butts. And then they threw grenades. At four in the afternoon people from other hamlets came to bury the dead and look for survivors. I was badly wounded in the head and unconscious all that time. I was covered with my blood and the blood of all the others. They were all dead. In the whole village, those who survived were protected by their dead, who lay on top of them."

The custodian, a minor Communist party functionary, lapsed frequently into the stale jargon of propaganda, which has indoctrinated him all his life — one version until 1975, the opposite since the Communist victory. But the events he described, reliving their pain as he spoke, were exactly those that the elders of My Lai breathlessly poured forth for me, the first American to whom they bore witness, on my first visit in 1969, after the atrocity had been brought to light in the United States. Unintimidated by the silent but attentive presence of officers of the Americal Division, who insisted on accompanying me in return for a helicopter ride to the resettlement area, inaccessible in those days by road, men and women from several hamlets of the village described in frightful detail the massacre. Were the officers acting when they allowed silent shame over what fellow officers and soldiers had done to show on faces that worked hard to appear stolid?

At My Lai today Vietnamese take pains not to make an American ashamed. "Today the nation is of one opinion: not to remind people of the past," said Cong. "I think the people of the village know that what happened did not represent America. When Americans come here to pay their respect, they are received like all others. There is no anger against them."

Is the caretaker, a loyal party member, just parroting the line that has come down from Hanoi? Higher party and government officials in the capital and towns and villages throughout Vietnam, in their stiffly formal reception rooms (one is never allowed to see them in the offices where they actually work), over cups of tea that are rarely allowed to go empty, deliver sermons of the same content, sometimes read from prepared notes with no effort to simulate spontaneity. Seated under the obligatory portrait of Ho Chi Minh, the national coat of arms, plastic roses, and little flags presented by delegations from East European countries while they were still flying Communist colors, the officials preach their dutiful lessons in the ideological argot that Communist "cadres" all over the world learned from their Soviet teachers. The ever-present note taker rises silently now and again to fulfill his secondary function of refilling the cups.

Vietnamese functionaries are among the scarce surviving practitioners of the mind-dulling rhetoric that until the demise of the Soviet realm made a homogenized, indigestible pap of conversations with officials and supervisors of many nationalities, Estonians sounding like Mozambicans, Laotians like Albanians. Vietnam survives as a kind of museum of oral history of the cant that was.

For the "cadres," embarrassment is evident. Whatever they really believe, they have to profess goodwill toward those whom they still identify as ideological enemies. Vietnam must look for help wherever it can find it, now that its principal source of foreign assistance has run dry with the debacle of the European Communist regimes. But most Vietnamese, north and south, sound convincingly sincere when they say that no resentments born during the war shape their attitudes today.

"No, what I answer is what I think," Cong said. "I consider Americans as people like all others, as friends. What happened was in the past. I hated the American soldiers who came to Vietnam and wanted them driven out. But that was then. After the war I tried to forget those feelings. Now my feelings are normal." He admitted to one exception: "I can't understand the trials and the pardons." Only Calley ever saw the inside of a jail, and that for less than five months, although a court-martial sentenced him to life imprisonment. The sentence was reduced, and the convicted mass murderer freed to run a family jewelry store in Columbus, Georgia. Others of Charlie Company faced trials; all were either acquitted or had their cases dismissed. Killers of Vietnamese children went unpunished to help the

United States overcome the rancors among Americans that the war had provoked. "Healing the wounds of war," this contribution to reconciliation among Americans was called. The wounds America inflicted in Vietnam, infinitely greater and deeper, go untreated.

The survivors arrived to be interviewed. Used as they evidently are to their role as witnesses, the two women quietly took their places at a large conference table and waited for a ritual they had performed many times. Even as they sat in silence, their tense, tired faces and frail bodies, held determinedly upright, spoke clearly of the lives of hardship of their generation, particularly of the people of the countryside in the zones of unending warfare. My Lai lived one day of particular terror — worse, perhaps, than any act of war elsewhere in Vietnam — but women and men who seem infinitely older than their years are more commonly encountered in Vietnam than in other poor Asian countries, Cambodia always excepted; its suffering surpasses all measure.

Truong Thi Le and Ha Thi Quy spoke without observing political codes, from wounded but unbitter hearts. Even the memorial's official interpreter, a woman whose cold and lifeless English could have turned a baby's babble into the jargon of the party daily's editorials, did not deprive me of the simple sincerity of their words.

Mrs. Quy, sixty-nine years old and nearly toothless, was badly wounded, and her daughter and only grandson were killed in the massacre. Her son lost a hand, a leg, and an eye in the artillery barrage that preceded the landing of Lieutenant Calley and his men. "When I see him working in the field I feel sorry for him," Mrs. Quy said. "He has an artificial leg, but no hand." Her husband was spared because he took their buffalo to the field especially early that morning. "I think the bullet is still inside," she said, straining to touch her own wound. "My back feels very hard there."

Mrs. Quy was examined by a doctor shortly after the awful day, but that was the only time. She said she had lost the document that he had given her, so she thought it of no use to ask for further medical attention. Has she burned a certificate issued by an official of the Saigon government, probably a South Vietnamese army doctor, for fear of its being seen by the new authorities? In the early years after their victory the powers then installed made people fearful of disclosing any connection with the old regime. In a society bound and stifled by red tape, in which simple people feel guilty for not possessing the right papers bearing the correct official stamps, Mrs. Quy may be afraid of seeking treatment. It is a question I cannot pose, and which she probably would not answer truthfully if I asked. Certainly not in an official place, through an official interpreter.

Mrs. Le is younger by five years. Her losses that day included her husband, her six-year-old son, her mother, and a brother. She never remarried and lives with a stepson, an orphan of the massacre, whom she brought up. She suffered not only a serious leg wound but, what is worse, psychological shock that, she said, has kept her from doing anything but light work ever since. ("Light work" for a Vietnamese peasant woman, in an agrarian country whose women bear the brunt of the workload, would qualify as heavy labor almost anywhere else.) "My daughter-in-law is unhappy with me because I can't work like I could before," she said. "She doesn't understand, but my son does."

"I want to put aside everything that happened in the past," said Mrs. Le. "We must have good relations so we can keep the peace forever. No hate, no anger, no war." She insisted that she was saying what she really felt. "Those are my true feelings," she said. "Sometimes, when I think of the dead in my family, I feel anger. Sometimes. But most of the time I look toward the future."

"If the Americans want to have normal relations we are very happy," said Mrs. Quy. Her anger, she said, is limited to those Americans who murdered the people of My Lai. "I can draw the line between people," she said. "There are some bad Americans, but I respect the American people. If they admit their mistakes, I can forgive what happened in the past."

Forgiveness is perhaps also needed for the American voluntary organizations, mainly of veterans or Protestant churches, that have on occasion raised hopes for badly needed human-itarian assistance in Vietnam that they never realized or, perhaps worse, began to fulfill only to stop far short. My Lai offers an example, far from the only one. A two-story clinic, large for so small a village, stands near the memorial. Its many rooms were empty when I visited but for patients awaiting the attention of the sole nurse. The nurse seemed embarrassed when asked about the bareness that surrounded her. She said all the needed equipment had been promised by the American group that funded the construction, but for four years nothing further had been heard from America. Still, the clinic is equipped with a stately plaque in its lobby. It reads: "International Mission of Hope, Cherie Clark, Director. Finished 1990." Since then they have run short of hope in My Lai.

Foreigners seem far more conscious of Vietnam's past than its present, greatly more so than the Vietnamese. "Vietnam" evokes to Americans and others not so much a country, a South-east Asian nation of nearly seventy-three million people, but the very idea of war, a half century of conflict, foreign and civil: French colonial war, Japanese occupation, American interven-tion, and Vietnam's own invasion of Cambodia, which brought on a brief but destructive incursion by China's People's Army and a dozen draining years of fighting against the Khmers Rouges. Most of today's Vietnamese have no direct share in that grim past except for the war in Cambodia; they were too young or yet unborn during the fighting on their country's soil and have consigned their parents' memories to the trove of national history.

Yes, the Vietnamese have indeed borne anguish, death, and destruction, more than a single nation's cup should hold, or heard their elders recall dire memories. But, perhaps because of the pervasive burden of poverty, they live determinedly in the present, with their eyes fixed on the future. Their energy is tiring just to watch as they scramble, against many obstacles, for what they hope will be a better tomorrow. They do so painfully conscious of the burden imposed by starting recovery from war fifty years later than most of their equally energetic neighbors, and of the weight of the same regime that until yesterday condemned the road toward prosperity that it has now chosen.

Yet in the world beyond, particularly in countries that intervened to shape by force a Vietnam of their own devising, the very name "Vietnam" evokes mainly the anguish that others inflicted on themselves by their interference. Vietnam is rarely spoken of as a real, living country. To most Americans it seems a remote region of the nation's mind, which for a decade or so was attached to America as a kind of temporary fifty-first state. They resent the great harm that this connection did, not so much the harm suffered by Vietnam as that suffered by America: the enduring, obsessive illness that Americans call simply "Vietnam." The name means the war, not the country. The country it denotes seems today mainly the site of a far-flung and costly archeological dig for American skeletons, the remains of those still listed as "missing in action," not a complex society organized for better or worse by those who defeated all intruders.

"Five Years after Vietnam" read a *New York Times* headline over an article on the anniversary of the Communist victory in 1975. "The Tragedy and Lessons of Vietnam" is the subtitle chosen by Robert S. McNamara for his 1995 book of remorseful retrospection. The former secretary of defense does not mean the lessons that we can all learn from an ancient nation of high civilization and admirable traditions, but from "Vietnam," the event in recent American history — the war. What would a Vietnamese make of a phrase that uses the name of his country to stand, not for his nation, vibrantly alive even if not well, but for a debacle in another nation's history? I have not heard Vietnamese measure time from the same war, which many Vietnamese also see as their debacle, as so many years "after America."

Nor have I, in many visits after the Communist triumph, heard many Vietnamese criticize American actions toward Vietnam, except the twenty-year wait before the establishment, in 1995, of normal relations with the country the United States could not defeat. The astonishing absence of postwar hostility is no less remarkable in the "enemy" north, Communist since 1945, than in the "friendly" south, the main theater of war. It holds for officials of the all-powerful Communist party and government as well as those who would like to see them go the way most Communist parties and governments have gone. The same refusal to speak ill prevails in Hanoi as in Saigon — the southern capital that the victors humiliated by making it bear the name of its posthumous conqueror, Ho Chi Minh, the patriot who linked the irreproachable struggle for independence to the dubious cause of communism.

2

An Accident at Christmas

Bach Mai Hospital in Hanoi, with its one thousand beds, is the largest in the capital and, said Dr. Tran Quoc Do, its vice-director, the place where Vietnam's finest specialists practice. it is our doctors who treat them," Dr. Do said.

But it was not for its medical excellence that Bach Mai was once a name meaningful round the world, and continues to hold a place in Vietnam's anguished history. Just before the final phase of the nearly five war-filled years of Vietnamese-American peace negotiations in Paris, when stalemate had once again been reached, President Nixon ordered the war's most intensive bombing of the north to bring North Vietnam back to making peace. The raids struck particularly at the densely populated region that stretches from Hanoi to Haiphong, the main port, sixty miles to the east. The savage bombing lasted from December 18, 1972, until December 29. Although Nixon, a Christian, gave Vietnam a day of grace on December 25, the air attacks entered history under the sardonic name of "the Christmas bombing."

Civilian areas were meant to be exempted; Bach Mai was one of the mistakes. "We were bombed three times," said Dr. Do, sounding apologetic for mentioning a matter that might make an American uneasy. "I was here for all three. But all this is in the past. I shouldn't mention this. Let bygones be bygones. All this suffering took place in the past.

"Half of this building was destroyed," Dr. Do said reluctantly when pressed for his recollections. He escaped injury because he was performing surgery in an underground operating theater. Much of the hospital's work was being done in shelters that had been dug earlier in the war, when air raids on the capital began. Dr. Do said twenty-two doctors, hospital workers, and patients were killed in the final raids, which preceded by only a month the "peace" agreement that allowed the United States to withdraw from the war and leave its South Vietnamese allies to their fate.

"But we shouldn't mention this again," he said firmly, ending his terse account. "Let the young generation look forward to close cooperation with America. Our tradition is, when something lies in the past, don't keep talking about it. Our people are ready to forget the past."

Dr. Do, a soft-spoken man, became reflective and earnestly sought to ease an American conscience by ranging the United States among other nations that had warred in or against Vietnam and belittling the importance of historical memory. "History is good for children starting to go to school," he said. "We have had so many enemies in history. China for such a long time. France later. Although the war with the United States was atrocious, it was a short war. Today, when Chinese, or French, or Americans come here, we consider them all as friends." The doctor, who wore his navy-blue blazer, gray slacks, and blue-and-white striped tie with casual elegance, as though they were not almost as uncommon in Hanoi as a Vietnamese mandarin's silk tunic and headdress would be in New York, spoke persuasively. He did not appear to be repeating a prescribed line, although what he said fit seamlessly into the official view.

The party line was provided, as it has been for years to any foreigner who requests it, by Major General Tran Cong Man. This amiable old soldier entered the armed resistance to Japanese occupation and French colonialism at the age of eighteen in 1944 and joined the Communist youth movement the following year. He spent one month at military school in Hanoi before entering active service in an army in which even generals had never received formal military training. At the decisive battle of

Dien Bien Phu in 1954 — which put an end to France's colonial rule in Vietnam, Laos, and Cambodia, once jointly called French Indochina — Man served as commander of an engineering regiment.

He spent the next decade teaching economics, "and of course philosophy, too," at the military academy. This, again, was typical for a country that had to improvise the institutions that go with statehood as it went along and staff them with largely untried men and women. In 1964 Man, then a colonel, reached his vocation. He was assigned to *Quan Doi Nhan Dan,* the daily newspaper of the armed forces of North Vietnam, first as deputy editor and from 1978 until his retirement in 1990 as editor in chief. This made Man, in effect, the voice of the Communist party organization in the military. Since then, in his formal capacity as deputy secretary-general of the Journalists' Association, the general has continued to serve as an unofficial but thoroughly authoritative voice of the Communist party's leadership.

A slight man of gentle, avuncular charm and almost deferential modesty, the general commands an unflappable mastery of ideological jargon to justify, apparently to his satisfaction, the profound shifts in party policy that followed the collapse of the Soviet Union, Vietnam's chief ally and provider of essentials. Man receives with tea and courtesy in the association's headquarters, a handsome but mildewed villa in the heart of what was once Hanoi's French administrative quarter. He delivered his explanations and commentaries in a language that is rapidly vanishing — the French spoken by the Vietnamese who were educated in colonial schools or worked for the French.

Southeast Asian indirection, flowery formulations, occasional archaically poetic turns of phrase, and avoidance of words that might shock give the French of elderly Vietnamese, Cambodians, and Laotians a particular pleasing softness; its inevitable passing will mean the demise of a language that is precious in an age that mistakes blunt, raw speech for a higher truthfulness. "It is not yet complete," said a hungry Cambodian encountered on a Phnom Penh street shortly after Vietnam liberated his country from Pol Pot's reign of terror and starvation, when I asked him whether there was enough to eat. I was embarrassed to ask a question whose answer was painfully evident, but Indochinese people do not volunteer to tell strangers their troubles, and journalists need to let those about whom they write tell their truth in their own way for the eyes of distant readers, rather than substituting an outsider's description. "A little enough," said another, equally eager not to offend the questioner with the harsh words of the palpable reality. "It is still a little miserable," said a third, a teacher.

In Hue, the last imperial capital and a city that took kindly neither to the French nor the Americans, I drew into reluctant conversation one day well before the end of the war an elderly man standing in front of his store. It specialized in vegetable and flower seeds. His English was weak, and I asked whether he spoke French. At that he brightened remarkably; our conversation became animated. He expressed his nationalist dislike of France and came as close as courtesy would allow to indicating his equally strong objections to the United States presence in Vietnam. But he was glad to speak French, he said. "You know, even today, a group of old friends and I get together one evening a week. We eat something and we speak French."

While there is no such nostalgia for English, it is the language through which the Vietnamese are making their entry from their past of isolation into the world of their future. From north to south, in the big cities and rural market towns, private schools teaching English are a growth industry. A chance to learn English is the one luxury that countless Vietnamese parents believe they must offer their children.

General Man learned his French at the Lycée du Protectorat in Hanoi, a high school that trained many of the future elites of Tonkin, the north, and his native central region, the colony that France called Annam, which later lay on both sides of the political fault line that fractured Vietnam in 1954. Tonkin and Annam were colonized as "protectorates," while Cochin China, the south, was an unvarnished French colony.

"I think we can put the past aside," the general said of the puzzling absence of residual hostility toward America or Americans. "From the historical point of view one can't totally forget. But from the point of view of relations with the world, one can put it aside. The Vietnamese harbor no hatred of America or France, no hatred whatsoever. That is not a political line, those are our sentiments. We are very patriotic, but the others are also human beings. I think there are no extremists among us." There is an admitted practical aspect to the official attitude. "We think of the United States first of all as an economic power," General Man said. "And if Vietnam wants to be more highly developed, it must not think of doing that and at the same time exclude another state. What we want at the moment is cooperation. No hatred for America, China, France, Japan. We forget the past to discuss the problems of the future."

As we left the general's reception room, the official guide-interpreter, a required attachment to any visiting writer — no meeting with any authority can be arranged directly — excused himself for a minute, stepped back into the room, and discreetly handed Man an envelope. It contained a few dollars' worth of Vietnamese *dong,* payment for the general's time with the visitor. Vietnam's somewhat Communist interpretation of its capitalist market economy, to which it switched when the Soviet Union stopped paying to make up for the failings of the the Communist system, means that the Foreign Press Center of the Foreign Ministry, which supplies the guide-interpreter, is obliged to share some of its daily fee in dollars with those, like General Man, who help the center earn precious hard currency.

Why the attitude toward America is one of the few subjects on which official pronouncements correspond to popular sentiment is a question to which the Vietnamese offer only vague and tentative replies. Are the Vietnamese so pragmatically Confucian that the realities of the present can force them to place a final seal on even their most recent history and its pain? Vietnam is indeed very poor and America very rich, and the tragic connection that joined them in bloody war has forged a link that causes the Vietnamese, with perhaps one million of their relatives living in the United States, to look hopefully toward continuing American involvement now that war no longer separates them.

Or does the answer lie in the collective memory of a people whose history has known so much war that death and destruction are taken for granted with much fatalism and sorrow but little lasting rancor?

Bitterness over the war that was lost is far greater in the United States than in Vietnam, which suffered infinitely higher human loss, as well as the destruction of serving as the battlefield. Is it because for many Americans, perhaps most, the war their country waged in Vietnam meant the death of an illusion? Until America by gradual steps, rejecting every chance to reverse them, erred into war in a distant land whose complexities its leaders had not bothered to study and understand, Americans harbored the self-flattering illusion that their country fought only just wars — and won them. There were no illusions in Hanoi or in Saigon. The Vietnamese, not only the northern "enemy" but also the southern "friend," never assumed that the United States sent its unknowing men and mighty arms for any other reason but that which had so often brought bigger countries to its shores — assertive pursuit of self-interest that had little to do with Vietnam's interests. It mystified many ordinary South Vietnamese throughout the war, seeing the hundreds of thousands of Americans among them, just what the American interest in their country might be. "Poor boys!" a Saigon woman with no affection for the American role said her wartime thoughts were. "So young, so naive, and coming here to be killed. What for?"

It is possible, of course, that Americans today benefit from a dubious distinction drilled into North Vietnamese minds by insistent wartime propaganda, intended to exploit for Hanoi's purposes the massive opposition to the American involvement within the United States. The line was that the American people bore no responsibility for the war: the bellicose government in Washington was a separate power, unconnected with the American people, who were said to be as peace-loving as the North Vietnamese and their government. In fact, Americans, of course, are a great deal more responsible for the actions of their governments, which they freely choose and reward or punish at the next election, than North or South Vietnamese, who enjoyed no such right.

SOUTHEAST ASIA

CHINA

Kunming

Nanning

Mandalay

Hong Kong

MYANMAR

Red River

Hanoi

Red River Delta

LAOS

N

Vientiane

HAINAN

Mekong River

Paracel Islands

THAILAND

South Ch

Bangkok

VIETNAM

Sea

Andaman
Sea

CAMBODIA

Phnom Penh

Gulf of
Thailand

Ho Chi Minh City

PA
(Ph

10° N

Phu Quoc Island

Spratly Islands

Mekong Delta

BRUNEI

MALAYSIA

SUMATRA

Kuala Lumpur

Kuching

SINGAPORE

EQUATOR

BORNEO

INDONESIA

0   KILOMETERS 500

0   MILES

100° E

110° E

3

Losses and Gains

Vietnam today is what the collapse of the Soviet Union forced it to become.

Its rulers remain as intolerant of critical views and vindictive against the handful who dare express them as they can afford to be. There are limits, now that the Politburo heads a country that needs the help and cooperation of nations and organizations that disapprove of dictatorship. The leadership, believed to be a collegial board of directors headed since 1991 by the party's seventy-seven-year-old general secretary, Do Muoi, has liberalized the formerly sterile, centrally commanded economy with considerable success and prevented it from collapsing after the Soviet benefactors of its old ways went out of business. But the superannuated men in power have been as successful in limiting to the irreducible minimum the political and cultural spillover from these measures as in reforming the economy to the general satisfaction of the International Monetary Fund and the World Bank. The narrow-minded and stiff-necked old Communists continue to rule much as before, their monopoly of power undiminished.

Moscow used to pay the bill to maintain Vietnam as a thorn in China's south. In the Soviet strategists' view of the world, Vietnam was to China what Cuba was to the United States — a friendly and destitute outpost, worth keeping afloat even at great expense because it lay at the border of a feared adversary. The total cost was ten to fifteen billion dollars from 1975 until the Soviet collapse, according to Dr. Do Duc Dinh of the

Institute of World Economy, an official Hanoi think tank. "Their debt to Russia is ten billion transferable rubles," a Russian diplomat said and added with a shrug, "Who knows today what that is worth?" In addition, the Soviet Union's European partners, the late German Democratic Republic in the involuntary lead, were obliged to pour considerable amounts — particularly after Vietnam joined Comecon, the Soviet-dominated economic bloc, in 1978 — into what they sourly regarded as a country of no importance to them, as well as a bottomless pit. None of the creditors has illusions about repayment.

While the bounty lasted, Vietnam could afford to be exactly what its leaders wanted: an authentic Communist country, far truer to the Marxist-Leninist faith in its rigid practice than Moscow itself. Dogmatic orthodoxy ruled long after it had progressively wilted in the Soviet Union, leaving bare there after Stalin's death in 1953, under the mounting pressure of its economic and technological uncompetitiveness, a crude police state with little ideological costuming to hide its true nature. Hanoi, at the same time, continued to nurture its Stalinist paranoia toward its own people and the world beyond and to strengthen the doctrinaire regimentation of its economy, bankrolled by an ally that had for its part been obliged to forswear the most dogmatic of these practices.

Long after Stalin had become an "unperson" in his own country and its other dependencies, he remained an idol in Vietnam. It was paradoxical, yet significant in relations between countries that attach great weight to political symbolism, that the continued cult of Xta-lin, as the name is transcribed in Vietnamese, was one way in which Vietnam asserted its relative political separateness from the Soviet Union despite its economic dependence. Only China and the two Communist mavericks, North Korea and Albania, still honored the Georgian despot so long after his decline in the land he ruled. Xta-lin portraits retained a spot of honor in Vietnamese public places into the 1980s. They were not as large as those of Ho Chi Minh, but no smaller than those of Cac Mac and Le-nin as the names transliterate into Vietnamese, the other bearded icons. Stalin's translated collected works filled shelves of required reading in Hanoi's main bookstore.

In 1979 I asked a school principal in Haiphong, the northern port city, why Stalin portraits still decorated classrooms long after they had been taken down by all the other friends of the Soviet Union. "In our history lessons we still study Stalin," he replied. "He is still a great revolutionary and a great Marxist. In World War I, he was a great leader in destroying the German fascists."

In Haiphong, too, at that time, the malignant fear of the most innocent contacts with foreigners painfully recalled the worst of Stalin's days. Strolling with Nicholas, my fourteen-year-old son, I noticed out of the corner of my eye a thin, elderly man, wearing the pith helmet that in Vietnam has been transformed from the symbol of colonialism that it represents in India and Africa to a mark of the triumphant liberation struggle. He fell into step at our side and regarded us intently. I greeted him; he replied in a whisper, "bonjour." He walked with us, biting his tongue, while his eyes spoke volumes he didn't dare give voice to. I stopped at the next corner, to give him a chance to break off gracefully an encounter that pained all concerned. He turned right, and we continued straight.

After a few steps I stopped and turned back toward him. He had done the same. "Au revoir," he murmured across the distance he had opened between us, sadly raising his right hand in farewell. I remember no more poignant encounter in the many years that I lived in the European Communist world.

In a side street, a middle-aged woman stood in her doorway. She smiled at the alien passersby and returned their greeting. But when they stopped, she said in fluent French that she didn't speak French. Again, "au revoir" ended a conversation that hadn't taken place.

Mikhail S. Gorbachev's rise to power in 1985, his substantial dismantling of the unproductive economic system under perestroika, and the political liberalization that came with glasnost sent a message that the Vietnamese leadership understood. The last Soviet leader's desire for better relations with

China and the United States deflated the value of the Vietname[se?]
and Cuban outposts, and his promises of a better life for his ow[n]
deprived people meant an eventual reduction of aid for the po[or]
cousins of communism. Moreover, in 1986 Le Duan, f[or]
twenty-seven years the doctrinaire general secretary of the Vie[t-]
namese Communist party, died, the first act in his long a[nd]
cautious political career to give impetus to liberalizing chang[e.]

At the end of the year the Sixth Party Congress, the kind [of]
event in which a Communist leadership feels free to make a 18[0]
degree turn in policy and present the new line as the right an[d]
logical continuation of all its previous contrary actions, decree[d]
doi moi, "change for the new." This catchphrase denotes th[e]
hopes of the Vietnamese for the better life that the party ha[s]
been promising since the end of the war in 1975. Making [a]
virtue of the necessity imposed by the defection of their seni[or]
partner and his hitherto indispensable contribution, the leade[rs]
loosened the economic dictatorship and largely freed Vietnam[s]
industrious and inventive people to provide for their own need[s,]
plus a little extra, by their well-tested wits.

Doi moi meant the scrapping of much of the centralize[d]
state command and control of the economy. It has been radic[al]
and beneficial. Agricultural collectivization has been undone —
the state still owns the land, but the farmers cultivate it as the[y]
see economically fit; retail trade has been largely privatize[d,]
most prices left to supply and demand, a more realistic valu[e]
imposed on the currency, inflation brought down from tripl[e]
digits, and real wages increased. The door has been opened t[o]
vitally necessary foreign investment and transfer of technolog[y.]
The Vietnamese no longer feel that they are completely left ou[t]
from the general Southeast Asian boom.

The opening of the economic door has breached the bar[-]
riers against foreigners. One encounters them all over, of man[y]
categories. Visiting Western bankers and businessmen are be[-]
trayed by suits going limp and wrinkled with the heat; residen[t]
Western bankers and businessmen bear up better. Both com[-]
plain of a pettifogging, obstructive, illogical, and corrup[t]
bureaucracy, ignorant of the ways of the world. Asian business[-]

men — Japanese, South Korean, or Chinese, from Taiwan, Hong Kong, Singapore, Kuala Lumpur, or Bangkok — seem more confident. Do they have fewer scruples about what it takes to gain the goodwill of local functionaries?

Business adventurers, hoping to occupy the ground floor of what they assure any and all will be Asia's newest tower of opportunities, a new economic tiger, speak of their permanently pending big deals as though they were in the bag. Diplomats from the new or expanding embassies and officials of the many branches of the spreading United Nations tree exude obligatory enthusiasm about their aid and cooperation projects to out-siders, reserving their more realistic skepticism for unpublished official reports. Wealthy tourists who have already "done" the rest of Asia in earlier journeys are eager to be among the first in exploring territory so long forbidden. But large tour groups of the unmoneyed classes, mainly French who have direct or indi-rect colonial links or whose nostalgia for where the French flag once waved has been stirred by a spate of romantic French movies about an Indochina that never was as romantic as all that, have come just as early.

Young world travelers of all prosperous nations crisscross, often on rented motorcycles, a cheap country tolerant of their Asia-on-next-to-nothing-a-day ways. They may not contribute much to the great economic boon Vietnam expects from tour-ism, for which it is woefully underequipped. To a country that has seen young Westerners largely on martial missions, how-ever, they display a more sympathetic and respectful face. They are received mainly with friendly bemusement, especially in the countryside.

Perhaps the oddest foreign travelers are small contingents of American soldiers, usually found mornings and evenings in the decrepit hotels of provincial capitals in the center and north, the regions where most bombs were dropped and planes shot down. During the days they scour the countryside, nearly a quarter century after American soldiers stopped killing and being killed in Vietnam, on a sad mission: the search for remains of comrades still listed as missing in action, the ghosts that a small but loud lobby trading on righteous or pathetic sentiment does not allow to be laid.

The Vietnamese are aware of how many hundreds of thousands of their own have never been buried in graves bearing their names — those acknowledged as missing because they died on behalf of the victors, and those cruelly ignored because they fell on the losing side. They recognize the injustice that allows the rich to go far afield, spending millions for disproportionately small results, while their own country will not or cannot give a decent burial to its own, of whom there are so many more. Yet the waitresses, interpreters, and drivers who are the principal contacts of the search teams during their leisure hours treat the foreign soldiers on formerly enemy territory with the same slightly condescending, bantering good humor with which their predecessors dealt with the American soldiers who had come in great numbers to fight, it was said, for the cause of Vietnam.

In fact, in a country where the graves of ancestors are worshiped and every house has an altar in their honor, where restless ghosts haunt places and things, people are sympathetic to the American search. Bao Ninh, author of the powerful and controversial novel *The Sorrow of War,* who fought as a North Vietnamese soldier for six years, spent four months at the end of the fighting gathering remains of fallen North Vietnamese in the Central Highlands, a main battleground. In a long conversation in his modest Hanoi apartment in a North Korean–built prefabricated tenement quarter, he reflected the anguish and conflicting emotions evoked by this painful subject.

"America is right to search for its missing," he said. "It may be politics, in order to delay normal relations with us, but the American wives and mothers, we understand them well. Our government is so poor. We have mothers and widows who know where their sons or husbands died, but they can't afford to visit their graves. Morally, the American mothers have a right to have their wish satisfied. We want Vietnamese mothers also to be able to put incense sticks on their children's graves, but the government can't afford it. Many Vietnamese in mourning feel sad and disgraced over that."

Bao Ninh laughed without glee at the ironic imbalance. "Our government is so kind to the Americans. It lets them use helicopters to go to check rumors. Vietnamese people are bitter about this. A Vietnamese mother who lost three or four sons in the war without knowing where they were buried may be helping to dig for Americans missing in action, because she knows where they were buried." Of course, the Vietnamese government may not be motivated solely by compassion for mourning Americans. It makes the United States pay dearly for the use of its Soviet-donated helicopters, as well as for the services of the many Vietnamese who participate in the searches.

The relatively open door for foreigners is, besides the economic relaxation, the most palpable innovation of *doi moi.* Most are Vietnamese who not long ago found asylum abroad from Communist Vietnam and return bearing the passports mainly of the United States, Canada, Australia, or France. The flow of visitors has opened a large breach in the wall of unnatural ignorance of the rapidly changing outside world in which the regime enclosed the Vietnamese. Unnatural, not only because Vietnam is full of people whose curiosity about the world is as eager as that of any in Asia but also because this thirst for contact derives from a more educated understanding of foreign cultures and history than one encounters in some countries with far easier access to the world. The long French presence and the shorter, but intense, contact with America have left not only scars, just as the decades of isolation — nearly four for the people of the north — impoverished the nation much more than just materially.

I asked Hang Ngoc Hien, a Hanoi literary critic and respected teacher of writers, which country he would choose if he were told that the next day he could visit any country he wished. "The United States," he replied unhesitatingly. His choice surprised me; Hien, whose knowledge of English and literature in English is excellent, speaks flawless French, and most of his cultural references have a French orientation. (Few seem to stem from his years of study in the Soviet Union.) "Because I don't want to be a country bumpkin," was his reply in astonishingly bookish English. "It is a major civilization," he continued in French. "Perhaps I'll be disappointed when I see it. But I have to see it at all cost, even to be disappointed by it." And France? "I know France without having seen it," he answered, reflecting the education of Vietnamese intellectuals of his generation.

Duong Tuong, an art critic who has assembled a fine gallery of nonconformist painting, was silent for a long moment when I asked whether there was a novel not to be found in Hanoi that I might bring on my next visit. So long, that I thought perhaps I had offended by suggesting a modest gift. But at last he replied. "What is the name of the author who wrote *The Man without Qualities*?" he asked. In so geographically remote and intellectually restrictive a country, a man curious about Robert Musil's magisterial, much-cited and little-read epic novel of the decline and fall of the Hapsburg Empire was totally unexpected, even in the unideological setting of Tuong's gallery of nonsocialist realist paintings.

Yes, he agreed, there aren't many in Hanoi with whom he could discuss this monument of the culture of Mitteleuropa, if he could ever get to read it. "I picked up my knowledge of literature wherever I could," he said. Some of it, he said, he gleaned from the French army against which he fought in Vietnam's war of independence, starting as a seventeen-year-old volunteer in 1949. "You know, whenever we captured a French post we gathered up the booty," he said. "And for me, the booty was books. I remember when we overran a post in Nam Dinh Province, I found a copy of *All Quiet on the Western Front* in French, and I said to myself, 'It wasn't for nothing that we captured this post.'" He laughed, relishing the bitter irony of acquiring Erich Maria Remarque's 1920s German best-seller, written in the fervent hope that World War I would be the war to end all wars, as a trophy of the hope's failure.

Tuong widened his literary horizon by steady visits to Hanoi's principal library, whose main stock right after the Vietnamese victory of 1954 was the books that the French left behind. His long-unsatisfied appetite for Musil's unfinished masterpiece was aroused by an article in a French Communist literary review. In the 1960s he read some of Franz Kafka's novels and stories, which were circulating in French among trusted friends. "I also got a copy of Orwell's *Nineteen Eighty-Four* in the 1960s," he said, still pleased at the exploit of thirty years earlier. "I read it in the open, and no one cared. Nobody here knew anything about Orwell or Kafka. You know, the politicians know nothing about anything."

The experience of free minds in unfree societies is independent of time or place. Almost thirty years earlier, I asked Jerzy Turowicz, the courageous Polish editor, how he managed so often in his weekly to publish articles critical of the current situation in his country, writing that stopped barely short of calling a spade a spade. "You shouldn't underestimate the stupidity of censors," he replied.

What did reading Kafka in North Vietnam in the 1960s mean to him? I asked Tuong. "I recognized much of my situation," he replied.

4

Heroes of War and Peace

Those who chafe under Vietnam's isolation, those whose horizons are wider than the primitive political orthodoxy that categorizes ideas, nations, and individuals crudely as friends or foes, are men and women who offered their lives in Vietnam's wars against France and the United States and the regime that it supported in Saigon. They include not only the usual out-of-step elements, questioning writers and artists who shun binding political affiliation, but also many loyal Communists occupying high positions of trust, which they would never betray.

Professor Tu Giay left medical school and went into the jungle at the end of World War II, when Ho Chi Minh after the defeat of Japan called for a general uprising against the return of the French colonial power. "You know, at that time it was a general movement," he explained, as though justification were needed. "The young are enthusiastic. It was the revolution, and later came independence. At that time we didn't have the idea of communism, of socialism."

Tu Giay is the much-honored — People's Doctor, Medal of Labor — founder of the National Institute of Nutrition in Hanoi, a vital organization in a country that still suffers from much malnutrition and is not sheltered from recurring local plagues of hunger. He retired officially as its director in 1993, but at the age of seventy-four he continues to work and receive visitors in his old office. He speaks the flowery French of his youth and often in conversation underscores points by lovingly citing passages of French literature. His eyes closed, he appears to be reading pages of the past with his mind's eye.

"Anatole France, I think," he said one day when asked whom he was quoting, modestly feigning uncertainty, after what must have been two pages, verbatim and flowing. "But my real love is French poetry." Two romantic poems followed, no longer pertinent to the issue that had brought on Anatole France.

"You know, the poet I love the most is that German who wrote in French," he said, glowing with literary élan, after he was complimented on his impressive performance. He closed his eyes once more and offered two verses from the *Buch der Lieder* of Heinrich Heine, who lived the last years of his life in Parisian exile but continued to write only in his native tongue. While the lyrical doctor lovingly recited translations of the German's songs of unrequited love, no doubt memorized from a schoolbook without the italic note of the translator's name, I pushed aside the fleeting idea of diminishing by a cavil his love of French, and Heine's, poetry. Heine's place as Tu Giay's favorite French poet remains secure.

The doctor's love for French culture has passed through periods of testing. For nine years, until the decisive battle of Dien Bien Phu in 1954, he was in the front lines of the war against France. A third-year medical student in the capital when the conflict erupted, he was sent to the front in the center of the country, around the coastal city of Nha Trang, and began his professional practice by learning on the job as assistant to a surgeon. He served throughout Vietnam, north as far as the Chinese border and west to Dien Bien Phu, in the inhospitable green mountains near Laos.

Twice during the fighting Dr. Tu Giay met with one of his old professors, Dr. Pierre Huard, a surgeon who had been dean of the medical faculty of Hanoi University. Teacher and student faced each other in the role of foes. The first time was in 1950 near Cao Bang, where a major French base on the Chinese border had been annihilated. "He came to get the French wounded while I was there," Tu Giay recalled. "He recognized

Bao Ninh, who won Vietnam's highest literary award in 1991 for his harrowing portrayal of combat in *The Sorrow of War.* (Photo © by Rémy Gassm-bide.)

General Pham Xuan An, a correspondent for *Time* magazine during the war and one of the boldest undercover Communist intelligence agents in Saigon. (Photo © by Le Minh, Time magazine.)

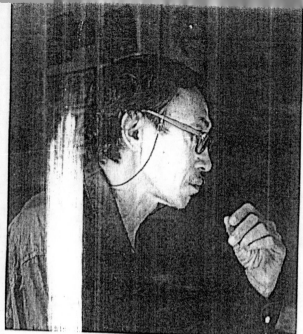

Duong Tuong, art critic, poet, literary translator, and the founder of an art gallery in Hanoi.
(Photo by Joren Gerhard.)

Duong Thu Huong, a novelist and Vietnam's closest equivalent to the dissidents of Soviet-bloc Europe, shakes hands with French culture minister Jacques Toubon in 1994 after her election to the Order of Arts and Letters in Paris.

Trinh Cong Son, whose widely popular antimilitarist songs were once banned by the Saigon regime.
(Photo by Henry Kamm.)

Cao Giao, a journalist and *Newsweek* reporter during the war.
(Photo by T. Terzani, © 1985 by Der Spiegel.)

Dr. Duong Quynh Hoa, a founding member of the Viet Cong and director of the Center for Pediatrics, Development and Health in Ho Chi Minh City.
(Photo by Henry Kamm.)

Bao Dai, last emperor of Vietnam, rev... is French-trained paratroopers
after an attack on Communist forces in ... (UPI/Bettmann)

Ho Chi Minh at a
Communist party
gathering in 1966.
(AP/Wide World Photos)

Pham Thi Trinh, a survivor of the My Lai massacre, stands next to a marker commemorating the American military slaughter of Vietnamese civilians there in 1968.
(AP/Wide World Photos)

Henry Kissinger with North Vietnamese leader Le Duc Tho during the peace talks in 1972 that would later earn them the Nobel Prize for Peace.

American marine threatens a South Vietnamese climbing over the wall of the U.S. Embassy to join evacuation flights before the fall of Saigon. *(UPI/Bettmann.)*

South Vietnam's last president, Duong Van Minh, walks out of Independence Palace after surrendering to Communist forces in 1975

Vietnamese boat people arriving in Hong Kong in 1989. *(AP/Wide World Photos.)*

U.S. Vietnamese excavation teams searching for traces of U.S. servicemen still listed as missing in action in 1994. *(Reuter/Bettmann.)*

A marketplace in Ho Chi Minh City, formerly Saigon. (AP/Wide World Photos)

Billboards along the Saigon River in Ho Chi Minh City. *(Reuters/Bettmann.)*

The Continental Palace Hotel and the Opera House on Dong Khoi Street, formerly rue Catinat, in Ho Chi Minh City. *(UPI/Bettmann.)*

...ench colonial-era villa in Hanoi. *(UPI/Bettmann)*

A street in Hanoi's old city center.
(Reuter/Bettmann)

Youngsters run to jump aboard an overcrowded streetcar in Hanoi. (AFP/Germain.)

The Bach Mai hospital. A wing of the building is left unrepaired to remind

Tomb of Ho Chi Minh.
(AP/Wide World Photos.)

Hanoi Opera House, decked
out with hammer and sickle
on the opening day of
Vietnam's Communist
Party Congress.
(Reuter/Bettmann.)

me. I had known him as my professor. He said, 'There have been many changes.' He was very friendly, very friendly." Even nearly a half century after the encounter, Tu Giay appeared to cherish the friendliness that surely the Frenchman, who had come on behalf of the vanquished, was obliged to show the former student who represented the victors. Dr. Huard was known as a friend to many Vietnamese, but would he have received Tu Giay with the same generosity had the roles been reversed?

"And the second time we met at Dien Bien Phu," Tu Giay continued. "Again, he came to see the wounded. It was always in the same spirit. I had respect for my professor. We were friendly, like colleagues. It was not a problem for us. I retain respect for the men who did me good. They were men like me; they had to follow military orders." Certainly not all Vietnamese officers and soldiers proved capable of the same magnanimity as Dr. Tu Giay, a man of exceptional kindness, in their treatment of the vanquished; the war was a bitter colonial struggle, and much of the campaign was spearheaded by the Foreign Legion, manned extensively by German and foreign hirelings of the Wehrmacht and Waffen-S.S. who avoided trial for war crimes by escaping under a nom de guerre into the next war.

The old soldier could not resist sharing the painful images that calling on memory had brought to his mind. "At Dien Bien Phu I was the first to enter the French underground hospital. You know, the hospital was made for eighty beds, and there were three hundred wounded in that hospital. There were three tiers. They could no longer get care, and urine and all that was dripping down. And you know, I felt pity, pity for these people. They are human beings, and now they are like that. It was a tragedy."

Tu Giay is one of many of his generation of Vietnamese who rallied voluntarily to arms because of the humiliation of colonialism, and fought a long, vicious, and bloody war, but prefer today to speak only of the good they have chosen to retain. And yet what France gave him was modest. A poor village boy brought up by his mother, who was widowed at the age of twenty-two, he won an essay contest after completing at age fifteen the six years of free education provided by the colonial regime. "I received a prize of fifty *dong; piasters,* we said then," he reminisced. "But you know, that was a big sum, because to enter the lycée here in Hanoi one had first to take an exam. For all the north there were only 120 places in the Lycée du Protectorat, 120 for all of Tonkin. I passed, but you know, one had to pay. Four *dong* every month. So without the prize I couldn't have paid."

He was enabled to complete high school because he received a free-tuition scholarship and one daily meal as reward for academic excellence. "After the baccalaureate, there were only two choices for Vietnamese who wanted further study — law, and in three or four years you could become a mandarin, or medicine. I preferred the seven years of medicine. I started in 1943. Then there was the revolution, and we left for the jungle." Tu Giay must have been a brilliant student to make it in the French system, which was designed to limit sharply the number of "indigenous" graduates. "There was a very radical elimination," he said. "I entered as one of two hundred, but after the exam at the end of the first year only forty remained. At the end we were only six or seven."

Dr. Tu Giay makes ritual references to the teachings of Ho Chi Minh, without which few conversations in Hanoi with men and women of his age go very far. He recalled that Bac (Uncle) Ho — as the late leader is commonly called, using a title that denotes in one word utmost respect for a public man and the familial love due to one's father's older brother, a combination made possible by the richness of the Vietnamese language in subtle designations of family relationships — taught his compatriots to distinguish between "the French colonialists" and the "French people, who are the children of the French Revolution and of liberty, equality, and brotherhood."

But Tu Giay sounded less dutiful, more his romantic self, in describing his personal motivation for joining the ranks of the independence struggle ("There was one thing — my mother. You know, I'm an only son. So my mother didn't know.") "Why did we go into the jungle?" he asked rhetorically. "It was the communion with the pain of the stricken, with the pain of the people who had lost their independence. These are the humanitarian ideals we learned in French schools. What remains for us from that past is the ideal of brotherhood."

The professor grew lyrical once more as he remembered those who were his professors. "For others there was perhaps a problem, I don't know," he said, speaking of how the French were perceived during the war. "But for me it was clear, because I had those professors. I can still cite from memory what they taught. You know, even today I remember Professor Blondet. Ah, he gave marvelous lectures! And when he raised his voice for the conclusion — at that time we still used fountain pens — we all closed the fountain pens and laid them down, to be ready to applaud. I still have his conclusions in mind. I remember how he described the treatment of cardiac insufficiency."

Tu Giay recited the description at length, lovingly making medical injunctions sound like another poem. Words and phrases like "heroic," "astonishing simplicity," "a triad," abounded, uttered ringingly and underlined with eloquent gestures. "You know, it was poetic. These are conclusions that you remember all your life. You see, this was magnificent! How can one harbor hatred against professors like that? How can I feel bitterness? To feel bitterness against such people would not be just. We should not hate the French or the American people."

To Brigadier General Pham Xuan An this would be an understatement. General An, one of the boldest undercover Communist intelligence agents in Saigon throughout the war against the United States and South Vietnam, loves America and Americans and ascribes his "political awakening" to the compassion that stirred him when he saw Japanese occupation troops mistreat and humiliate the same French who not much earlier had mistreated and humiliated his compatriots.

If this is puzzlingly complex and seemingly contradictory, so is An, a frail man, bent but unlikely to break, like a tree in a tempestuous landscape. I have known him — I once thought well — for a good quarter century. Not for a moment did I suspect him of being, throughout the war, a colonel of the National Liberation Front's army, the Viet Cong, as they were called by their enemies. I knew him as a generous, informative, and gently witty colleague, the only Vietnamese employed by the American press to be given by his employer, *Time* magazine, the status of a full-fledged correspondent, not a mere local assistant to his American colleagues sent out from New York to cover the war. His other employer promoted him to general after the war.

Now, sixty-eight years old and still, at least nominally, on active service, An receives old friends and colleagues. Until *doi moi*, he was rarely allowed to be at home for those who requested to see him. In the book-filled living room of his modest Saigon villa — a general of the former South Vietnamese army would never have lodged so humbly — An, much frailer than in his journalistic days, his voice dim but his mind vital with restrained passion, explains. "Mine has always been a paradoxical life," he began a long conversation, in an understatement singular even for so understated a man.

An's father, a land surveyor and customs agent in French service in the southernmost Mekong Delta, punished him for a failure in school at age nine by sending him to live with relatives in a village near Hue, the imperial capital, in central Vietnam. Failure in education even at an early age is a cardinal sin in a traditional family like An's in so Confucian a society. An's father wanted his son to learn how well off he was by making him experience the poverty of rural life in one of Vietnam's enduringly poorest regions. "It was so poor we had no oil for the lamps and used a wick dipped into a plate of rat fat as a candle," An remembered. When he failed again the following year, his father brought him home to supervise his education himself.

An's first realization of the paradoxes of his nation came at age thirteen, in 1940, when the Japanese occupied Vietnam after France's surrender to Hitler. In the southern port town of Rach Gia, An's home at the time, the conquerors rounded up the French men and in the central square chained them together under the merciless sun. The purpose was to humiliate the former white rulers in the eyes of the Vietnamese and so accredit Japan's grand vision of a new, triumphant Asia under Asian — Japanese — auspices.

"I never liked the French, because the French colonialists' children mistreated us Vietnamese children," An said. "But the Japanese cruelty disgusted me. The Frenchmen were thirsty. I went to ask my father, and he said, 'Boil some water and take it to them.' When I did, the Japanese slapped the Frenchmen in the face.

"I still don't like Japanese officials," An continued. "Before 1975 I never accepted invitations from their embassy because of that." It was the only time in many conversations on his turbulent life, so placid on the surface, that I detected an edge of vindictiveness sharpening An's voice and equanimity. The Frenchmen's fate aroused his sympathies for the underdog. Another factor in his early decision to take sides actively, he said, was Vietnamese injustice to Vietnamese. He saw landowners, his classmates' fathers, mistreat their tenants. "They tortured them," An said. "They forced their daughters and even their wives to sleep with them.

"That's why I have such respect for America," said the Vietnamese general. "They are taught to help the underdog."

An joined in clandestine military training organized by the Viet Minh, the Communist-led armed movement that drove out the French. He was rejected at his first attempt because his father was a landowner and worked for the French regime, but in October 1945 he was accepted. The political instruction that was given along with the military training emphasized independence, not communism. "I was a young patriot and felt strongly about social injustice," An said. He had his baptism of fire in jungle warfare against the French army. "The Viet Minh didn't have enough rifles, about fifty for more than a hundred troops, and after firing you had to pick up the cartridge cases to make new bullets," he recalled. At nineteen he was a platoon leader, but he was soon sent back to his family, in territory fully under French control. He organized student demonstrations in Saigon against French rule — "independence was my sole goal" — but nonetheless was drafted into the colonial army in 1950 and sent briefly to officers' school. A deferment demobilized him. In 1952 his Viet Minh commanders summoned him to a jungle command post near Saigon and assigned him, over his protest against becoming a stool pigeon, to work for what they called the "strategic intelligence" branch. "I was the first recruit in intelligence," An said. The following year he was made a member of the Communist party. "I was given the classic Communist texts to read, in French, and found good ideals in them," he said. "I became a Communist."

In 1954, as the French departed, South Vietnam gained the independence that it owed largely to Ho Chi Minh's armed victory. An was drafted into the new army being formed under American guidance and made a warrant officer in the psychological warfare branch of the general staff. His first assignment was to act as liaison officer between the Saigon command and the American and French officers who carried out the turnover from French to American responsibility for organizing, training, and supplying the armed forces of the new state. An, who had begun studying English with a Vietnamese Protestant minister in 1945, speaks with convincing affection of the members of the military and intelligence team headed by Colonel — later General — Edward G. Lansdale, the principal American organizer of "counterinsurgency" warfare, under CIA sponsorship, against Southeast Asian Communists. It was these men who laid the basis for the unequal American–South Vietnamese military alliance, which at its peak brought a presence of more than a half million Americans to a country they little understood.

An insists he never felt that his positions created a conflict of interest. "These two things are completely different," he said. "My actions were completely compartmentalized." No doubt he means that his personal friendship for his American and South Vietnamese colleagues was genuine and quite separate from what must have been a constant flow of his rich knowledge of their activities into the Communist "strategic intelligence" compartment.

Among An's duties was to advise on the recommendation

of officers for training courses at American military staff colleges. It is not the least irony in a life rather rich in ironies that it was An who passed favorably on the application of the young Nguyen Van Thieu, South Vietnam's last military dictator, to pay his first visit to the United States for a course at Fort Leavenworth.

"I learned a lot from the Americans," An said, his appreciation of American ways unfeigned. "I was obtuse before; they enlarged my horizons." Clearly the affection was mutual. Officers of the Military Assistance Group continued to teach An English, and in 1957 they sponsored an official visit to the United States for the young South Vietnamese liaison officer. Recommended for a scholarship by Lansdale, he enrolled at Orange Coast College, a junior college in Orange County, California, as a journalism student. "I was the first Vietnamese to settle there," said An, in ironic allusion to the predilection of postwar Vietnamese refugees for Orange County. In 1959, before returning to Vietnam, he served as an intern-reporter on the *Sacramento Bee*. An wants it clearly understood that he was a genuine journalist and did not only use his jobs with Vietnam Press, an official news agency, then with Reuters news service, and finally with *Time* as a cover for espionage. "Journalism helped me to be objective," he said. "I'm sad I'm not free to do it any more." His commanders were sufficiently sophisticated, he said, not to use his position to plant fake stories.

"They were decisive years for me," An said of his American stay. "I learned about American culture, the American mentality." What the Vietnamese general says about American virtues, eyes aglow with admiration, could pass muster at an American Legion Fourth of July celebration — honesty, hard work, fairness, a sense of justice, openness, and kindness. "I like the United States," he said. "The Americans did a lot of good here. They trained a generation to work, to be more realistic. They gave us some notions of liberty and respect for human rights. The GIs treated the people who worked for them well. They even got a day off every week. They showed me how to see things the other guy's way, to criticize yourself first. I would like my children to be educated there."

A son, Pham Xuan Hoang An, has returned to Saigon from nearly three years at the University of North Carolina, which were preceded by six years of study in the Soviet Union. He works as a press officer for the Saigon branch of the Foreign Ministry, speaks with equal fondness of his friends in Moscow and Chapel Hill, and hopes someday to return to the United States for a Ph.D. His father, no doubt because of the secrets to which he is privy, has not been allowed to accept invitations to visit American friends.

"I always hoped the United States would open its eyes and help the real Vietnam," An said. "I tried to help the Americans to understand Vietnam. They were too influenced by the French and supported the Catholics from the north too much, not the people of the south. The northerners were bitter refugees, who lost everything they owned when they fled to the south in 1954."

An makes light of the difficulties of his extraordinary existence on both sides of the divide, but if pressed will admit that he lived in terror. "But I'm a fatalist; God decides," the Communist general said wryly, without apparent irony. "I didn't even know my rank; I never think of such things." He disclosed his promotion to general with self-mocking embarrassment, and noted, as if in extenuation, that even at that rank his monthly pay was well below one hundred dollars.

An said he met his ever-varying Viet Cong contacts by appointment in equally varying locations in Saigon, delivering his intelligence orally, rarely putting anything into writing. Since very few even among his comrades knew him, identification was usually only by items of clothing. But not infrequently he would slip out of the city into the nearby "liberated zones" for longer debriefings by senior commanders, usually in tunnels to shelter from bombing. Crossing the undrawn lines was frighteningly dangerous, since both sides naturally were intensely suspicious. All Saigon governments dealt harshly even with innocents whom they suspected of Communist sympathies. Only An's wife and mother knew of his perilous double life.

And a double life it truly was, until its very last moment, Saigon's surrender, when An for the first time put on the uniform of the army he had served secretly for so long and continues to serve. His ultimate act in the final stage of the American evacuation was to save the life of an old friend, desperate to make his way to one of the last helicopters but trapped and unable to force his way through a panicky and hostile crowd into the building whose roof was the evacuation pad. An bluffed and bullied his elderly companion into the place of rescue. Both cried at the moment of their hasty parting. The friend was no less a figure than Dr. Tran Kim Tuyen, chief of the feared secret police under the regime of Ngo Dinh Diem, the South Vietnamese dictator overthrown and murdered in a 1963 coup, and a longtime associate of the American Central Intelligence Agency. Perhaps Tuyen would have suffered no more than long or permanent imprisonment in a concentration camp — euphemistically called "reeducation" in Communist Vietnam — had An not made possible his escape, but on that cataclysmic April 29, 1975, when nothing was certain but the Communist victory, both had reason to fear the worst for so marked a figure of the old regime and the Viet Cong colonel who helped him to escape from "revolutionary justice."

Five years earlier An had risked his precarious status on behalf of an American colleague. A rash young reporter for *Time* was captured in Cambodia, the graveyard of most journalists who fell into the hands of the Khmers Rouges irregulars fighting then alongside North Vietnamese troops, who had an interest in hiding their presence on foreign territory from the outside world. An succeeded in persuading the Vietnamese to release the American, Robert Sam Anson. It was only when Anson met An again many years after the war that An, still reluctantly, acknowledged his life-saving role.

"I was sad on April the thirtieth," said An of the day of his army's victory. "I said good-bye to Tuyen. Most of my friends left, and I knew those who didn't would be in trouble." He was sad also because he had sent his wife and four children to the United States on an evacuation flight organized for *Time*'s

Vietnamese staff, to spare them what might have turned into a bloody battle for Saigon. They returned after the dust had settled.

Although An is too loyal to say so, his loyalty has not been rewarded with the full confidence of the men from the north who rule the country. Shortly after what in today's politically correct language is called "the liberation," An was sent north for a period of "reeducation" organized for those whose service to the cause had exposed them to the life and ideas of the enemy. On his return to Saigon he was offered the job of press censor, which he declined.

Pham Xuan An's life, with all its bewildering ambiguities, can serve as a paradigm for a people that in modern times has continually had to confront a multitude of painful choices, which tragically never included one that most could whole-heartedly embrace. Most did no more than the minimum that the varied, frequently changing powers in control exacted from them, and even this minimum compliance cost countless lives. An, not a man who shirks ethical choices, chose.

"There were true patriots on both sides, despite their differences," he said. Reflecting on the aggressive influences that for better and for worse went into the making of the minds of South Vietnamese of his age, he acknowledged a debt to all. "There are three cultures in a Vietnamese like me," he said. "And there is a little communism, too."

5 ·

Guardians of the Grail

Not long after the last stirring of the Soviet Communists — the abortive Moscow coup of August 1991 — the Institute of Marxism-Leninism in Hanoi, the Holy Grail of the received truth, expanded its name. The new shingle at the gate of the old French villa now announces, "Institute of Marxism-Leninism and the Thought of Ho Chi Minh." What's in a name? In this case, job security.

The guardians of the Grail, the doctors of Marxism-Leninism who received their degrees at the Moscow fountainhead and used to be called derisively "party doctors," are preparing for the dire eventualities that the future may hold. The values of Marx and Lenin have proved elsewhere not to be as eternal as they are still taught to be at the institute. If, even in the few places where their sanctuaries still stand, the old idols wither away more quickly than the state, whose withering Marx foresaw, their passing won't find the party doctors of Hanoi unprepared; they have taken out insurance. In Vietnam, Ho Chi Minh and his thought can be counted on for a longer shelf life than that of the German and Russian idols, even if not for eternity, as is still affirmed. With the extended name, the institute and the doctors' jobs have gained a new lease on life, good, they hope, for some time to come.

Always ready with an answer based on dialectical materialism, Hanoi's party doctors have come to believe that the collapse of European communism proves the correctness of their theories. "In those countries Marxism-Leninism was wrongly applied," said Professor Vu Huu Ngoan, the deputy director. "If they had applied it correctly, they would have survived. Their collapse is proof of the correctness of Marxism-Leninism." This is difficult to argue with.

If the institute's sages are guilty of a weakening of the historical optimism that their creed prescribes, they are not alone. Vietnam's leaders have suspended the beliefs that they have lived by for so long. The Socialist Republic of Vietnam today is socialist in name only. It has abandoned the achievements of which Communists were proud — doubtful benefits like the collectivization of agriculture and central control of most of the economy, but also such real gains as free medical care and education. The people must pay now for going to the doctor or sending their children to school. As a result, fewer Vietnamese go to school or to the doctor. Only primary education remains free of charge. "Free education was possible in the past," said Professor Vu Van Tao, a senior assistant to the education minister. "Today it would be utopian. Our former policy was ultraleftist."

Instead of the egalitarianism that was preached before socialism was pronounced utopian — and actually rather puritanically practiced in Vietnam, contrary to most other Communist countries, whose "establishments," called "nomenklatura" locally, enjoyed life on the rich side of a hypocritical gulf between theory and practice — the party has pinned on its banner a new motto: Getting Rich through Individual Enterprise Is a Good Thing, even if it undoes the social leveling that for so long spread poverty fairly evenly. In Do Muoi's policy statement before the party's Central Committee in 1994, the general secretary said, "We should consider the fact that a portion of the population will get rich before others as a necessity for development." The underlying implication that eventually all will be rich seems no more justifiable in what remains one of the world's poorest nations than in any other country, but it suggests that late in life Vietnamese politicians have learned not only from capitalist economists but also from political demagogues of the democratic persuasion.

A friend who is a Russian diplomat with a wide range of personal friends and political contacts, built up over a long stay in Hanoi, is perhaps best placed to consider the depth of the Vietnamese leadership's late conversion to reform and ideological renewal. "Vietnam is gradually going away from socialism," he said.

> Socialism here has become a tradition that is more rhetorical than real. But contrary to us Russians, who have always been bothered by the gap between ideology and real life, the Vietnamese have known how to live with both and their contradiction. I believe even today there is more socialism in Russia, in the bureaucracy and the minds of the people, than here in Vietnam. In the Vietnamese mind, there is a peaceful coexistence of the old Communist gods and the pragmatism of a nation of peasants and traders. Now they are leaving Marxism-Leninism behind on the altars of their ancestors. When they feel the need, they pray to these gods at night, but during the day they do business. I think they are in the process of replacing the Western gods, like Marx and Lenin, with national gods. They are living by the ideas of Ho Chi Minh now, ruling their own nation. The main slogan of the party now is, Rich People and a Strong State. There is nothing socialist about that, but they do have the strong state.

The Russian recalled that in the first days of the Moscow coup many party officials in Hanoi expressed their support for those who hijacked Gorbachev and set out to reverse his reforms. "I told them not to hurry to recognize the coup," he said, pleased with his sound advice. But he pointed out that even after the coup's failure, some Vietnamese continued to sympathize with the plotters who wanted to restore the old Soviet ways; "Many in the old generation here want to see the reestablishment of the Soviet Union and wish for a rebirth of socialism." And he noted that the leadership was of that generation. They knew the reforms were a necessity for survival, but in their hearts they wished it weren't so.

What remains in this land run by reluctant reformers of the customs of the countries that affixed "Socialist" to their official names is a state intolerant of divergent views or any challenge to the ruling party's singular power, with a potent secret police as the enforcer. The arrogance of power is still what it was: the state and party may admit their fundamental and damaging "errors" in past policies but do not for a moment allow that having committed such errors should disqualify them from continuing to govern. They are ready to give perestroika a chance; but glasnost, an opening for free thought and speech, no thanks. How to encourage free, enterprising economic initiative while denying intellectual freedom is a circle they cannot square. The leaders' fear for their unlimited power has placed too low a ceiling on Vietnamese hopes and chances.

The secret police controls the lives of ordinary citizens through a fine-meshed network of spy-on-your-neighbor informers that reaches down to every village hut and cubicle apartment in cities and towns. Vietnamese suspected of holding independent views are entitled to far closer observation and occasional summonses for "informal" chats with police or party officials, and the very few who have voiced unpopular opinions are subjected to imprisonment, threats, loss of job, undisguised surveillance, ostracism, and other forms of open intimidation. These practices, of course, are not covered by law; some, in fact, are open violations. One-party rule, on the other hand, is enshrined in the constitution.

The latest of the four constitutions of the Communist state, adopted in 1992 and hailed as the most liberal charter, says, in the official translation, in Article 4: "The Communist Party of Vietnam, the vanguard of the Vietnamese working class, the faithful representative of the rights and interests of the working class, the toiling people, and the whole nation, acting upon the Marxist-Leninist doctrine and Ho Chi Minh's thought, is the force leading the State and society."

Freedom of expression in culture and the arts is covered by Article 30: "The State undertakes the overall administration of cultural activities. The propagation of all reactionary and depraved thought and culture is forbidden; superstitions and harmful customs are to be eliminated." This creates a worrying ambiguity: "superstition" is what religion is often called in the wooden language of the Institute of Marxism-Leninism and the Thought of Ho Chi Minh. Still, the constitution warrants religious freedom in Chapter 70. Article 33 covers press freedom: "Shall be strictly banned all activities in the fields of culture and information that are detrimental to national interests, and destructive of the personality, morals and fine lifeway of the Vietnamese."

"They are free to say what they want, as long as they don't attack the government," said Nguyen Phuoc Tuc, an official in Hue, in praising the liberties enjoyed by the city's students. In Saigon's main post office, a sign over a counter announces bluntly what most countries that indulge in the unpleasant practice disguise under euphemistic labels. "Culture Censorship," it proclaims in Vietnamese and English. No book or other printed matter, video, or cassette may be packed in a parcel until an officious guardian, who is gloomily earnest about her job, has leafed through the pages or sampled the sound of the potentially subversive material and added one more stamp to the many that must be gathered at various counters before a parcel can be mailed from Vietnam.

The constitution also confers on the state vast and ill-defined powers over the citizen that can make anyone subject to punishment at any time. Article 13 declares, "All machinations and acts directed against the independence, sovereignty, unity and territorial integrity of the motherland, against the construction and defense of the socialist Vietnamese motherland, shall be severely punished in accordance with the law." The power of definition is left to the state.

These are the limits within which *doi moi,* the renewal of Vietnam, fitfully proceeds. Within their far too narrow confines, officials in Hanoi and in government offices throughout the country must do verbal acrobatics to explain how they manage to practice both socialism and *doi moi,* under which socialism is being virtually dismantled. General Tran Cong Man, as ever the voice of the party, makes an arduous effort, but at times even his perennial professions that, whatever the party's policy today, it is good and of a piece with the policy that preceded suffer strain. It is a credit to his Communist steadfastness that he is uncomfortable dethroning the men and ideas that have been the lodestars of his life.

"For a long time we followed the Soviet model," Man said. "It was our unique model. Now we find that it was a false model. It was a bad application of Marxist-Leninist ideals, perverted by Stalin. We feel Stalin didn't understand Marxism-Leninism." Not much earlier, the general would no more have been capable of such blasphemy than Saint John the Baptist of declaring Jesus weak on Christianity. He noted his listener's surprise, smiled shyly, and explained. "There were two sides to Stalin. He was a leader against Hitlerism. He was a hero who achieved important exploits. But ideologically he committed important errors."

The general explained the negative effects of transferring these "errors" to Vietnam. "This was not suited to the needs of a developing economy. There were objective and subjective errors. There were errors in the management system. There was a lack of democracy. Totalitarianism destroyed the people's initiative. Yes, we committed errors. Collectivization of agriculture; now we apply another policy. Priority was given to heavy industry. This was a grave error; it misdirected investment. Almost all enterprises were state-owned. Now there are all types."

But, unsurprisingly, Man reconfirmed his loyalty to the regime's surviving undemocratic view of democracy. "There is a difference between totalitarianism and a power monopoly by one party," he said. "One can have democracy with a single party. It wasn't the Communists who destroyed other parties, but colonialist repression. Only one party survived it — the Communist party." He said that after the colonial period all other parties lost popular support because only the Communists had been ready to make the sacrifices necessary to achieve independence. "The others died of old age," he said. "They proposed their own dissolution. It was we who emancipated the nation."

General Man said this emancipation freed all Vietnamese. Those who disagree also? "We don't punish those who have different opinions," he said. "The discussions in our meetings are keen. We punish those who engage in activities against the stability of our country, who organize subversive groups." This apparently covers Buddhist monks and Roman Catholic priests who defend the independence of the practice of their faiths from state control and novelists whose works create discord in the unanimous chorus of enthusiastic approval, as well the few who were accused of forming cells of resistance, or the foolhardy Ly Tong, a former South Vietnamese air force pilot in exile in the United States, who dropped antigovernment leaflets from a commercial airliner over Saigon and then parachuted to be arrested, tried, and jailed.

Such was General Man's explanation in 1992. Two years later, the general had progressed further in avowing reality while clinging as firmly as ever to his party's claim to full power, at least for "a few years" more. "Naturally, democracy has not yet been established here," he said. "We have to learn democratization. We must arrive step by step at a democratization that will be better and better organized. I think this cannot be done in a few days or even a few years. We are not afraid of democracy. We think that the European model of democracy is not entirely favorable for us. Naturally, democracy has some good sides. But if we apply it without selectiveness, it can cause disorder, as for example in the ex–Soviet Union. I think our people are afraid of this disorder, because such disorder would not bring about social and economic development. And for that reason we want the country to remain stable."

Social and economic development is what Vietnam has chosen as its present target, and thus it has strayed from the path to socialism. The terms in which the spokesman described this ideological transformation are clearly those in which the party leaders have passed it down through the ranks and propagated it through the monotonous chants of press, television, and radio. On a twelve-day drive from Hanoi to Saigon, with many stops to meet local officials, it was not only the ideas that were predictably unvaried from town to town but, more disconcertingly, also the words in which they were couched. In a nation so rich in strongly individual men and women, so varied in the way in which great distances between regions shape regional character, it was disappointing and somehow unnatural to discover so little difference in the way in which intelligent people from the north, center, and south described the state of their nation, and the dreary sameness of their vocabulary.

There is a remarkable similarity about the senior functionaries of the system, clearly the result of a process of human homogenization that has virtually erased distinctive personalities in that caste. At the level of provincial leadership, as well as with top officials in the big cities like Hanoi, Saigon, Da Nang, or Haiphong, I found myself facing men — no women, despite the dynamic role in public life that women have played throughout Vietnam's history — well past the prime of their years, who were either natives of the former North Vietnam or southerners who in 1954, when the country was divided, were part of the comparative trickle of about 100,000 who chose — or were chosen — to go north from the south (while at least 800,000 went the opposite way) and became part of the military or political organization of North Vietnam. Those who occupy these powerful positions, not subject to the critical eye of an opposition or a citizenry accustomed to civil rights, have rarely had the training and experience for the complex task of revolutionizing the centralized, state-owned economy. They owe their dominant roles to merit in war two decades ago and loyalty to the party.

Surely not all are mere party hacks, despite the deadening sameness of their discourse on any issue, but all know that their positions depend on the survival, as intact as they can keep it, of the system that put them there. Their interest lies in the preservation of the status quo, and the result is widespread passive resistance and foot-dragging. And since even at the top the leaders' hearts are not quite in the liberalization that circumstances have forced on them, change comes so haltingly that many well-trained younger officials, academics, and social scientists fear that it will get permanently mired in a morass of ill will and bad faith motivated by the massive preservation of personal interests.

An academic of the middle generation overcame his well-founded timidity in the presence of a minor official accompanying me to our meeting to speak frankly, but, as he said with a wink, only because we shared a language that he hoped the official, dispensed from interpreting duty, didn't understand.

"So much is outdated in official thinking," he said, shedding his reserve as he spoke.

The party retains all of its Marxist and Leninist doctrine, the teaching of capitalist exploitation, Marx's theory of surplus value, etc. Above all, the leadership retains its cold-war posture. Foreigners are coming here because they think this is a country that can offer profits on investment; they don't come bearing arms. But the leadership's receptiveness to them is zero point zero. Some people here still think that Vietnam is the navel, the center of the world, the center of subversive activities, all activated by the CIA. And the leaders have, because of their concept of the class struggle and ideological discrimination, developed no national reconciliation, no concept of development, no unity of all forces in Vietnam.

They don't permit democratic discussion. At this most hopeful point in Vietnamese history, the leadership clings to conservative, restrictive, and administrative regulatory measures. Our reform is in great difficulty as a consequence. Local authorities have every intention of keeping reform stalled in this twilight phase. Why? Things are different today from 1986, when reform was initiated. Then those in power were in danger. They knew that if they didn't reform, the country would collapse. They had to find strength in our own force. Then the local authorities urged reform, the development of the private sector, a market economy, opening to the world, greater foreign trade. Today those in power are the greatest beneficiaries of reform. This is not a state of laws; there are no democratic controls. They can dispose of everything — land, resources, the smuggling trade. All are involved, all the authorities, including the army and the police. They can speculate on real estate. It is corrupt government employees who support this system.

Where will the model for further progress come from? How can the party reform itself while retaining its claim to be the leading power? How can new concepts be created? To lead a country one must have a theoretical concept. In the middle range there is an intelligent and capable group of people who know the world, who can take on this challenge. But they are not allowed to. One's heart bleeds.

The closing remark was no mere figure of speech; it vibrated with angry frustration. The academic delivered his passionate plaint in deliberate, carefully chosen language, with only an occasional precautionary glance at the idle official, who assured me afterward that he had not understood a word but hoped the meeting had been useful. But his critical main themes — the party's determination not to let economic liberalization weaken its stranglehold on independent thought and intellectual initiative, and its fear of the corrupting effect of liberalization — were forcefully restated in a major pronouncement by General Secretary Do Muoi's 1994 policy declaration to the Central Committee.

The document, a thirty-eight-page state-of-the-nation message delivered to the leadership's main sounding board, reflected above all the party's anxiety over the unsettling potential inherent in loosening the reins in any field and opening their once-isolated country to influences from the non-Communist world. It echoed similar pronouncements by the Chinese leadership and adopted for Vietnamese use a Chinese ideological bugaboo, "peaceful evolution," as a principal danger to be guarded against. (A number of Chinese ideological texts devoted to the struggle against this menace have been published in Vietnamese translation.) Far from being the desirable development the words suggest, "peaceful evolution" is a catchphrase for what the party fears the most: that the foreign influences to which it had to open the door from economic necessity will peacefully evolve toward a dilution of its total power. "We will carry out an all-people, comprehensive and long-lasting struggle to foil all schemes and acts of 'peaceful evolution,' sedition and subversion," Do Muoi announced, according to the official translation into the unidiomatic English of a Soviet language institute, which trained the regime's translators.

The speech, a summation of themes that since the collapse of the Soviet Union have persistently recurred in statements and articles from all levels of leadership, was studded with dire warnings based on real or simulated fear of the outside world and with references to unspecified hostile acts. It reflected what the academic described as the party's continuing "cold-war posture." Without troubling to cite an example, Do Muoi declared: "Hostile elements have carried out strenuous activities against our people's work of national construction and defense. Once more, our revolutionary cause undergoes acute challenges."

Despite the evident absence of opposition, the leader evoked a need to restore "order and discipline within the Party." He seemed to be praising the work of secret-police surveillance when he said that the party had "obtained better results in getting information about activities of hostile elements and combating them efficiently." But, said the general secretary, "The leadership quality and work efficiency of many Party committees are still poor and, in some places, deviate from the Party lines." He accused party "cadres and members and the people" of not being vigilant and of failing to recognize the dangers: "Profound perceptions are yet to be formed on the schemes and activities of sabotage by hostile forces in an attempt to abolish the Party and the socialist regime in our country."

Too much democracy, Do Muoi warned — evoking what does not seem a present danger — would be a bad thing. "We should establish social order and discipline, oppose all manifestations of extremism in democracy," he said. "We must use dictatorship against all elements acting against the Motherland and encroaching upon the interests of the people."

Turning to a real problem, the general secretary said, "Corruption and smuggling keep developing seriously, causing high indignation among the people and greatly eroding their confidence in the Party and the State." It could not have been said more forthrightly by a more objective observer than the general secretary.

Corruption and smuggling are not the only consequences of economic relaxation that are eroding the image of party and state. The more or less legitimate business activities of party and state bodies do their share. Since it was these bodies that "owned" everything before *doi moi*, it is they who have become its principal beneficiaries. There are practically no private savings to be turned into investment; thus the breaking up of large state enterprises has not meant privatization. Local officials have "privatized" enterprises that were under their control as though they owned them. The military, who occupy much real estate, are renting it out for their own benefit. The Vietnamese navy has signed joint-venture contracts with foreign tourism investors to develop resorts on some of the finest beaches, which it "owns." The military are active also in the construction business and renting "their" large fleet of trucks for business ventures. "The state apparatus will stay for a long time," the resident director of a French bank said. "Just about all the enterprises are run by ministries. The big state enterprises have been divided up, not among the public but among state organisms."

And because it is officials who conduct the negotiations with foreign businessmen and investors, it is they who reap the benefit of the goodwill gestures that are not uncommon to lubricate deals. It is often their relatives who are hired for the highly desirable jobs with foreign or joint-venture offices; it is their sons and daughters who receive the foreign scholarships or training courses that most Vietnamese dream of for their children. The party, which owns many houses confiscated from their owners in the major cities, converts them into small hotels. "Everyone has dollar signs floating before his eyes," a British banker said of the officials with whom he negotiates.

"This is a feudal system," a French banker of long experience said. "The leadership is collegial, and every one has a separate regional power base. In their region they do what they want.

You go to get a license to do business in Hanoi, but if the province where you want to set up doesn't want it, it won't work."

The symptoms look like those of the terminal illness of Communist rule in those countries of eastern and central Europe that were engaged on a hesitant course of reform to revitalize their creaking economies. But Communist rule came crashing down not because of the progress of reform but because of the "Gorbachev factor," the Soviet leader's withdrawal of the Russian protective hand over those who held power. They held their power because they exercised it in the interest of the Soviet Union's strategic posture rather than the well-being of their own countries. As the Soviet role in their countries diminished, for the first time the Communist rulers in Warsaw, Budapest, and Prague stood alone, facing nations that had tolerated them grudgingly, bowing to the reality of Soviet might. In the waning days of the 1980s, the handful of dissidents who had kept the spirit of independence and freedom flickering in what Lennart Meri, a dissident who became president of his nation, Estonia, called "the cosmic darkness," found that their voices, always heard but rarely followed, were stronger than those of the faltering dictators. They did not bring down Communist rule, but they had kept alive a possibility of change, whose time had come.

The "Gorbachev factor" operated in Vietnam as well, but only so far as to impose a need for economic reform. The Vietnamese Communists have a legitimacy far greater than that of the Soviet Union's European dependencies. Their power does not derive from foreign backing; they installed themselves as the leaders of Vietnam in three decades of armed struggle. And they rule over a country with a great tradition of resistance against foreign domination but none of internal opposition. Confucianism has instilled acceptance of a hierarchical order that provides stability and order. The regime may not be loved, but it is not opposed, because few Vietnamese believe that those not of the mandarin class have a role to play in affairs of state. Dissidence barely exists. Change will come as it must, because those who rule are a handful of old men, but it is likely to be shaped by the party mandarins who enjoyed the old men's favor.

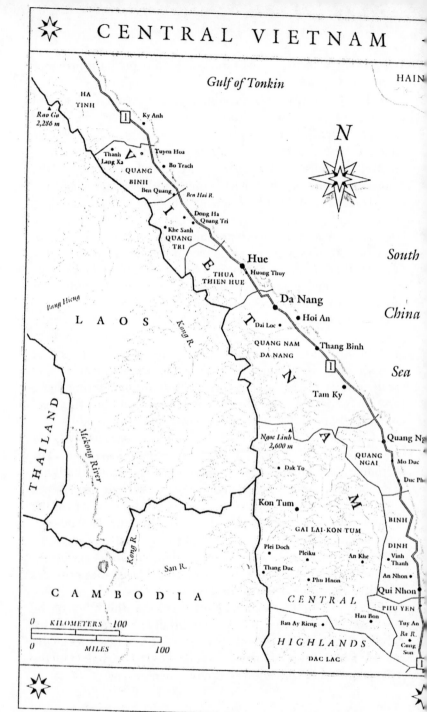

CENTRAL VIETNAM

Gulf of Tonkin

HAIN

N

South

China

Sea

LAOS

THAILAND

CAMBODIA

Mekong River

HA TINH

Rao Co 2,286 m

Ky Anh

Thanh Lang Xa

Tuyen Hoa

Bo Trach

QUANG BINH

Ben Quang

Ben Hai R.

Dong Ha

Quang Tri

Khe Sanh

QUANG TRI

THUA THIEN HUE

Hue

Huong Thuy

Da Nang

Hoi An

Dai Loc

QUANG NAM DA NANG

Thang Binh

Tam Ky

Rang Hieng

Kong R.

Ngoc Linh 2,600 m

Dak To

Kon Tum

GAI LAI-KON TUM

Plei Doch

Pleiku

An Khe

Thang Duc

Phu Hnon

San R.

Kong R.

Quang Ng

QUANG NGAI

Mo Duc

Duc Ph

BINH DINH

Vinh Thanh

An Nhon

Qui Nhon

PHU YEN

CENTRAL

Hau Bon

Ban Ay Rieng

HIGHLANDS

DAC LAC

Tuy An

Ba R.

Cung Son

KILOMETERS 100

MILES 100

0

0

6

Two Cities, One Nation

Twenty years after its humiliating defeat, Saigon looks and feels much as it did before. The southern metropolis has cast off the dour sackcloth the victor forced it to wear. That it has been able to do so with such aplomb is not really surprising. The hair shirt never fit.

Not that Saigon ever had all the glamour that its romantic French designation "Pearl of the Orient" conjures up; the great majority of its Vietnamese and Chinese citizens worked far too hard at far too stingy wages to make the city a romantic idyll for most of its people. Sentimental postcolonial hype has focused on the lives of the privileged elites — the colonialists, other foreigners, the Vietnamese aristocracy, and the top of the Chinese and Vietnamese business classes. Not insignificant in numbers, but not much in the total of about 250,000 inhabitants in the 1930s. The big war, with American participation, removed whatever residual glamour might have survived France's exit. By 1975, with the steady inflow of refugees from the war zones and the magnet of job opportunities, the population had grown in malignant prolixity to probably around three million. The paddy land around the city had turned into endless shantytowns, and even the lovely, well-laid-out old French quarter had lost most of its Europe-in-Asia charm. Barbed wire and other unsightly defenses ringed villas and government buildings; many of the trees that lined the streets had fallen victim either to the ax to ease the passage of the bulky American vehicles of war or to asphyxiation from their exhaust fumes. The victims of wars and hangers-on of armies, particularly those of rich nations in poor countries, had aggressively taken over the sidewalks. Rotting garbage filled gutters and blocked sewers, and rats no longer shunned daylight. The pearl had lost any pretense of luster.

But even if it lacked glamour, Saigon vibrated with energy. It was Vietnam's principal economic center. Its people hustled too fast, yelled too loud, insulted too readily, laughed and jeered too much; the city lived at full tilt. Commerce was its main reason for being, and it threw itself into it with a raucous energy exhausting to behold, particularly under its year-round humid tropical heat. The Central Market and the streets surrounding it were a beehive of getters and spenders, ringing with the shouts of offering and the rude but friendly jibes bandied among the competing traders. The vulgarity of the brash raillery among the fishwives, speaking in the most slovenly tones and accents of the south, as far a cry as possible from the more classic, elegant Vietnamese spoken in the north, still brings blushes to the cheeks of Saigon women in foreign exile, long after the insults have blended into a many-stranded tapestry of nostalgic memory, of fond home-thoughts from abroad. Saigon has drawn life and liveliness also from being a port, not on the sea but linked to it by the navigable Saigon River, and beyond it to a much larger world. Above all, the city reflected the general character of the South Vietnamese — unrestrained to the point of undiscipline in the eyes of others, dedicated to commercial gain but not at the expense of its single-minded pursuit, ready to laugh or to cry, quick to flare in anger and almost as quick to forgive and forget, easy of approach and little given to pretense.

Saigon is modern, as cities go. It was not occupied in the course of the steady Vietnamese expansion southward until 1674, and until the eighteenth century it was still a small settlement of fishermen, known by its Cambodian name of Prey Nokor.

How different is Hanoi! It has been settled since at least the seventh century, when Chinese invaders of the Sui dynasty established an administrative capital nearby and called it Tong

Binh. In 1010 King Ly Thai Tho was traveling on the Red River from his capital, Hoa Lu, seventy miles to the south, when, approaching the town then known as Dai La, he saw rising from a lake and soaring high into the sky a great golden dragon. Unlike the dragon in Western mythology, a fear-inspiring monster to be slain by heroic knights liberating fair damsels, the dragon in Asia is a symbol of might and majesty and is often linked to royalty. The king, transfixed, followed the golden dragon's flight with his eyes until it disappeared in the heavens and decided without hesitation that he had been sent an auspicious omen from above. He moved his capital to the site from which the dragon had risen and called the city Thang Long, "Ascending Dragon." It did not become known as Hanoi, meaning "this side of the river," until the capital was moved to Hue at the beginning of the nineteenth century.

Although greatly transformed under French rule when Tonkin, the northern third of colonized Vietnam, became a protectorate in 1883, Hanoi is as distinctly Vietnamese as Saigon is cosmopolitan. The French modernization turned the city into an unusually harmonious blending of surviving ancient pagodas (although many were sacrificed to make room for buildings the French considered more important), handsome seats of colonial power, elegant French residences, and large new commercial and residential quarters in an attractive local architecture, more solidly and painstakingly built than is common in the region. The total of these ingredients is more than the sum of its parts; the mix has turned into something specifically Vietnamese. Saigon invites comparison with other Southeast Asian metropolises; Hanoi with none.

No doubt the long years of war and enduring poverty have prevented "developers" from doing their worst in the heart of the city. North Vietnam has had other priorities than refurbishing its capital. The few representational structures built since independence — Parliament, City Hall, Ho Chi Minh's tomb — make one thankful that they are so few. However much Vietnam has to be grateful for to the Soviet Union, this debt does not include the Soviet influence on modern Vietnamese architecture.

(Similar horrors have been inflicted, no doubt with the best Soviet intentions, on traditional dancing. Acting on a conviction that every Communist country requires a national troupe of folk dancers, Soviet instructors trained any number of lithe and graceful young Vietnamese, Laotians, and Cambodians to don Cossack-like boots and invented "traditional" costumes, stamp the ground, and clap their hands to the rhythms of synthetic "folk" music, in rollicking, thoroughly inauthentic dances celebrating the rice harvest or similar paeans in praise of labor.)

Fortunately, nothing seems to have been added to or subtracted from the most original part of the old Hanoi, a wonderfully lively quarter off the Lake of the Restored Sword in the center of the city, in which every street of two- or three-story narrow traditional shop houses bears the name of the goods that were sold or manufactured there in the past. Reminiscent of the cohesion of the members of medieval guilds that helped to shape cities in Europe, the section recalls Hanoi's village origins. Craftsmen or traders in a particular commodity from one village reconstituted their old communities in one street when they moved to the capital, sometimes bringing with them even their village shrines. Surprisingly, some of the streets still live up to their names, but most now offer a variety of wares. It adds something to the flavor of the dish to taste a bowl of noodles on Pho Hang Bun, "street of the thin rice noodles."

Hanoi has retained much of its old cityscape. Having until recently lacked the affluence of private cars, it is a city whose many trees are far healthier than those of Saigon. But the lack of means has prevented Hanoi from maintaining most of its houses and streets in livable condition. Except for the buildings in which a state represents its grandeur, the capital of Vietnam is a shabby and run-down city. Most of the more than three million inhabitants of the city proper and its extensive immediate surroundings live in tiny, mainly one-room compartments of crumbling, mildew-eaten old buildings or in somewhat more spacious apartments in jerry-built, rapidly decaying newer houses. A distinguished academic, for instance, lives in the center of town, two flights up a dark and dank stairwell. The single room that he shares with his wife has only minimal furniture, so as to leave room for cooking, washing, the clothesline, and the family vehicle, a bicycle. Daylight barely penetrates through the two windows, facing out onto the narrow space that separates the house from its neighbor. The couple share a toilet with many other tenants. Hanoi's streets and sidewalks are rutted and potholed; one has to fix one's eyes firmly to the ground to keep from tripping or stumbling into uncovered sewers.

The differences in brick and stone that distinguish Hanoi from Saigon subsist, but since the introduction of the new economic policy both cities have been turned into places in transition. Saigon is taking the changes in its stride; they are a reversal leading the city back to familiar ground and old ways. But the city has grown even bigger since 1975; the present population is estimated at 4.5 million. The streets have exploded once again into frantic commercialism. The return to private agriculture and pricing determined largely by supply and demand have raised production and put money back into the pockets of farmers and shopkeepers and commodities back into the commercial circuits. The chronic food shortages of the earlier years no longer plague the city. Money, in the form of gold and dollars, that went into hiding in 1975 has come back into circulation. The masses of overseas Vietnamese, obeying the Confucian rules of responsibility toward the family, are pouring in remittances at a rate that has been estimated at six hundred million dollars a year. And as restrictions on tourism have been lifted, the sisters from California or nephews from Paris are bringing in with them large amounts of cash not only to help their relatives to survive but also to give them a start in founding small businesses.

Probably the largest wellspring of the revival of trade in Saigon has been an inflow of investments by Chinese from Taiwan and overseas Chinese from all over Southeast Asia — Singapore and Malaysia in the lead — through their family connections in Cholon, Saigon's revitalized Chinatown, which no longer shows the deadening effect of the expulsion of many ethnic Chinese in the late 1970s. The overseas Chinese continue throughout Asia to form the most cohesive and efficient network of fruitful business connections, the locomotive of the regional economies. The bulk of the investment fueling the economic revival of Saigon is in trade and services, not in labor-intensive manufacturing, much as in the pre-Communist past. This makes for highly visible business activity but creates little employment, so it may give a deceptively positive picture of economic well-being. So does the proliferation of advertising displays for Japanese and Western goods, which now outnumber the posters exhorting the Saigonese to do many high-minded things to make their city worthy of the name of Ho Chi Minh, clamped on it by the victors in 1975. Great progress has been made in linking Vietnam to the world by a well-functioning international telephone and fax network.

But the social ills that go with a superficial and uneven economic upswing are equally visible. *Doi moi* has opened a huge economic gap between on one hand the small class of the newly rich and a larger one of people earning a decent living for the first time since the war, and on the other the great majority, who remain poor in an economy of rising prices. Under-employed day laborers constitute perhaps the largest group in Saigon's labor force, and long-term and medium-term unemployment, officially estimated at 300,000, is doubtless much higher. It is family cohesion rather than any social welfare programs in the socialist state that keeps the masses of jobless and their families afloat. The economic gulf is widened by a large inflow of foreign businessmen, mainly from Southeast Asia, shopping for the opportunities presented by a late starter in a booming region. That this late starter offers a domestic market of seventy-three million eager would-be consumers makes Vietnam's attraction to such shoppers even more tempting; it is the most populous nation in continental Southeast Asia and second only to Indonesia in the region.

So Saigon today has recovered, for better or worse, its old air. The street scene is as varied and rich in color as it ever was, and women have rediscovered style, makeup, and the ministrations of beauty parlors. Private cars are back, and so are the death-defying and earsplitting hordes of men and women on motorcycles and scooters. Traffic is at least as chaotic as it was in the earlier days, and Communist rigor has not prevailed against the penchant of the Saigonese to break the social contract for mutual safety symbolized by traffic lights or one-way street signs. The young have revived the grimly unromantic pre-1975 Sunday-evening mating ritual, in which endless swarms of boys drive their girlfriends on their two-wheelers, at maximum speed and noise levels, from the square around the Roman Catholic cathedral down General Uprising Street to the riverfront and back up the parallel one-way streets. Then on for one, two, or three more rounds, until a couple tires of the noisy cavalcade. Then they may stop for the rest of the evening in the park between the cathedral and the former Presidential Palace, lean the cycle against a tree and themselves against the cycle, and exchange confidences or act out within the strict limits imposed by conservative social mores the sentiments that the joyride may have inspired.

In this period of transition from communism to the next stage of Vietnam's travail, interregnum scenes full of paradox occur. I spent a Sunday morning with an old friend of pre-1975 days, then a prominent pro-peace and persecuted politician. Now a reputable private entrepreneur, he has built a tennis court on his factory grounds, and a good-sized swimming pool was under construction. His guests for tennis, drinks, and lunch included the swimming-pool builder from France, another former politician released after many years of "reeducation," two resident French businessmen full of tales of woe about the red tape and corruption that make doing business in Vietnam arduous, and a former Saigon businessman and professional tennis coach, recently returned from America and now doing business in his old country. He was sternly coaching his thoroughly Americanized preteen daughter, who seemed headed toward a rich future among the next crop of tennis child prodigies.

Foreigners are no longer assailed by young and old beggars, hawkers, or prostitutes with rudely pointing fingers and brash shouts of "lien xo, lien xo!" — "Soviet! Soviet!" — many of them have reverted to the "hey Joe!" of the American days. In fact, the most effective way of shaking the more persistent beggars is to reply "lien xo," which is taken as a pauper's oath. Sadly, as in the old days, many of the beggars still gesticulate with their stumps or wooden limbs to extract sympathy and contributions, and many of them bed down for the night on the sidewalks on which they ply their calling, as do hordes of street children. Bars are flourishing again in the same parts of town where in the past American soldiers and civilians found easy company. To emphasize the sense of resumed continuity, some have chosen sardonic names like B 4 75 or Apocalypse Now, with a martial decor recalling the war movie that inspired the latter name.

Vice today is casting its net wider than in the past. Prostitutes are no longer only women from the poorer districts of the city or the countryside. Educated call girls have become part of the scene. An American teacher of English recognized one of her better students peddling herself on the street. Shocked, she told her school's director what she had seen. His cynical reply deepened her shock: "I'm surprised she is working on the street. With the good English that she speaks, she could be earning a lot more money doing it in a hotel."

The problem, whose existence used to be puritanically denied, is officially recognized now that some realism has entered into the way the authorities view Vietnamese society. Trinh Van Le, a director in the Ministry of Labor, Invalids and Social Affairs, said: "We had largely eliminated this problem before *doi moi*. We used to assume that the war and the puppet regime were the main causes of prostitution. After the liberation of Saigon, we thought we had cured the problem. We brought the number of prostitutes in Saigon down to three, maybe only two, digits. Now there are tens of thousands in Saigon, and even in Hanoi there are now thousands where there used to be tens, at the most hundreds. And they exist even in the provinces." (I refrained from saying, "You're telling me." I had spent a sleepless night in the desolate, utterly provincial town of Quang Ngai in the center of the country, fending off a concentrated, long-lasting siege by women who banged on the door of my room in the sordid hovel that is Quang Ngai's best hotel, tried to enter through the transom, and managed even the ultimate achievement: making the mute telephone ring and speak, all for the sake of proposing their services.) The official cited what he considered the principal causes. "There is a small number of women who want the high life that has now become possible. More turn to prostitution because of the hardships of life, unemployment, the need for money to pay for medical treatment for their families. There is also an ignorant perception of what a market economy is. Some believe anything is now allowed to earn money. And there is an inadequate legal system. The law punishes only brothel keepers or procurers, not the women." Nguyen Son, a spokesman for Saigon's City Hall, was cynical. "Our girls sell themselves cheaply," he said. "They are pretty, and they are cheaper than those of Bangkok or Hong Kong. With the coming of a market economy, naturally social injustices are reborn. As a Communist, I am very pained by this problem. The prostitutes violate the traditions of Vietnam."

Truong My Hoa,* who as a member of the Communist party secretariat and president of the Vietnamese Women's Organization is probably the highest-ranking woman in the country, said that a survey by her organization had indicated that there were as many as eighty thousand prostitutes in the country. "There is a looser morality now," she said. "We don't think we have a perfect society. The government has relaxed its tight controls over national life. Our economic standards are very low; we cannot satisfy all the needs of the people. Some women cannot find work."

What is a return to the norm in Saigon, however negative some of its symptoms, is new to Hanoi, a city that has always reflected the more traditionalist character of the North Vietnamese. A softening of its hard ways had been going on gradually even before *doi moi*. Time had caused a significant shift. In the early years following the Communist victory, it was Hanoi that had imposed its ways on Saigon and made the conquered city resemble its conqueror's capital. But in the 1980s, with the waning of the victors' will to punish the losers for having for so many years enjoyed an easier life than they, a natural kind of osmosis was at work. The comforts and pleasures of the more relaxed city, its more modern ways, and its greater openness to what is happening outside Vietnam had made inroads among northerners, particularly the young. The first "video cafés" opened in Hanoi, T-shirts and jeans became the preferred dress, and Western popular music conquered one of the last remaining bastions of commendable resistance to the worldwide twang of the electric guitar. English rather than Russian became the foreign language that the young and less young wanted to study.

As Hanoi had been the imposed model for Saigon, Saigon became the model of choice for many in Hanoi. The Western visitors who used to admire the Spartan austerity of Hanoi and its people's discipline, praising them as the opposite of what they discovered in Saigon, began to see that these qualities were not necessarily the people's choice. Southerners were asking sarcastically whether the south was not after all emerging as the winner in what the American sponsor used to call "the battle for the hearts and minds of the Vietnamese."

Doi moi gave official blessing to the greening of Hanoi. Independent trade, in newly opened shops or sidewalk stands, began to flourish. The government, in its determination to make the world recognize that there is only one capital of the Socialist Republic of Vietnam, requires all foreign business and banking offices to base themselves in Hanoi before opening branch offices in Saigon, where business is done. As a result, a sizable moneyed foreign community has established itself in the city. In the past it was mainly Communist diplomats and technical-aid advisers, paid poorly and in currencies that could not be exchanged for moneys of universal acceptance, who represented the world at large in Vietnam's capital. To accommodate the new flow of foreigners, many buildings have been being converted into small hotels and guesthouses. Since most of them had been confiscated by the government either from the French or members of the "exploiting class," it is party and government officials who have the inside track in turning them into profit-making enterprises. This has given rise to a general suspicion, probably well founded, that it is they who have become the new exploiters.

Restaurants, pizza parlors, and piano bars are opening their doors in a city that was woefully short of evening entertainment of any kind. Because they are an innovation, these have an innocent charm that is quite absent in brassy Saigon. The young waiters and waitresses may lack all professional skill, as do, unfortunately, many cooks, but they confess their failings with disarming naïveté and engagingly profit from the opportunity to practice their beginners' English with their customers, who are in their great majority foreigners. In the present stage of their venture into the free market, the people of Hanoi have not yet acquired the aggressiveness or refusal to take no for an answer that can make a walk through downtown Saigon trying. Shoeshine boys keep smiling through refusals of their services and try again with equal timidity the next time the foreigner passes their way. And when I allowed one to go to work on my shoes on one of Hanoi's busiest corners, he was soon joined by a friend, who helped, while assuring me that there would be no extra charge. A woman selling fruit at the same corner brought her stool and insisted that the foreigner sit during the operation. Soon a crowd gathered to observe what is still a new spectacle. The onlookers commented on the quality of the work, urged the boys to put more muscle into their efforts, and scolded them severely when at the completion of a brilliant shoeshine they requested a modest sum. They urged the customer to pay only half and remonstrated with him when he paid what was asked.

The social ills that have reappeared in Saigon are no longer absent in what used to be the puritan, virtually crime-free north. The shock of this unfortunate fact of life in a less-regimented society to party functionaries causes many of them to voice thinly veiled doubts over *doi moi*. "Moral standards are declining," said Nguyen Ba Du, who is deputy chairman of the People's Committee of the port city of Haiphong, the equivalent of assistant mayor. "There is robbery, thieving, murder, other violence, prostitution, and black culture." By that dark phrase, Du meant specifically the coming to Haiphong of pornography and the business of sex, but his strictures extended to most of the innovations that slipped in with *doi moi*. "We opened the window for some fresh air, but others are also taking advantage of the opening. Our girls are tempted; they want to try something new," he said of the oldest profession, which clearly has as long a past in Haiphong as in any other major port city. "They imitate the lifestyles of other countries. It affects girls rich and poor, unemployed or working. Our control was better in the past; we confined the seamen to their ships. Now the crews and all those businessmen are all over the hotels. There are private hotels and restaurants now. We cannot supervise them as we did before. The police has less power; we respect human rights. The young people are absorbing new things like freedom, dancing, singing, films, videos, all kinds of new things." The deputy chairman left no doubt that he found life preferable before *doi moi*.

Nghiem Xuan Tue of the Ministry of Labor, a man of rigid dogmatism, was predictably firm in voicing dutiful support of the party's policies, whether he liked their results or not. After he had discussed the negative consequences of *doi moi*, I asked whether he would have preferred that the liberalization had not taken place. "I cannot say whether I like it or dislike it," he replied. "Vietnam is now following an open policy, and we all support it. *Doi moi* definitely will continue, despite the high social cost."

Hanoi remains a decorous place. But today it is capable of providing small shocks to the unsuspecting that not long ago were unimaginable in its prim setting. The Lake of the Restored Sword — named for a legend that a magic sword, with whose help Emperor Le Loi freed Vietnam from Chinese rule in 1428, was one day snatched from the emperor's hand or from its sheath in its place of hiding, it depends on the version, by a large tortoise and carried back to the bottom of the lake — is a romantic, if thoroughly dirty, attraction in the center of Hanoi, a place for strollers and lovers by day and by night. It is regrettable that nowadays after dark it has also become a hunting ground for prostitutes. So I was not surprised to be approached one evening in 1994. But when the lisping lady on second look turned out to be a transvestite, a further advance in Hanoi's aping of Saigon, I felt for the first time a twinge of sympathy for Tue's lack of enthusiasm for *doi moi*.

☀ SOUTHERN VIETNAM

LAOS

THAILAND

Mekong River

Kong R.

San R.

QUANG NAM
DA NANG

*Ngoc Linh
2,000 m*

Qu

QUANG
NGAI

• Dak To

Kon Tum
•

GAI LAI-KON TUM

BINH

Vinh
Thanh

Plei Doch •   • Pleiku   An Khe •

DINH

• Thang Duc

C A M B O D I A

Son R.

Tonle Sap

*CENTRAL
HIGHLANDS*

PI
Tuy

Y I

Tuy

• Phu Nhon

Hau Bon •   *Ba R.*

Ban Ay Rieng
Ban Don
Ban Me Thuot
•

Cung
Son

Buon
Mrong •

Nha
Trang

Kampong Cham •

Mekong River

Duc Lap •
Chu Yang Sin 2442 m •

DAC LAC

Dien
Khanh •
KHANH
HOA

Phnom Penh ●

• Kien Duc
• Gia Nghia

Dalat
•

Phu Hoi •
Di Linh •

SONG BE

Dong River

LAM DONG

Du Long

Phan Rang

TAY

V I E T N A M

Tay Ninh •

NINH

Bien
Hoa
•

DONG NAI

B'nom M'hai 1642 m •
• Xa Vo Dat
THUAN
HAI

Chau Doc •

LONG AN

①

Ho Chi Minh City
•

Phan Thiet

AN
GIANG

DONG THAP

Mekong R.

Tan An •

Go Cong •

HO CHI MINH

Long Xuyen •

Rach Gia •

TIEN
GIANG

My Tho
•

Vung Tau

*Phu Quoc
Island*

Kien Thanh •

Can Tho •

Vinh Long •
BEN TRE

Ben Tre •

KIEN GIANG

Tra Cu •   • Tra Vinh

Ap Luc •

Soc Trang •

CUU LONG

N

*Gulf
of Thailand*

Tho Binh •   • Ca Mau

Bac Lieu •

HAU GIANG

Mekong Delta

MINH HAI

South China Sea

0 ___ KILOMETERS 100

0 ___ MILES

☀

7

The Legend of the Lord
and the Queen

Four thousand years ago Lord Lac Long Quan, offspring of a long line of dragons, drove out an invading army from the north. He captured and took as his spouse Queen Au Co, an ethereal being, a fairy from the realm of spirits and the wife of the monarch of the invaders. She bore him one hundred sons, but one day Lac Long Quan said: "We are incompatible. I am Lord of the Waters and belong to the race of dragons. You are a Fairy, born from Fire. We must separate. But if need arises, we shall join forces."

They went their separate ways. Lac Long Quan, followed by fifty of the sons, headed eastward toward the seacoast and settled the fertile plains; Queen Au Co led the other fifty sons westward into the mountains. The dragon installed one of his sons on the throne of the kingdom of the plains, called Van Lang. He was the first in a dynasty, the Hung, which counted eighteen hereditary monarchs.

The eighteenth king had a beautiful daughter. Two princes sought her hand: Son Tinh, the Spirit of the Mountains, and Thuy Tinh, the Spirit of the Waters. The king promised to give the princess in marriage to the prince who would be first to lay wedding presents at his feet. Son Tinh did and carried his bride off to the mountains. Furious, Thuy Tinh sent the waters to assail the mountains. The Spirit of the Mountains drove them back. And every year, at the same season, the assault begins anew, the spirits give battle, and year after year the waters are made to recede.

This is the legend of the birth of Vietnam, in the version retold by Nguyen Khac Vien in his officially sponsored history of Vietnam. (Since then Dr. Vien, a physician and Communist party member and propagandist to the outside world, has on several occasions demanded democratic reforms and is therefore unlikely to be allowed further official publications.) Like all legends of the birth of nations in times too distant to have left substantial archeological traces, it exists in many variants. But these variants do not differ in essence.

The scene of the legendary birth of a nation is the northernmost part of today's Vietnam, well above the course of the Ben Hai River, which flows from the mountains to the South China Sea and served as the embattled border that from 1954 until 1975 divided the country into hostile halves, until the northern victory healed the rift.

As the legend tells it, the inhabitants of Vietnam spring from varied ethnic roots. The Lac Viet, the sons who followed their father, are the people of the plains, today's ethnic Vietnamese, their country's dominant tribe. The mother's children, called the Au Viet, are the forebears of the varied and distinct mountain tribes, who to this day must fight off the predators from the plain, who have never ceased making inroads into their lands. "The Americans bomb us, the Communists take away our sons, and the government steals our lands," a mountain tribeswoman said in a far-off village in South Vietnam near the Cambodian border during the war. As she spoke, she slowly and rhythmically swayed back and forth to rock the baby that she carried in a broad sling around her waist. And every year in the season of the monsoon, the floodwaters of the rivers of the plain threaten the crops and homes of this rice-growing nation and cruelly test its people's endurance in the face of the ever-recurring menace and its resilience in the unending battle for life.

Vietnam emerges from the land of legend into recorded history at the end of the third century before the current era, in the year 208. Significantly, this first appearance was chronicled by a Chinese scribe and records a Chinese conquest. Trieu Da, a Chinese general, led an invasion from the north and, having conquered the kingdom of Au Lac, betrayed his emperor and established himself as emperor in his own right of a realm that he called Nam Viet, the Viet people of the south. People of the same ethnic roots lived to the north, in today's southern China.

Independence did not last. In the next century the powerful Han dynasty unified China, recaptured the secessionist land, and incorporated it as the province of Giao Chi. For nearly two thousand years to follow, until the eighteenth century brought invaders from more distant lands, this land's history is that of a constant struggle against the giant to the north. It ebbs and flows, with massive invasions and centuries of occupation, rebellions that succeed briefly, only to be cruelly put down, and periods when the Chinese emperors, preoccupied with struggles to preserve the core of their realm, let its border marches be ruled by indigenous monarchs or warlords.

The first and most celebrated of the rebellions exploded in the year 40. Two daughters of a military officer named Trung, Trung Trac and Trung Nhi, led a rising in their region northwest of today's Hanoi. It spread rapidly to most of the national territory. Many of the local insurgent leaders were also women. Trac was acclaimed as queen and quickly dismantled the Chinese structure of rule, beginning with the system of taxation. It took the dispatch of an army commanded by the Han emperor's most trusted general, Ma Yuan, to quell the rebellion two years after it erupted. The Trung sisters, according to Chinese annals, were captured and executed. But Vietnamese legend has it that the heroic pair chose death at their own hands. To this day, the sisters who defied China remain the most honored national heroes or heroines. Even during the war between north and south, when the two Vietnams agreed on nothing, both Hanoi and Saigon, and all other towns on either side, named a principal street Hai Ba Trung, "two Trung sisters."

In 248 it was another woman, Lady Trieu, who led a rising. "I want to ride the great winds, strike the sharks on the high seas, drive out the invaders, reconquer the nation, burst the bonds of slavery, and never bow to become anyone's concubine," she said, according to Nguyen Khac Vien's translation into French. She rode into battle at the head of her army, clad in golden armor and mounted on an elephant. Legend has made her a giant of wondrous beauty, with breasts so ample that she had to swing them out of the way over her shoulders as she faced the foe, a voice as mighty as the largest of temple gongs, capable of eating a mountain of rice every day and marching toward the enemy at a pace of five hundred *li*, about two hundred miles, a day. Lady Trieu, as the legend tells it, was not defeated by Chinese might but by treason in her ranks. A turncoat disclosed to the opposing general that she abhorred all that was dirty and vile. The general ordered his men to shed their clothes and attack her forces naked, shouting obscenities at the top of their voices. Her troops fled in horror and fright, and Lady Trieu chose death by plunging into a river. And ever since, the Vietnamese endow themselves with a claim of being far cleaner, physically and morally, than their mightier neighbor.

Although in 679, under the Tang dynasty, the country was officially named An Nam, "pacified south," insurrections marked the centuries. Always the great power to the north clenched its fist and struck down the vassals who took so much of China's culture but refused to surrender their sense of separate national identity, their language, and their stubborn claim to independence.

It was a naval battle in 938 in the Bach Dang River estuary northeast of Hanoi that for the first time established Vietnam as a sovereign state. The rout by a small fleet of junks, commanded by a military mandarin, Ngo Quyen, of an armada dispatched to reestablish Chinese rule after one more rebellion was a triumph of cunning and daring compensating for weakness in numbers and muscle, qualities that time and again have undone Vietnam's antagonists, Asian, European, and American. Ngo Quyen seeded the shallows of the estuary with spikes tipped with iron. At high tide the Vietnamese fleet sailed out to sea, as if to engage the foe. Suddenly the vessels turned, feigning retreat before the great Chinese fleet and drawing it into the estuary and the trap. Low tide impaled the invaders' craft, leaving them at the defenders' mercy. The following year Ngo Quyen proclaimed himself emperor of a country free of imperial domination from the north, the first truly independent Vietnamese state. He named it Dai Viet, or (land of the) "great Viet." He ruled for five years, but at his death in 944 a dozen rival warlords fought bitterly for the succession.

In 967 one of them, Dinh Bo Linh, reunited the realm. His reign lasted for only one decade, but its achievement was great: he won for the first time Chinese recognition of Vietnam's sovereignty and established a tributary relationship similar to the loose ties that secured the independence from China of other states south of her frontier. Paying regular tribute did not shield Dai Viet from frequent incursions and two major wars. The first, from 1075 to 1077, ended in a negotiated peace in which Vietnam gave up some border areas. It regained them in renewed negotiations two years later.

The menace was greater when in the thirteenth century, after the Mongols under Genghis Khan had established their dominance in China, they turned an aggressive eye southward. A first invasion was repelled in 1257, when the hot and humid climate proved the greatest foe to the men of the northern steppes and their mounts. But in 1282 the armies of Emperor Kublai Khan descended once again, spreading fire and devastation through the land. The invaders occupied most of Dai Viet. But adversity gave birth to one more great hero of resistance to China: General Tran Hung Dao, to whom King Tran Nhan Tong entrusted the general command. Under the shock of the first assaults, Tran Hung Dao ordered the evacuation of the capital and was summoned by the king. Should Vietnam not surrender to spare its people destruction? he asked his general. "I understand the humane feelings that inspire Your Majesty's heart," Tran Hung Dao replied. "But what will become of the lands of our ancestors, the temples of our elders? If You wish to surrender, order my head to be severed first." Instead, the king ordered his general to organize an all-out defense of the realm.

Tran Hung Dao's order to hold or recapture the land at all cost has become a classic text of Vietnamese history. "Through the day, I forget to eat; through the night, I forget to sleep. I cry; my bowels are as if they were slashed. I want to devour the flesh and the liver of the enemy and drink his blood to quench my hatred." His soldiers, their passions roused, tattooed on their forearms the motto, Death to the Mongols. The land was laid waste and most of it occupied, but the invaders' troops were spread thin and subjected to hit-and-run attacks by guerrillas who gave them no respite. As the harassed Mongols gathered to withdraw across their borders, Tran Hung Dao attacked frontally. The rout of the demoralized invaders was complete, and an army of a half million was beaten; survivors were allowed to straggle back to China.

Revenge was not long in coming. Two years later a Mongolian army of 300,000 and a fleet of five hundred vessels renewed the war. "The people of Giao Chi hid the rice and fled," a Mongolian chronicle of the campaign recorded. Once again, the invaders seized much territory but could not hold it under continuous harassment and ambushes and the anger of the population. Peasants rose against the marauding enemy troops, who despoiled the countryside pillaging for food. The climactic battle took place, as in 938, in the Bach Dang River estuary. Tran Hung Dao staged a confrontation modeled on Ngo Quyen's strategy. Again iron-tipped spikes were planted in the estuary, once more a decoy flotilla of Vietnamese ships went out to lure the enemy, and as they had been three centuries earlier the invaders' vessels were trapped by the receding tide. One hundred junks were destroyed, four hundred captured. The news spread panic among the Mongolian troops and set off a hasty and disorganized retreat.

Wisely, King Tran Nhan Tong took some of the sting away from having vanquished a mightier foe by sending a peace mission bearing tribute to the Peking court in 1288. In another gesture of reconciliation the following year, he ordered all captive Mongolian officers to be freed. Nonetheless, Kublai Khan was preparing a new punitive expedition against Dai Viet at the time of his death in 1294. His son and successor, Timur, called it off, and Vietnam agreed to pay an annual tribute in return for peace. Tran Hung Dao died in 1300, taking his place in the national pantheon next to the Trung sisters. As the protector of the nation he is the object of a veritable cult, which reaches its peak every September in a pilgrimage to his shrine in the northern village of Kiep Bac and has continued throughout the Communist era.

The peace held for a century, but with the consolidation of the Ming dynasty, successors to the Mongols' Yuan dynasty, China's emperors once again found the existence of an independent state of a related people that owed so much to Chinese cultural roots intolerable. The Ming invasion began in 1406; by the following year Dai Viet had once again become Giao Chi, an integral part of the Middle Kingdom. For two decades its people were subjected to the most repressive alien regime Vietnam had known. Chinese administrators and soldiers held sway throughout the country, heavy taxes weighed even on the poorest, forced military and public works service made the able-bodied neglect their families' interests. Not only raw materials and cattle were confiscated for shipment northward — even skilled craftsmen were banished from their homeland to work for China. The ways of the conqueror were imposed; war was declared on the culture and religion of the occupied land. Wherever works of Vietnamese literature were found, they were carried off or burned; only Chinese gods could be worshiped.

Uprisings punctuated the Ming occupation. The rebels found their leader in Le Loi, a landowner from Thanh Hoa Province south of Hanoi, who proclaimed himself king in 1418. A major Chinese offensive launched in 1427 was disastrously defeated, and the invaders sued for peace. Le Loi not only granted it but, with the shrewd and self-serving magnanimity of a small nation that has defeated a much larger neighbor, also provided the horses, boats, and provisions for the Chinese retreat to their homeland in 1428.

Le Loi's victory achieved lasting independence from the most persistent enemy. Only once again, in 1788, during a fratricidal struggle among the Vietnamese, did China briefly invade with the intention of annexing Vietnam. It was defeated the following year. Le Loi established his capital on the site of Thang Long and named it Dong Kinh, "eastern capital," the original form of the name that as Tonkin designated the northernmost of the three territories of French colonial rule. In the nineteenth century, when Hue was the capital of reunified Vietnam, Emperor Minh Mang renamed the city Hanoi.

The millenary, eventually successful liberation struggle from Chinese physical dominance on its soil is the central pillar of Vietnamese national consciousness. Other dominant foreign powers have come and gone; gone forever, the Vietnamese believe. But China continues to cast its huge shadow and, at times, makes even its substance felt, most recently in mounting a punitive incursion across their border in 1979, after Vietnam toppled Pol Pot, China's Cambodian client. The great power that has weighed so long and so heavily on Vietnam, greatly shaping its being and fate, remains a dark, unsettling, and menacing presence in the minds of Vietnamese.

The dynasty that Le Loi founded based itself on a redistribution of the large landed estates of the Ming officials, their indigenous collaborators, and aristocrats. The beneficiaries were either the state or its senior public servants, the mandarins. However, the new landholders did not rule over peasants as serfs; the peasants were placed directly under the authority of the state. A tightly organized central administration, directly under the king's control, was established, the army reduced in size and assigned to agricultural labor when not engaged in assuring national security, and an elaborate legal code promulgated, which for the first time established considerable rights for women. The original architect of this work of nation-building was Le Loi's indispensable Confucian counselor in military and civil affairs, Nguyen Trai, a poet both in Vietnamese (the first whose work survives) and in classical Chinese. His advice to Le Loi when he offered to serve him was, "It is better to conquer hearts than citadels." National history holds him in highest esteem as the greatest mandarin Vietnam produced. His reward was betrayal through court intrigues, years of isolation to a hermit's hut, and finally, in 1442, execution. The Le dynasty, particularly the reign of Le Thanh Tong, from 1460 until 1497, ushered in what has come to be regarded as a golden age of Confucian rule, marked by stability, high agricultural productivity through guaranteed land and property rights, the founding of corporations of craftsmen, and a strong development of domestic commerce through the establishment of a network of regional markets.

Nonetheless, only the early period of the long rule of the Le kings was a golden age, and even that was not entirely a time of peace and internal stability. Although the mountain tribesmen of various ethnic groups had fought alongside the majority lowland Vietnamese, known as the Kinh, against the Ming rulers, in fulfillment of Lord Lac Long Quang's promise that in time of need his descendants and those of Queen Au Loc would stand together, the mountain people were not allowed to share in the fruits of victory and peace. Instead Kinh mandarins subjected them to oppressive rule, intrusion on their traditional lands, and heavy taxation. In consequence, the reign of the Le kings was marked by continual revolts in the mountain regions, usually severely repressed. This left a legacy of open minority resentments that subsisted through the centuries until the full imposition of Communist rule put an end to all expression of opposition to central power.

These antagonisms were ruthlessly exploited by the Western powers that most actively interfered in the affairs of Indochina. Through the French and American wars in the region, the Communist armies met no more determined resistance than that of the montagnard minorities enrolled against them by France or the United States. In the war in neighboring Laos the brunt of the fighting on behalf of the American-supported royal government against the North Vietnamese and their Laotian allies, the Pathet Lao, was borne by the Hmong, or Meo, tribesmen, who live on both sides of the Vietnamese-Laotian border. These tribesmen were easily encouraged and exploited by the Central Intelligence Agency to take arms, as an American-organized force only nominally under the Laotian military high command, against the Vietnamese, whom they regarded as their people's perennial enemy. Many refused to lay down their arms even after the North Vietnamese victory in 1975 and the end of American support, carrying on clandestine resistance well after the official end of fighting. Similarly, the Cambodian Khmers Rouges found ready allies among the mountain tribes on both sides of the Cambodian-Vietnamese border in their silent border war against Vietnam, which provoked the Vietnamese invasion of 1978–79 that toppled their murderous rule.

The Le dynasty ruled, at least in name, until 1788, but its long decline began with the end of Le Thanh Tong's reign in 1497. Vietnam expanded inexorably southward, at the expense of the kingdom of Champa — a state founded at the beginning of the modern era and inspired by Hindu thought although never under Indian dominance — and later of the Khmer kings of the present Cambodia. As it did, territorial antagonisms and local secessions, together with rivalries among mandarins and popular resentment over their arbitrary exercise of power, undermined the Le kings' hold over their country. As Nguyen Khac Vien observes, with the lengthening of internal distances in the expanding kingdom, royal orders often failed to reach their destinations, and taxes and other contributions from the provinces no longer reached the royal court. The northern regions of the kingdom fell under the authority of the lords of the Trinh family, while in the southern realm the Nguyen lords held sway. Through the seventeenth and eighteenth centuries a Le king sat on the throne in Thang Long, not yet called Hanoi, while their country was a battleground for the Trinh and Nguyen vassals. The kings became figureheads in the hands of the Trinh, under whose domination stood the throne of Vietnam.

As was to happen again, the country was effectively divided. There has always been a strong sense of common nationality, but Vietnam has also too often been cursed with antagonistic leaders ready to go to the extreme of war to assert their claims to be its sole legitimate representatives. The mandarinate, a respected hierarchy at the outset and a source of administrative strength and stability, grew increasingly venal and oppressive; peasant risings and court intrigues sapped the power of the Trinh, and as the eighteenth century drew toward its close, their rule was shaken and ready to be toppled.

Those who overthrew the Trinh came from the south, where the power of the Nguyen, centered on the city of Hue, then called Phu Xuan, was suffering the same rot that had weakened their Trinh adversaries. In 1771 arose the rebellion that in short order overthrew the Nguyen lords, repelled a Siamese invasion aimed at reinstating them, and finally also defeated the Trinh lords, restoring national unity for the first time since the decline of the Le dynasty. The peasant rebellion was mounted by three brothers from the village of Tay Son, near the town of Qui Nhon on the central coast, and in this century the Tay Son rebellion became the movement that Ho Chi Minh's Communists proclaimed as their model. The three brothers changed their original family name of Ho to Nguyen, no doubt to reinforce a claim to be the rightful successors to the feudal overlords whose corrupt and oppressive rule had made both the lowland peasantry and the mountain tribes ready for insurrection. The brothers from Tay Son quickly succeeded in capturing several provinces and the town of Qui Nhon. The troubles of the Nguyen feudal rulers tempted their Trinh adversaries to march southward and capture their capital, Phu Xuan, in 1774. The Tay Son brothers concluded a temporary agreement with the Trinh, leaving the northern invaders in possession of the capital, while the Tay Son brothers spread their rebellion southward.

There, in the Mekong Delta, a last Nguyen prince, Nguyen Anh, led a strong resistance movement against the rebels. The Tay Son army, under the command of the most gifted of the brothers, Nguyen Hue, defeated the prince's forces in 1783. Nguyen Anh took refuge on the island of Phu Quoc, off the southern coast where Vietnam and Cambodia meet, from where he sent a call for assistance to the kingdom of Siam, modern Thailand. A large Siamese army, carried by a fleet of three hundred ships, landed in the west of the Mekong Delta, where it was disastrously defeated by Nguyen Hue's forces in 1785. The victor quickly turned northward and recaptured Phu Xuan from the Trinh the following year. A month later, Nguyen Hue reached the Red River Delta and the capital, Thang Long. Having defeated the Nguyen and Trinh rivals, he restored the Le dynasty to royal powers and as a reward was given a daughter of King Le Hien Tong in marriage.

The new peace did not last. The king died, and his successor, Le Chieu Thong, turned against Nguyen Hue. Defeated and expelled from his capital, Le Chieu Thong called for help from the Chinese emperor. In 1788 an army of 200,000 Chinese invaded Hanoi and restored the king as a figurehead monarch under their control. In response Nguyen Hue formally declared the Le dynasty deposed and proclaimed himself king under a third name, Quang Trung. In a fiery speech to his troops, he called up the memory of the Trung sisters, General Tran Huong Dao, and Le Loi, those who had expelled earlier Chinese invaders, and promised to liberate the country within a month. After having defeated the Nguyen, the Siamese, and the Trinh, King Quang Trung, always referred to as Nguyen Hue and regarded by all subsequent regimes as one of Vietnam's greatest heroes, drove the Chinese back across their border in a lightning campaign and obtained China's recognition of the independence and unity of all Vietnam under his reign.

The Tay Son reign, which the new king began with a farreaching, liberal land reform that made property owners of many landless peasants, was short-lived. The brothers no longer saw eye to eye, and Prince Nguyen Anh took advantage of Nguyen Hue's preoccupation with the Chinese invasion to regain a foothold in the south. Nguyen Hue died in 1792, leaving the throne to his six-year-old son; one of the two surviving brothers died the following year, and Nguyen Anh steadily advanced northward. He seized Phu Xuan, the modern Hue, in 1801 and declared it his capital. The following year he proclaimed himself emperor under the name of Gia Long, and less than two months later, as the resistance of the Tay Son forces crumbled, he occupied Thanh Long, shortly to be renamed Hanoi. Gia Long was the first of the Nguyen dynasty, who reigned over the country that had been reunified by the Tay Son brothers. It was to be Vietnam's last imperial dynasty.

8

"To Love Our Domination"

Gia Long and the Nguyen emperors who followed him on the throne in Hue modeled their reign on the nearest example — China. Soon after crowning himself emperor in 1802, Gia Long paid the customary tribute to Beijing and obtained recognition of Vietnam's sovereignty and his rule. He established an absolute monarchy served by a mandarinate of the strictest Confucian observance, chosen by competitive examinations and motivated by a rigid conservatism. The seat of his reign was a miniature version of Beijing's Forbidden City. Chinese-inspired formalistic court ritual was slavishly followed, and the appalling cruelty of the rule of the Qing dynasty also found its reflection at the court of Hue. Gia Long settled his score with the Tay Son rebels by having Nguyen Hue's remains exhumed, to be urinated on by his soldiers in the presence of the late emperor's captive son, the boy emperor Quang Toan. Then Quang Toan was drawn and quartered by elephants, to which his limbs were bound. The Qing dynasty that served as example for the Nguyen emperors was ravaged by the corruption, court intrigues, factionalism, and abandonment to self-indulgent luxury that marked its gradual decadence and eventual fall in 1911. The course of Vietnam's final dynasty, confronted with a nation that was far from being consolidated or at peace and faced with an aggressive new challenge, was to be no different.

The new threat was European expansionism into a world Europe considered infidel, uncivilized, and undeveloped. In Vietnam the menace of foreign aggression was posed by a particularly unholy alliance led by the Roman Catholic Church, which found no difficulty in aligning itself with the military, commercial, and eventually political establishments in France. There had been occasional visits by missionaries beginning in the fourteenth century, and in the seventeenth century the Society of Jesus, after its expulsion from Japan, looked toward Vietnam as a possible new field for proselytism. The first mission was established in 1615 at the Portuguese trading post of Faifo, today the lovely little town of Hoi An, just south of central Vietnam's largest city of Da Nang.

Nine years later, with a group of six Jesuits dispatched to reinforce the mission, arrived for the first of many sojourns a remarkable thirty-three-year-old French priest, who was to leave an enduring mark on Vietnamese civilization and bear a measure of indirect responsibility for the colonial future that lay ahead. He was Alexandre de Rhodes from the Provençal city of Avignon, whose ancestors had sought refuge there when Ferdinand and Isabella, the "Catholic Sovereigns," expelled the Jews from Spain. The "Rhodes" in his name was not the Greek island but derived from the Provençal word *rode,* the small "wheel" that medieval Jews were forced to wear on their clothing to identify them, much like the yellow star of a later age of inhumanity. Alexandre was a Marrano, offspring of Jews forced to convert by the Inquisition.

On arrival in Vietnam, he was at first taken aback by the language, which, he wrote, made him believe he was "hearing birds chirp." But six months later he reported that he was preaching "in the language of Cochin China." ("Cochin China" in the seventeenth century was a term that the Portuguese had given to the region that is today's central Vietnam, not the country's southern region, as it came to mean under French colonial rule. In those years today's southern Vietnam was still part of the waning Khmer empire.) Alexandre's linguistic gifts were such that he, who had just learned Vietnamese, completely revolutionized its writing in a way that Chinese intellectuals envy to this day. With extraordinary ingenuity the missionary devised, no doubt with the help of his Jesuit colleagues, a system of writing Vietnamese, until then written in Chinese ideograms, in the Latin alphabet and rendering its complex system of six tones, each conferring a different meaning on the identically spelled monosyllabic word, through accents and other diacritical marks placed over or under the vowel. He also compiled and published in Rome a dictionary and a grammar of the language. His purpose was, of course, to facilitate the propagation of the Gospel, but the result was to make reading and writing far simpler and more adaptable, benefiting all Vietnamese arts and sciences and enabling the Vietnamese to acquire foreign languages with greater ease. (Pasteur and Alexandre de Rhodes were the only French street names in Saigon to survive decolonization after 1954. The priest's name did not vanish from the small street near the cathedral until the Communist conquest of the city, but Catholic intellectuals are hopeful that in today's more liberal atmosphere the man who revolutionized Vietnamese reading and writing will regain this modest token of recognition.)

Father Alexandre's indirect responsibility for the coming of French colonialism was rooted in his discontent with the ineffective way in which Portugal carried out its responsibility, bestowed by the papacy, for evangelization in Asia. Consequently he embarked on a lobbying campaign in Paris, after the last of his many expulsions from the land he had grown to love and where he wanted to stay for life. (There were also some arrests and at least one sentence of death, par for the course for the intrepid early missionaries to Asia.) Alexandre beseeched the princes of the French church and state, including the king, as well as French overseas traders, to direct their attention to a country that he deemed ready to become Christian and that could make French Christians rich. The creation of the French Society of Foreign Missions, as well as the Compagnie des Indes, a major government trading organization, followed his lobbying efforts. By then Alexandre had died, far from Avignon and from Vietnam, banished to Persia by the Jesuits because of the delicate diplomatic problems his political activism had caused the society. But the Society of Foreign Missions and the

Compagnie des Indes became major bearers of the French flag to Vietnam.

Catholicism took deeper root in Vietnam than in any other country on the Southeast Asian continent, perhaps because the Vietnamese lacked the deep attachment to a faith that distinguishes to this day the Theravada Buddhists of the other nations of the Indochinese peninsula — Cambodia, Laos, and Thailand — but no doubt also because its missionaries, coming from technologically advanced countries and cunningly using this to proselytizing advantage, often proved helpful in advising rulers on the contemporary world or even procuring for them coveted supplies of contemporary arms. Moreover, the French missionaries pursued a successful policy of creating many indigenous catechists, later also priests, which brought their faith closer to the Vietnamese people. It was the link between a missionary and a man destined to become emperor and founder of the last dynasty that led to the entry of the French state into Vietnam and its eventual colonization. The missionary was Pierre Pigneau de Béhaine of the Society of Foreign Missions, the titular bishop of Adran, a formerly Christian city then under Ottoman rule; the emperor was Gia Long.

As Nguyen Anh, the prince on the run from the Tay Son rebels, the later emperor had found refuge on Phu Quoc Island, where the priest directed a seminary in which he schooled youths from neighboring countries in the Catholic faith. The bishop persuaded him to appeal to France for assistance and was authorized to plead the prince's case with King Louis XVI. In 1787 he arrived in Versailles, accompanied by Anh's seven-year-old son, entrusted to him by his father as a token of the prelate's right to speak for the prince. The result of the negotiations was the first official international engagement linking France to Vietnam. Louis XVI agreed to help "the King of Cochin China" to regain his realm by furnishing 1,650 troops and four frigates. In return Nguyen Anh would grant France a concession at Da Nang, which the French called Tourane, and ownership of the island of Poulo Condor, as well as exclusive trading and shipping rights for French citizens. The agreement never came into force. Shortly before the French Revolution, the government revoked it. Bishop Pigneau, a man of action at least as much as a man of the cloth, decided to lead his own military expedition in aid of a monarch he wanted to enthrone, raised money from merchants in France's Indian concessions, chartered two ships and hired crews and a band of mercenaries, and set sail for Cape Saint-Jacques, today's Vung Tau, southeast of Saigon. But when he landed in July 1789, the month of the French Revolution, Nguyen Anh had already led his own troops in the reconquest of the Mekong Delta from the Tay Son rebels. Pigneau's men trained Anh's soldiers, created a navy, and oversaw the building of fortifications in the style of Vauban, the great French military architect, aiding significantly in the campaign that carried the pretender to full military victory and his coronation as Emperor Gia Long in 1802. But by then the bishop had been dead for three years.

Gia Long's son and successor, Emperor Minh Mang, who mounted the throne in 1820, felt no inherited obligation either to France or the church. He refused any grant of trading privileges and in 1825 decreed a ban on foreign missionaries, who, he said, "pervert and seduce the hearts of men and weaken the morals of the people." As missionaries ignored the edict and continued to land in Vietnam, often in disguise, he issued harsher prohibitions, culminating in 1833 and 1836 in a general ban on Catholicism and its foreign and Vietnamese priests. As local rebellions, provoked largely by economic misery and resentment of oppressive mandarins, erupted with mounting frequency, Minh Mang's campaign against the church began to make martyrs, including French priests who had links to rebels. They were executed in the sadistic ways of the day. The clergy in France, making a political comeback after the decline of religion during the revolutionary and Napoleonic eras, created considerable public opinion and political pressure on behalf of the persecuted French missionaries. Minh Mang's son, Emperor Thieu Tri, reaffirmed the anti-Catholic edicts, while the missionaries, clearly intent on provoking a French military intervention, continued to defy them. The first French shots fired against Vietnam resounded in 1847.

Learning of the arrest of a French bishop in Da Nang, a French fleet in the South China Sea dispatched two vessels to demand his release. By the time they anchored off Da Nang, the bishop had already been freed, but the naval commanders were unaware of this. Angry talks ensued that deepened the misunderstanding. Who fired the first shots will never be known, but before setting back out to sea the French sank several Vietnamese ships, and their cannon killed many ashore and devastated harbor installations. The consequence of this first overt act of imperialism was heightened persecution of Vietnamese Catholics and edicts against missionaries, and in France an intensification of Catholic demands for a massive military intervention. Emperor Tu Duc, who succeeded his father in 1847, mounted an even more vehement campaign against the Catholics, ordering punishments that ranged from branding their faces to death by various cruel methods for native and foreign priests. Under the pressure of the church and military and political personalities who were alive to the imperialist tendencies of the epoch throughout Europe, Emperor Napoleon III issued an order in 1856 for a naval task force to sail to Da Nang and demand the port's surrender to France. But the diplomat entrusted with the mission stopped off first in Siam and Cambodia; one of the warships reached Da Nang before him, and its commander sent a company of troops ashore to destroy its defenses. This persuaded the Vietnamese to agree to negotiations, but there was no one at hand with whom to negotiate. The diplomat arrived only after his ships had left, having run out of supplies, and found it difficult to practice gunboat diplomacy without gunboats.

The first full-scale imperialist expedition, with the mission of capturing Da Nang and imposing on Tu Duc the acceptance of a French protectorate, ended in fiasco followed by unexpected gain over the long term. A fleet of thirteen vessels, carrying 2,300 French and Spanish troops, easily captured Da Nang after shelling it heavily and reducing much of the small town to ashes. But the uprising of Catholics that the main militant, Bishop Pellerin, had foretold did not ensue, and the small occupying force found itself pinned down and under constant harassing attacks. The commander, Admiral Charles Rigault de Genouilly, acting on his own, changed targets and, leaving a small, beleaguered force behind in Da Nang, set sail for Saigon to claim the rich and less well defended Mekong Delta for France. He captured the city in a day's fighting on February 1, 1859. But, as in Da Nang, the expeditionary force proved not strong enough to enlarge upon the initial capture of the city, and Paris refused a dispatch of reinforcements. Typhus and cholera were meanwhile taking more victims among the French than their skirmishes with the defenders. The admiral resigned his command and left for home, bitter over a victory that was beginning to resemble a defeat. In March 1860 his successor, Counter-Admiral Page, ordered the evacuation of Da Nang, leaving behind to the vengeance of the mandarins the Catholic Vietnamese who had put themselves under his troops' protection, as well as a town in flames. The sad symmetry of foreign intervention is fearful. It was in Da Nang that the U.S. Marines began the full-scale American engagement in Vietnam in 1965, 105 years later. And from Da Nang, ten years after that landing, came the first shocking images of Americans pushing off from their departing planes and helicopters many of the Vietnamese who had aligned themselves with the forces of intervention.

But in Saigon a garrison of eight hundred invading troops held out against insistent Vietnamese attacks until relieved by reinforcements that were sent by Prosper de Chasseloup-Laubat. A grandmaster of French colonialism in Vietnam, Chasseloup-Laubat was minister of both the navy and the colonies. The combination of the two ministries in one man's hands indicates the spirit of the times; Chasseloup-Laubat's mission was one of imperialism, and he was a missionary of that cause. He perceived it as a God-given and mystical task and made himself its dithyrambic minstrel, even in bureaucratic instructions to his subordinates. "A difficult task," he wrote to his officers in Saigon on the subject of how to deal with the Vietnamese. "We must on one hand in large measure respect their morals and laws, but at the same time lead them little by little to love our civilization and our domination." In a later letter he wrote, "I want to create for my country a veritable empire in the Far East. I wish our Christian civilization to have in our new conquest a formidable establishment, from which it will send its rays to all its regions, where such cruel morals still exist. There is in this sentiment of being useful to a task of which God alone knows the grandeur and the mystery, there is in this sentiment that one has when one serves this great cause of civilization and the Good, a joy, a force, that make up for all the sacrifices."

Whatever sacrifices the minister imposed on himself, the greater sufferings were borne by his troops in an alien and hostile land. He sent Vice-Admiral Leonard Charner to relieve Saigon and capture the surrounding regions, so that France would be in a position of strength in proposing a peace treaty to Emperor Tu Duc. Charner and his successor, Admiral Bonard, despite heavy losses inflicted by fierce Vietnamese resistance and the difficult terrain of jungle and waterlogged paddy fields crisscrossed by rivers and canals, expanded their conquests into the rich rice-growing provinces of the Mekong Delta until Tu Duc, in March 1862, sent his emissaries to Saigon to plead for peace. This act of surrender has never been forgiven by Vietnamese nationalists of all political persuasions; all the emperor's subsequent recorded utterances are steeped in anguish and remorse at not having found another way out of a tragic dilemma. The price Vietnam paid in this first submission to colonial power was full French sovereignty over the three eastern provinces of the Mekong Delta, including Saigon, and Poulo Condor Island, and the occupation of a fourth province. An "indemnity" to France and Spain of four million dollars, an astronomical sum for the period and for a poverty-stricken nation, was imposed on Tu Duc. Freedom for Christianity was guaranteed.

In one of the most cynical effusions that colonialism has produced, Admiral Bonard, named governor of France's new colony, addressed these words of consolation to Vietnam's emperor in the name of the emperor of France: "The cession of the provinces that the sovereign of Annam made to His Imperial Majesty is like a marriage in which the bride who is given to her fiancé, while owing him obedience, does not deny her father. The wife that is well treated by him who protects her and fulfills her needs soon loses all apprehension and, without forgetting her parents, ends by loving her husband." The excellent French historian of Indochina, Philippe Franchini, son of a Vietnamese mother and of the man who founded Saigon's Hotel Continental Palace, remarked that the "marriage" resembled rather an act of rape, accompanied by a ruinous dowry and humiliating conditions. Following this surrender, French imperialism set out on its inexorable march of conquest over Indochina. Cambodia bowed to a protectorate in 1863; in 1867 the neighboring provinces of Vietnam were occupied, placing all of Cochin China under French rule.

France's next imperialist temptation was to open the Red River of Vietnam's north as a trade route to China. Tonkin at the time was riddled with popular risings against the increasingly unpopular Tu Duc and the corrupt and arbitrary mandarinate. The unrest was heightened by the marauding presence of Chinese bandit gangs fleeing into Vietnam after the suppression of the Tai Ping rebellion in China, as well as regular Chinese troops carrying out banditry on their own account rather than putting a halt to the rebels' pillaging. In 1873 Jean Dupuis, an adventurous French trader of arms and other commodities for the Chinese army fighting rebels in Yunnan Province in China's south, was blocked in a dispute with the Hanoi mandarins, who refused to let him sail northward with a cargo of salt. Boldly, Dupuis with his crew of mercenaries occupied a part of the city and called on Admiral Jules-Marie Dupré, the governor in Saigon, for help. Although instructed by Paris not to intervene in a part of Vietnam whose sovereignty France still recognized, Dupré, who had long sought a pretext to extend France's possessions, sent a particularly venturesome naval lieutenant, Francis Garnier, at the head of a force of 188 French troops and twenty-four Vietnamese to "mediate" between the mercenaries and the mandarins. With superb arrogance, and clearly assured of Dupré's support, the junior officer arbitrarily proclaimed the Red River open to all commerce. A few days later he led his small troop and Dupuis's mercenaries in an assault of Hanoi's Citadel; it fell in an hour's combat, with the loss of one man, a Chinese in Dupuis's pay. The commanding general of the defenders, Nguyen Tri Phuong, wounded and captured, refused all dealings with the French and starved himself to death. But the people of the Red River Delta, who had never reconciled themselves to the ouster of their kings of the Le dynasty and suffered under the greedy and unjust mandarins sent by the court of Hue, offered little resistance as Garnier expanded the French hold through most of the Red River Delta, including the port of Haiphong. Fittingly, the exalted young conqueror was killed as he advanced alone, ahead of his troops, in an ambush outside Hanoi before the end of the year that had brought him such victory.

France, still under the shock of its defeat by Prussia in 1871 and not eager for dangerous new foreign adventures, acted quickly to renounce Garnier's conquests and open negotiations with Tu Duc. The emperor formally recognized French sovereignty over all of Cochin China, opened the ports of Hanoi, Da Nang, and Qui Nhon to France, with the right to establish consulates there and station troops to protect the consuls, and confirmed Garnier's declaration that the Red River was an international shipping lane. He agreed also to receive a high-level French "resident" at his court and to guarantee the freedom of Catholic practice. In return France recognized Tu Duc's sovereignty in Tonkin, relieved him of the unpaid balance of the four-million-dollar ransom, and undertook to furnish him with ships and arms to combat bandits and pirates. Once again, an evacuation of foreigners who had rallied Vietnamese to their side left them, Catholic Tonkinese on this occasion, as scapegoats at the mercy of their foes. Tu Duc, regarding the French concessions in the treaty as signs of weakness, sought revenge in massacres and persecutions, particularly of Christians. Further bandit incursions from China made null and void the opening of the Red

River to commerce. Tu Duc called on China to help him keep order in Tonkin, which threatened to collapse into uncontrollable anarchy.

In Paris a great debate raged about the question of further intervention. Despite eloquent opposition by the World War I prime minister, Georges Clemenceau, who wanted France to concentrate on the recovery of Alsace-Lorraine, recently lost to Prussia, the imperialist strivings of Prime Minister Jules Ferry won the day. A naval officer, Captain Henri Rivière, was sent at the head of a contingent of five hundred men nominally to reinforce the Hanoi garrison but in fact to repeat Garnier's earlier exploit. Rivière succeeded in imitation beyond his wishes: in 1883, after duplicating Garnier's conquest of much of Tonkin, he, too, was killed in an ambush near Hanoi. That was pretext enough for Ferry to dispatch a major expeditionary force to complete the conquest of Vietnam and submit the emperor to French control. A direct seaborne attack on Hue brought the capital into French hands on August 20, 1883. Tu Duc had died a month earlier, cursing the French, and a struggle for succession had just placed a new emperor, Hiep Hoa, on the throne, after another prince had reigned for three days before being deposed. His first act was to sign the surrender, accepting the French protectorate over all parts of Vietnam that were not under outright French sovereignty. The surrender cost the emperor his life; he was assassinated three months later. War continued in Tonkin, with the French opposed by Chinese troops fighting alongside Vietnamese. An undeclared war with China raged until 1885, with fighting in Tonkin, on the Chinese coast and Taiwan, and on the Pescadores Islands. It was only after Ferry's government fell over the Tonkinese adventure that two war-weary countries concluded the Treaty of Tientsin. China recognized French possession of Vietnam.

The emperor in Hue at that time was Ham Nghi, thirteen years old. A regent who exercised his power for him, Ton That Thuyet, humiliated by the arrival in Hue of General Roussel de Courcy, a new and particularly assertive French commander and "resident-general," ordered an attack on the French forces.

It was put down with great violence and followed by an act of the crudest vandalism, the destructive sack of the Imperial Palace. Thuyet escaped to the mountains of Laos, taking with him the boy emperor Ham Nghi, and for the first time France used its power to install a monarch in Vietnam: the fugitive's older brother, the compliant Dong Khanh. From his mountain hideout, Ham Nghi called for resistance. What followed was the unpeaceful process called "pacification," by which France solidified, without ever making complete, its control over all of Indochina, rounded out in the last decade of the century with its extension over all of Laos. Betrayed by a montagnard chief, Ham Nghi was captured in 1888 and deported to Algeria.

The attitude that shaped the violence of "pacification" was expressed by a contemporary account in the leading Paris newspaper, *Le Temps,* unearthed by the historian Franchini: "Profoundly egotistical and cowardly, this vicious and degraded race will not get used to our domination until we hold it on our leash. To apply French laws to a people that has always marched under the cane, to address it with proclamations while it never received anything but orders, is to make a mockery of our system and to destroy our influence."

France's enterprise of bringing its "civilizing mission" to a country with a civilization at least as old as its own went through all the phases of the failure of colonialism. There were frequent local rebellions, which found support because of the oppression of a nation of peasants, not all illiterate and passive, by foreigners and those who had compacted with colonial rule. The French judiciary exacted draconian punishments; the guillotine was a major tool of colonial policy. Another was daily humiliation by crude arrogance or kind condescension. There was economic oppression and the reduction to cannon fodder of men who had no stake in France's conflicts. Nguyen Khac Vien, the Communist historian, says that 50,000 Indochinese soldiers, mainly Vietnamese, were made to fight for France in World War I, and 49,000 workers were mobilized to work in French factories. The French had their collaborators — many for convenience, profit, and status; others from a sincere belief that a highly developed Western power would help Vietnam out of its material underdevelopment and that the well-meaning Frenchmen who proposed assimilation and eventual equality to the colonized nation could make this progressive view prevail in Paris. There were anticolonial nationalists — some who believed naively that there was a French left on whose support they could count, and others who were Asian chauvinists and believed, particularly after Japan's defeat of Russia in 1905, that with Japan's help they could drive out the white man and restore their country to Asian rule. There were nationalists who drew their support from the Chinese Nationalists of Chiang Kai-shek. And there was Ho Chi Minh.

Much of Ho's life is intentionally obscured by the disguises, noms de guerre, and deceits of the life of a professional revolutionary driven into permanent clandestinity by the forces that he contested and by the conspiratorial life of a functionary of the Comintern, the secretive machine by which Stalin directed the international Communist movement and made it serve Soviet national purposes. More is hidden by the legends that were fashioned to envelop the idolized founder and leader of a liberation movement. These legends were kept alive even after Ho's death and his movement's victory because of the fear of transparency that may have been a necessity in the years of struggle against forces intimidatingly superior in arms and equipment. What is certain is his single-minded passion for the independence of his people, by peaceful means if possible, by war if necessary. Rightly or wrongly — but his success deprives the argument of substance — he convinced himself after reading the anticolonialist writings of Lenin in Paris that Vietnam's road to independence could only be Communist.

The man who led his nation's fight for independence was born in 1890 as the son of a minor mandarin and teacher in Nghe An, an impoverished and rebellious province in central Vietnam. His education ended in high school in Hue. In 1911 he left Vietnam, having signed on as a galley boy on a French freighter, no doubt not knowing that he would not return until thirty years later. He never disclosed whether he left with the intention of getting to know the enemy and preparing for struggle or to satisfy his questing mind by seeing the world. Between voyages, which kept him at sea for about three years, he spent time ashore in France, England, and the United States. Settled later in Paris, he read widely in many fields and many languages, attended political meetings, wrote for varied publications, not only on political subjects, and earned his keep on a variety of odd jobs. In London, for instance, he is said to have worked in the kitchen of the Carlton Hotel as a pastry cook under the great chef Escoffier. On the fringes of the Versailles peace conference of 1919, at which he tried in vain to petition President Woodrow Wilson to advocate democratic reforms in Vietnam, he met important French Socialist leaders. They invited him to represent the Indochinese colonies at their 1920 party congress, the occasion at which the Socialists' left wing split to form the Communist party. Ho sided with the left, becoming a cofounder of the party, but neither the French Communists nor the Socialists sided with him in his open confrontation with France after World War II. The Communists' patriotism, which failed them only when on Stalin's order they opposed the war against Germany until Hitler attacked the Soviet Union, proved stronger than the party's anticolonialist ideology. They made up for this failure of solidarity when Ho's enemy was the United States.

Ho moved to Moscow in 1923, probably after having been recruited by the Comintern. His first assignment took him to China, during the period of the alliance between Mao Zedong's Communists and Chiang's Nationalists. He returned to Moscow when Chiang turned murderously against his allies but was soon back in China, in Bangkok, in Hong Kong. He organized Vietnamese students into a Brotherhood of Revolutionary Youth in Guangdong, probably the first formal Vietnamese Communist movement. Its members became the first Communist organizers active inside Vietnam. The historian Nguyen Khac Vien reports that among the guiding principles in which Ho instructed them was that the Vietnamese revolution must be integrated into the world revolution, and that its supporters must act in concert with the policies of the Third International — in other words, the Comintern. Ho's unquestioning loyalty to Moscow probably saved his life during the paranoiac Stalinist purges of the 1930s, which took the lives of countless foreign Comintern agents.

Following a general Vietnamese tendency to political factionalism, suppressed only when a dictatorship takes hold, three Communist parties were formed in 1929–30. Ho united them at a meeting in Hong Kong, forming at the same time the full panoply of "mass organizations" that seem to have been part of Moscow's organizing kit. They represented labor, peasants, women, and youth. The party, named "Vietnamese Communist Party" at the outset, changed its name to "Indochinese" a little later, probably at Moscow's order, without apparently having recruited Cambodian or Laotian members. "Overthrowing French imperialism, feudalism, and the landlords" was the first of the party's founding theses, "supporting the Soviet Union" the tenth.

When war broke out in Europe in 1939, the party followed the line of the Soviet Union, partner in a pact with Germany and participant in the rape of Poland and the Baltic states. Having earlier called for a "worldwide anti-Fascist front," the Indochinese Communists now declared the war to be a "simple war between imperialists," in which they took no sides. But after the Japanese occupation of French Indochina following France's defeat in 1940 and the German aggression against the Soviet Union in 1941, Ho resisted the temptation of many Asian anticolonialists to cast their lot with Japan, the continent's conquerors. His strategy was to align the Vietnamese Communists with the eventual victors — France was a defeated and occupied country — and receive as a reward Vietnam's independence on Japan's defeat. In 1941 Ho returned to Vietnam, and in a meeting of the party's leadership in the mountains just south of the Chinese border, they formed the League for the Independence of Vietnam, the Viet Minh, whose soldiers thirteen years later achieved its aim.

The Viet Minh rose in open conflict with the Japanese army in March 1945, when Japan swept aside the colonial regime that they had left in place and made the last emperor, Bao Dai, declare Vietnam independent under its auspices. A government of Japanese inspiration was installed. The Liberation Army was formally brought into being in April, and Vo Nguyen Giap, a law graduate of the University of Hanoi, became a member of its commanding Military Committee. He learned military science by teaching it to his equally unschooled troops and proved his surprising military genius by devising victorious strategy while commanding the armies that defeated France in 1954 and America and its South Vietnamese dependents in 1975. By June most of the provinces between the Red River and the Chinese frontier were in Vietnamese hands. The guerrillas were inspired not only by the revolutionary fervor of their leaders but also by a catastrophic famine, which made the food stocks kept under Japanese control a necessary target. Japan had forced Vietnamese peasants to plant industrial crops for its war machine rather than rice, cassava, and sweet potatoes, the staples. Despite the Viet Minh's rapid successes, estimates of famine victims range as high as two million.

After the dropping of the atomic bomb on Hiroshima, when the Allied victory was assured, Ho acted to present the victors with an accomplished fact — Vietnamese sovereignty over Vietnam — to forestall a return to colonial rule. In this he hoped above all for American backing. His wartime contacts with American intelligence agents in southern China had convinced him of President Roosevelt's aversion to French rule in Indochina. On August 16, the day after Emperor Hirohito announced Japan's surrender, Ho convoked a national congress, which adopted his resolution "to seize power from the hands of the Japanese and the puppet government before the arrival of the Allied troops in Indochina, to receive as masters of the country the troops who are coming to disarm the Japanese." Ho was unanimously installed as president of a provisional government and proclaimed: "The hour is decisive for the destiny of the nation. Let us all arise and bend all efforts to liberate ourselves. Many people of the world are rising to conquer their independence. We cannot lag behind. Forward! Under the banner of the Viet Minh, let us march forward with valor!" It was a call for a general uprising. With many local differences, peacefully through well-organized mass demonstrations in some cities and regions, bloodily in others, with much settling of old political or private scores, the August Revolution in the north and center largely achieved the accomplished fact that Ho intended. Hanoi was seized on August 19. Six days later in Hue, Emperor Bao Dai abdicated. Dressed in full regalia, he handed over the imperial seal and symbolic golden sword to a delegation of the National Liberation Committee. He assumed the commoner's name of Nguyen Vinh Thuy and was appointed "supreme political counselor" to President Ho Chi Minh.

On September 2 Ho declared Vietnam's independence, in a speech beginning with the opening phrases of the American Declaration of Independence, whose correctness he had checked a few days earlier with Major Archimedes L. A. Patti of the Office of Strategic Services, the American he knew best and who headed the OSS team that had reached Hanoi on August 22. Was it admiration for the ideals of the United States? Only a pragmatic gesture to enhance his bid for American support? The legend of Ho Chi Minh permits either answer. If he did admire the notions of life, liberty, and the pursuit of happiness, what did he really think while he lived in the Soviet Union, whose praises he sang until his death in 1969, during the years of Stalin's great terror of the 1930s?

But in Washington, ten days before Ho's declaration of independence, General Charles de Gaulle had already issued France's declaration of war: "France's position is very simple," he told a press conference. "France intends to regain its sovereignty over Indochina." To confirm his intentions, he named Admiral Georges Thierry d'Argenlieu, a former monk who combined in one ascetic person the mystical and chauvinistic traits of the priests and admirals who conquered France's Indochinese colonies, as high commissioner for Indochina. De Gaulle instructed him to accept no foreign mediation in dealing with the Viet Minh. "We do not deal with our subjects through foreign channels," the general advised him. In a further signal of his aims, de Gaulle named France's war hero, General Philippe Leclerc de Hauteloque, the liberator of Paris, as military commander. Leclerc arrived in Saigon, where bloody clashes between French and Vietnamese had degenerated into massacres on both sides, in October and almost immediately led his troops into battle. He rejected the idea of negotiation. As he wrote to de Gaulle, he believed the Vietnamese were causing "troubles" because they still regarded France as a defeated nation. "How do we dispel this conviction? By showing our force." By February 1946 France had reestablished its positions throughout the south and in the Central Highlands, but those positions lived in the insecurity created by a constant guerrilla presence.

In the north the Viet Minh's authority was seriously sapped by the presence of an army of perhaps 200,000 Nationalist Chinese, sent by the Allies after their victory to demobilize the Japanese occupation troops. It was like sending the devil to drive out Old Nick. (British troops, mainly Nepalese Gurkhas, had the same mission in the south.) The Chinese presented a dual danger to Ho: the ill-paid, ill-nourished, ragged, and war-weary troops conducted themselves like greedy conquerors, and their political leaders, fearful of the example that a Communist government presented for Mao Zedong, strongly favored the anti-Communist Nationalist Vietnamese party that Chiang Kai-shek had nurtured in southern China. And for all Vietnamese, Chinese armies on Vietnamese soil raised the question of whether they would ever leave. With disorder raging, the menace of a lasting Chinese presence that would be worse than the French, and no international support for Vietnam's independence, even from Moscow, Ho accepted negotiations with France for a continued association — if Paris recognized independence. In March Ho and Jean Sainteny, representing France in Hanoi, signed an agreement under which France recognized independence within the French Union, the postwar name for the empire, which France was even less ready to abandon than the other colonial powers. Vietnam accepted the return of French troops to relieve the Chinese, and both agreed to negotiate on their future relationship. Leclerc, greeted by Giap, landed at Haiphong and, reaching Hanoi, declared to cheering French residents, in allusion to his liberation of Paris, "Hanoi, last phase of the Liberation!"

The French–Viet Minh negotiations reached stalemate even at a preliminary session in the hill resort of Dalat. The principal divergence centered on French insistence that the south — the colonial Cochin China — having been ceded to French sovereignty in 1862, could not become part of independent Vietnam. Ho Chi Minh countered, "Our brothers of the south are citizens of Vietnam. Rivers may dry up, mountains crumble, but that truth will remain forever." But even before Ho Chi Minh reached France for the full-scale negotiations, he learned that d'Argenlieu had formed a separate government for Cochin China. As the negotiations at Fontainebleau, near Paris, stalled from the outset, clashes in Vietnam quickened. Ho sent his delegation home but remained alone, finally signing, as a last resort to prevent a breakdown of negotiations, a modus vivendi that did not provide for French recognition of Cochin China as part of independent Vietnam.

Armed incidents multiplied throughout the country, climaxing in a particularly bloody French attack on Haiphong. In December major fighting broke out in Hanoi. Ho Chi Minh fled from the city and issued a general call to arms: "Let him who owns a rifle use his rifle, let him who has a sabre use his sabre, let those who have neither sabre nor rifle use spades, shovels, sticks! Let all rise to oppose colonialism and defend the fatherland!" While the Viet Minh forces left the towns and cities, which they could not hold against superior French arms, they mounted guerrilla warfare throughout the country.

In June 1949 France persuaded Bao Dai, who had settled in Hong Kong, to give up his long resistance to its appeals for his return to head a rival, pro-French government as head of state. Paris conceded the unity of all Vietnam, including Cochin China, and a circumscribed form of independence as an "associated state" of the French Union. Under this formula, France continued to control everything essential, above all Vietnam's defense and foreign relations. And little by little France persuaded the United States that its war to retain its empire was, in fact, a conflict in which France stood for the democracies threatened by a worldwide Communist conspiracy of conquest. The argument gained considerable weight with the Communist victory in China in 1949 and even more with the outbreak of the Korean war the following year. During the same period the Viet Minh, strengthened by the new China's active backing, raised the level of its aggressive warfare from guerrilla actions to a large-scale campaign against the major French bases in the north. By the end of 1950 the entire chain of French strong points in the mountainous region adjoining China had been overwhelmed or evacuated, and French forces in Tonkin were massed in the Red River Delta.

Another of France's World War II heroes, the imperious General Jean de Lattre de Tassigny, was sent out to be high commissioner, with the hope of rallying a faltering army to new offensives. He succeeded briefly in halting Viet Minh offensive campaigns, but when he died of cancer in 1952, not long after his only son, a young lieutenant, had been killed in action, the Viet Minh were again gathering strength. In 1953 the Liberation Army was on the offensive throughout Tonkin, in Laos, and in central Vietnam. Under American pressure, effective because by then the United States was paying for the greater part of the French campaign and for almost all of the cost of the growing army of the Bao Dai regime, the new commander, General Henri Navarre, drew up a plan to create throughout Tonkin and neighboring Laos a chain of strong bases from which the French forces would be able to mount offensive actions and regain the initiative that would force Ho Chi Minh to negotiate. It was Navarre who first professed to see light at the end of the Vietnamese tunnel.

One of these bases was an obscure village in a deep and narrow valley in the jungled mountains near the Laotian border. Its population, of the Thai montagnard minority, calls it Muong Thanh; its Vietnamese name is Dien Bien Phu. In November 1952 a small French garrison there was overrun by the Viet Minh, creating an opening threatening to the French hold over northern Laos. French and Vietnamese troops recaptured it in an airborne attack a year later. To the French command, Dien Bien Phu seemed a secure place for a major strongpoint. It was far from Viet Minh bases, making it difficult for General Giap to supply troops operating in the sector, whereas France could reinforce and supply its troops by air. Navarre thought it improbable that Giap could infiltrate enough troops to attack Dien Bien Phu, or that he could position artillery in the surrounding mountains to be trained on the base and make the all-important airstrip unusable. The Viet Minh commander, recognizing the probable reasoning of his antagonist, prepared for the very battle that Navarre had thought the least likely.

Beginning in December 1953, Viet Minh troops, aided by endless columns of men and women acting as porters, encircled the defenders, positioning troops and equipment in the mountains, installing heavy guns so high that all of the base lay within their range. Fifty thousand Viet Minh troops, often reinforced during the battle, surrounded the 16,500 French, Vietnamese, Africans, and varied European volunteers of the Foreign Legion who manned Dien Bien Phu. The assault, a total surprise to the defenders, began on March 13; by March 30 the Viet Minh had placed the airstrip within artillery range and made the garrison dependent on parachute drops of supplies. While the United States alternatingly raised and deflated French hopes that it might intervene militarily, at one point even considering the use of the atomic bomb, and Secretary of State John Foster Dulles failed to persuade Britain to join in intervention, Dien Bien Phu's defenders were being steadily reduced. The white flag went up over the French command bunker on May 7, to be replaced by the red flag with the yellow star of the Democratic Republic of Vietnam.

On the following day, in Geneva, a conference opened that had been convened earlier for the purpose of solving the problems of Indochina. France, the two Vietnamese governments, the United States, the Soviet Union, China, Britain, Laos, and Cambodia were the participants. The Final Declaration — unsigned because the United States refused to participate actively, mainly because of the presence of Communist China — partitioned Vietnam "temporarily" along the seventeenth parallel, with the French and pro-French Vietnamese forces to be withdrawn south of the line and the Viet Minh to the north, and called for general elections throughout Vietnam in July 1956. The United States and Bao Dai's Vietnam withheld their approval; Washington promised only that it would not use force to "disturb" the agreements.

France had granted Bao Dai's demand for independence within the French Union in June 1954 but retained a large expeditionary force in the new South Vietnam, which consisted of Cochin China and the southern half of Annam, central Vietnam. Two weeks later Bao Dai named an austere Catholic, strongly nationalist, anti-French and pro-American mandarin, Ngo Dinh Diem, as prime minister. In October, alarmed by the Geneva accords and a belief that further Southeast Asian "dominoes" must be kept from falling to the Communists, President Eisenhower wrote to Diem to inform him that the United States would accord him military and economic aid directly, no longer via France. In February 1955, in an agreement reluctantly acquiesced to by France, the United States took over the training of the South Vietnamese military. At the same time France, resentful of Diem's antipathy and believing that he would never willingly work for reunification, sought to persuade the United States to drop its support. In Saigon there were Vietnamese who warned against too close association with the United States, but Diem was adamant. (A fellow mandarin from Hue, who had known Diem all his life, recalled for me many years later that he had told Diem, "You were wise never to get into bed with the French mouse; you should be even more reluctant with the American elephant." His advice spurned, the mandarin withdrew from active life and never received an American in his home until sixteen years later a relative persuaded him to talk with me.) Diem alienated France further by refusing to meet with North Vietnamese representatives to prepare for the elections to be held in 1956. In October 1955 Diem, with American help, organized a referendum that deposed Bao Dai. He established the "Republic of Vietnam" and was proclaimed its president. In December he annulled the remaining economic agreements with France and left the French Union. The following March, France agreed to withdraw its troops.

America's twenty years of primacy had begun.

9

The War of the Dominoes

Minor acts of American hostility against North Vietnam began almost immediately after the Geneva accords. They resembled spiteful boyish pranks of sabotage of no military or political significance, carried out by dirty-trick experts of the Central Intelligence Agency. They ended with the closing of the American Vice-Consulate in Hanoi, accredited to the defunct French colonial regime, in 1955. After that the United States concentrated fully on efforts to build up the regime of President Ngo Dinh Diem to stand as a bastion against further Communist advances. It was clear that Diem had no intention of allowing the 1956 nationwide elections for a unified Vietnam, called for by the Geneva accords, to be held. Two separate states were taking root, distinguished in purpose by the evident desire of the north to continue the struggle for reunification, and the south's more defensive concentration on solidifying its existence as the anti-Communist Vietnam.

Ho Chi Minh set about creating a conventional state on the Soviet model at about the same time that tensions against that model were heightening in such countries as Poland and Hungary. Heavy industries were established to realize the romantic early Communist dream of strength and happiness deriving from possessing one's own gigantic steel mill rather than producing more of the goods that make the life of people in a poor agrarian country somewhat easier. A land reform program was put into effect, whose main aim was "to separate our friends from our enemies" through a "Population Classification Decree." This assigned all citizens by a kind of point system to one of five categories, ranging from "agricultural worker" to "landlord," categories that surprisingly also applied to the urban populations. Thousands of death sentences were carried out by summary "People's Agricultural Reform Tribunals" against those classified as landlords. Many of the victims were later acknowledged to have been worthy Viet Minh fighters. In August 1956 Ho announced that "errors" had been committed; in November the tribunals were abolished and a "Rectification of Errors Campaign" was initiated, rather late for those who had been killed, but freeing other thousands from prison camps. "One cannot wake the dead," said Ho in urging his countrymen to practice forgiveness. Unforgiving peasants in Ho's native province of Nghe An staged an angry rising, which was quelled by a massive and bloody military intervention. The crushing of the rebellion coincided with a similar event in Hungary but attracted no international attention. Nor did a concurrent wave of repression of critical artists and intellectuals, who had begun to raise their voices following the beginning of de-Stalinization in the Soviet Union and the brief policy of "letting a hundred flowers bloom" in China.

But whatever errors the harsh North Vietnamese regime committed, it did not offend Vietnamese self-respect by slipping from colonial status into a client relationship with a foreign power. North Vietnam received extensive assistance from the Communist world, but its will and ability to make its vital decisions independently were never in doubt. And the greater became the estrangement between Moscow and Beijing, the more shrewdly Hanoi exploited it by playing one off against the other to retain its own independence. Diem, the most independent-minded dictator to rule South Vietnam in its twenty-one years of existence, was never able to step out of the large American shadow that enveloped him. Under his successors, none of whom would have managed their coups or rigged their elections without American approbation, the sense of total dependence on the United States continued to increase, sapping the self-esteem of the South Vietnamese and with it their will to resist either their dictators or the advance of the more

"Vietnamese" of the two regimes that contended for control over their fates.

Diem ran an authoritarian and corrupt regime, in which most power was held by himself and his brother, Ngo Dinh Nhu, who became the most feared person in the country through his influence over his brother and control over the secret police. Their brother Ngo Dinh Can exercised even more autocratic power over the northern regions, and Bishop Ngo Dinh Thuc held his ecclesiastical hand over the family regime and its reputed riches. Nhu's wife promoted herself into becoming the ruling family's most public member, specializing in provocative anti-American outbursts, scorn of democracy in general, and an openly callous attitude toward the non-Catholic 90 percent of Vietnamese. She became Diem's confidante and elevated herself into the position of chief censor of morals, introducing an alien spirit of puritanism to a generally permissive society. Her 1962 law containing the flat phrase, "It is forbidden to dance anywhere at all," among other restrictions, is suggestive of her priorities in a country at war.

The Ngo family propagated a political philosophy of "Personalism," expressed in a tightly disciplined and secretive "Revolutionary Personalist Labor Party," whose members were rewarded with many key posts in the military and the public service, a boon not much different from that conferred in the north by Communist party membership. The creed originated among French Catholic intellectuals who, suspicious of parliamentary democracy, preached a doctrine closer to the "corporate state" that was an ideal of the Fascist regimes in Italy and Spain. The mismatch between this Catholic elitism and an overwhelmingly non-Catholic nation, and between America's aims and the intentions of its Vietnamese client, could not have been greater, nor could the alienation of the people from the government. The Diem regime, which in Washington's policy of containment was to constitute a democratic bulwark against the spread of communism in Asia, adopted police-state methods of rule that were almost as oppressive as those of their foes and leavened only by the greater corruptibility of its officials, as well as occasional formal obeisance to democratic custom in response to American admonitions.

Whatever doubts American officials harbored over the Diem regime, they were always put aside for the sake of not endangering South Vietnam's apparent stability. Diem and his family shrewdly exploited this reluctance in their maneuvering to turn aside all American pressures for reform to make his regime more responsive to the needs of the country and American ideas. In his masterly summation of Vietnam's recent history, Stanley Karnow cites an unnamed American official in Saigon, who described Diem as "a puppet who pulled his own strings — and ours as well." A military coup was put down with considerable bloodshed in Saigon in November 1960. The United States declined to intervene. A month later, as John F. Kennedy prepared to assume the presidency he had just won, the National Liberation Front was formed in an underground network of tunnels near Saigon, with the aim of expelling the American-supported regime and reuniting the country. It was a grouping that included non-Communist nationalists, but its directives throughout its existence came from Hanoi.

Under Kennedy, American support of South Vietnam, which had preoccupied his predecessor, Dwight D. Eisenhower, but not been at the center of his foreign-policy priorities, was moved into that position. Like his conservative predecessor, the young, liberal president saw, with astonishing oversimplification, a monolithic Communist bloc directed by Moscow challenging the West to global struggle, and the noncommitted or newborn independent nations of Asia and Africa as the looming battleground. Kennedy's ideological commitment to the notion of America's duty to defend everywhere the values that it professes, coupled with blithe disregard of Vietnam's specifics and complexities and of the deep rift splitting the largest European and Asian Communist powers, spurred him to decisive, ill-starred action. No doubt the hubris of American military supremacy contributed to excessive faith in its capacity to resolve complex conflicts. And was there an underlying, implicit belief that nations of modern Western civilization possess a superior sagacity that can resolve problems provoked by peoples deemed to be less enlightened? Despite often-conflicting advice from the foreign-policy intellectuals and national-security specialists whom he had drawn into his inner circle, Kennedy decided that Vietnam was the place in which America had to make its stand against communism, and Diem was the surrogate he had inherited.

Already in Kennedy's first year in office, the number of American advisers in Vietnam increased, and introduction of American combat troops was a subject of discussion. The president's favorite soldier, General Maxwell D. Taylor, advocated this, as well as American bombing of North Vietnam, should Ho respond militarily. The guerrillas of the National Liberation Front, called by their foes the Viet Cong, or Vietnamese Communists, which has a derisive ring to Vietnamese ears, stepped up their attacks on Diem's army, as Hanoi raised "American imperialism" to the status of principal antagonist and demoted the South Vietnamese army to the rank of "puppets." In February 1962, a United States Military Assistance Command was established in Saigon. Soon, in threadbare secrecy, American military planes and helicopters were flying combat missions in support of South Vietnamese units. The demise of the Diem regime was provoked by its violent reaction to Buddhist demonstrations, which had been caused by the authorities' blatant favoritism toward Catholics. The first incidents occurred in Hue but soon spread to other cities, including Saigon. When the first of several monks to do so immolated himself in protest against the government's repressive measures, Madame Ngo Dinh Nhu delicately called the tragedy "a barbecue." The ruling family ignored American pressure to strive for reconciliation, affirming that the Buddhists were being manipulated by the Communists. As the regime's unpopularity became increasingly evident, the Kennedy administration gave its approval to a cabal of generals who plotted its overthrow. The plot was carried out on November 2, 1963. Diem and Nhu were assassinated, a finale probably not included in the American-approved scenario. Three weeks later President Kennedy met the same fate.

Lyndon B. Johnson's first written order on Vietnam, at a

time when there were 16,300 American military advisers in the country, disclosed both his determination to pursue the war and the absurd Washington view of why there was a war. The United States, the new president ordered, would help South Vietnam to win "against the externally directed and supported Communist conspiracy." It was difficult to tell in 1963 who the external director might have been; China and the Soviet Union were in open conflict, and North Vietnam had no illusions about the larger global interests that limited the extent of both powers' commitment to Hanoi. The Soviet Union was pursuing "peaceful coexistence" with the United States; China saw no inconvenience in Vietnam's draining United States fervor for involvement in Asia by pinning it down in a long and unpopular war.

In Saigon, the fall of Diem was followed by political chaos. The original military junta that succeeded Diem, headed by General Duong Van Minh, lasted less than three months before being overthrown. It had convinced Washington by then of its hopeless ineffectualness. The next regime, under General Nguyen Khanh, quickly disappointed early hopes. Khanh's tenure was marked by unrest, plots, and coups; he resigned for a few days, returned to power, and installed a weak civilian government, only to stage another military coup to oust it a little later. In February 1965 Khanh was finally removed by the military and sent off to any destination he chose as "ambassador-at-large" without portfolio. He was given a tidy amount of money to cover his "ambassadorial" expenses and not much later opened a Vietnamese restaurant in the fashionable, very Proustian Faubourg Saint-Germain in Paris. "You remember me as a general and chief of state," he said when I visited him there. "Now you see me in the soup. And it's good soup, because my wife makes it, and I serve it." An extraordinary conspirator even by Saigon standards, he played for me a tape that he had surreptitiously recorded of an angry conversation with a hectoring Maxwell Taylor, then the American ambassador in Saigon and Khanh's bête noire. He took particular glee in telling me that it was Taylor himself who had supplied the American technology by which Khanh secretly recorded sensitive conversations in his office. His successor as

prime minister was Air Vice Marshal Nguyen Cao Ky, a flamboy-
ant air force commander who liked to show himself in public
with his glamorous wife, both wearing dashing matched,
custom-tailored, and richly zippered pilots' jumpsuits.

But 1964 was marked also by a dramatic escalation of the
war — the beginning of American air raids on North Vietnam.
Following a contrived naval incident in the Gulf of Tonkin in
August — no conclusive evidence that North Vietnamese patrol
boats had attacked two American destroyers operating near
their coast has ever been presented — carrier-borne American
planes attacked shore installations and ships. Two planes were
shot down; one pilot became the first American prisoner of war.
Johnson used the incident to obtain congressional approval for
a resolution giving him essentially unlimited powers to make
war "to prevent further aggression" against American forces.
The only aggression that had definitely been committed in the
gulf at the time had been daring South Vietnamese commando
raids in conjunction with the U.S. Navy.

While Saigon stumbled from coup to coup and the Johnson
administration wrestled with the dilemma of stiffening an un-
steady ally or taking over the war by engaging American combat
troops, North Vietnam and the National Liberation Front
greatly strengthened their highly disciplined forces by extensive
recruiting in the south and a growing flow southward of northern men and materiel supplied by China, the Soviet Union, and
its allies along the Ho Chi Minh Trail network. The jungle and
mountain trails were rapidly improved and expanded into a
broader logistical network linking North and South Vietnam
across sparsely populated mountain regions of Laos and Cambodia, whose consent for such use of its territory had not been
asked. Communist attacks and ambushes throughout South
Vietnam were taking a toll of the government army, and installations of American advisers in and around Saigon became targets. At that time, the number of advisers had risen to 23,300. In
February 1965 guerrillas attacked a major camp and air base of
American advisers at Pleiku in the Central Highlands, killing
eight Americans and destroying ten planes and helicopters.

The raid resolved a long-simmering dispute among Johnson's principal advisers and generals and precipitated a decision
that had been long in the making — the president ordered a
bombing campaign against North Vietnam. It began as a limited
series of retaliatory strikes and quickly lengthened into continuous, unlimited raids on what by then had become "the enemy."
The bombing continued without surcease until Christmas Day,
1965, when Johnson suspended it for five weeks in the hope of
bringing North Vietnam to negotiate. Inexorably, America's de-
scent into war in a country that presented no vital American interest had begun. A month after the first air raid, the first combat
troops came ashore on a beach at Da Nang, with the mission of
protecting the expanded American deployment of planes at the
airfield. More defensive troops followed, and by April their mission had been broadened on the tactical theory that offensive
patrolling was the best defense. Communist troops were on the
attack throughout the south, inflicting demoralizing defeats on
the government army. General William C. Westmoreland, the
American commander, advised Johnson that the war would be
long, and that more Americans were needed. He found a powerful supporter in Secretary of Defense Robert S. McNamara, who
urged what amounted to an all-out American war to be carried by
all means against all of North Vietnam. Three decades later,
McNamara pleaded guilty to having been disastrously wrong —
and knowing it — in a remarkable eleven-point mea culpa in his
memoirs. In July Johnson agreed to Westmoreland's demand for
more men to meet "mounting aggression." By the end of 1965
there were 184,300 American troops in Vietnam.

As the Americans poured in, there arrived not only troops
but also armies of engineers with construction equipment that
Vietnam had not seen before nor since, to build roads, ports, storage facilities, communications and electronic detection installations, and many structures without windows whose arcane
purposes puzzled not only the local population. The American
embassy and the agencies of the Pentagon grew vastly, implanting
throughout the country diplomats, intelligence operatives, and
technicians of all descriptions, who generally refused to describe

what techniques they practiced. The Americans, military and civilian, brought with them to a country of deeply rooted traditionalism and rural and urban poverty the garish gear of mass culture and the throwaway paraphernalia of a society of overstuffed consumers. They brought it not only to the cities but even more to a countryside where until then a bicycle had been the most modern known implement and a sign of relative prosperity. So alien were the Americans and so numerous, so apparently mighty the means they brought with them, that many of the people of South Vietnam felt that their fate had been taken out of South Vietnamese hands and naively trusted the Americans to achieve what they had come so far to achieve. Others felt that their land had been usurped and joined the Liberation Front or supported its fighters in secret with information, money, or food. Others yet realized that the powerful and rich American machine offered many opportunities for personal profit. But very few South Vietnamese gave to the Americans or their own leaders, about whose legitimacy, honesty, or competence they had few illusions, what the United States wanted above all — their "hearts and minds." Those were devoted mainly to fear and anguish over a war they never wanted and its countless victims.

Much of the South Vietnamese elite submitted all too willingly to American direction, as many had to the French before them, and were often rewarded with painful condescension. "An outstanding officer," an American infantry colonel once said, pointing to his Vietnamese "counterpart," whom he was introducing to me. "I'm proud to shit in the same crapper with him." As part of what was called "civic action," the American military took over more and more of what should have been South Vietnam's ordinary daily civil life. How absurdly far this had gone was made clear to me in 1969, when in the military part of Da Nang's airport I was privy to a conversation between a colonel and a lieutenant colonel, both proud to wear the colors of the U.S. Marines. They were comparing notes on their programs of increasing and improving the production of broilers in their respective areas of what was then called Eye Corps, the term by which Americans referred to northernmost South Vietnam, militarily designated with a Roman numeral as I Corps.

During the first half of 1966 South Vietnam continued to be a battleground of many risings against the regime, which featured the depressing spectacle of a virtual war between troops loyal to Ky and dissident units beholden to rivals of the prime minister — "a civil war within a civil war," as McGeorge Bundy, Johnson's national security adviser, had described this South Vietnamese tendency earlier. Militant Buddhists and students began demonstrations against the regime and its American backers in Hue in March; they quickly spread to Saigon, Da Nang, and other cities. Violent clashes occurred, monks and nuns immolated themselves, the American consulate and library in Hue were set afire. Again, the demonstrators were accused of acting on Viet Cong orders; many were jailed and released only in the exchange of prisoners under the 1973 Paris agreement. Embarrassed by its strong-arm client, the United States imposed national elections in 1967 under a new constitution of American inspiration. General Nguyen Van Thieu, until then a figurehead president, won the redefined presidency, which gave him the real power that he exercised in authoritarian fashion until he and his fortune fled abroad when defeat was certain in 1975.

The war went on, with little change for the Vietnamese people. Bombs continued to be rained onto the north at a rate far surpassing the explosives that the United States expended on all of Europe during World War II, to no more effect than they had had on Germany's power to carry on the war and its mass slaughter of the innocent. Young men continued the long and perilous trek down the Ho Chi Minh Trail, to remain in combat for years on end, enduring not only American firepower from the ground, the air, and the sea and the horrors of napalm and white phosphorus, but also the sparsest of rations, minimal medical care against wounds and the illnesses of the jungle, and endless separation, years without news, from their families. In the south the war continued to spread throughout the countryside, the pressures of the contending forces increased on villagers who tried to stay out of harm's way, and hundreds of thousands were uprooted by fighting or by South Vietnamese and American projects to put populations under strict controls to deny them to the opposing side. By the end of 1966 there were almost 400,000 American troops in Vietnam; by the end of the following year, 485,600.

At the end of January 1968, as Vietnam was beginning the celebration of Tet, the lunar new year festival, the war emerged from the jungles and rice paddies and burst upon the principal towns and cities of South Vietnam. The Tet Offensive, in which the Viet Cong penetrated even into the heavily fortified American embassy compound in Saigon and captured Hue, ended after a month of intense combat with the recapture of all previously held positions by the Americans and South Vietnamese. It caused enormous bloodletting to the Viet Cong, which in the long run cost the National Liberation Front most of its influence in Hanoi's decision making. But no matter how much the Johnson administration attempted to depict it as a victory, the Tet Offensive was a watershed for the dominant American role in the war. Military victory vanished as an objective, to be replaced by a search for what was called a peace with honor: for America, that is, not for its South Vietnamese ally. But public reaction to the Tet Offensive had shown that Americans would not indefinitely support the undeclared war, its mounting casualties, and the bitter, divisive recriminations over it that were envenoming public life. In March Johnson astonished Americans by declaring that he would not seek reelection and would devote himself to making peace in Vietnam. He announced a sharp curtailment in bombing of the north and his readiness to negotiate. There were more than a half million troops in Vietnam as he spoke.

On May 10 the Paris peace talks began. One point was implicit in this process, which went on for five years, with most of the killing still lying ahead: the talks were about an end to the American involvement, not about peace in a divided Vietnam. And there can be no doubt that the United States knew that this meant that the war it was still fighting had become a lost cause. Yet it went on fighting. Washington knew that, with the outcome left to be decided between Hanoi and Saigon, Hanoi was certain to triumph. In his last major presidential action on Vietnam, Johnson ordered a full halt to bombing on October 31.

With Richard M. Nixon's election in November, there began the new president's duplicitous course of seeking to withdraw America from Vietnam without being seen to be losing the war. To do so, he needed to persuade Vietnam's main sources of help, the Soviet Union and China, to weaken their ally by drawing nearer to the United States. With the help of Henry A. Kissinger, his national security adviser and later secretary of state, Nixon achieved what in the eyes of North Vietnam amounted to virtual abandonment of its cause by its two great friends. However ferocious American attacks in Vietnam, they did not divert Moscow and Beijing from responding favorably to American overtures.

To conclude what he could depict as peace with honor, Nixon, with Kissinger's assistance, was prepared to step up and widen the war to force concessions from North Vietnam. His first venture was to rise to a long-standing North Vietnamese challenge and join in violating Cambodia's neutrality by bombing North Vietnamese and National Liberation Front bases and supply routes in the neighboring country. Prince Norodom Sihanouk, who had largely succeeded in sparing his people the worst of the Indochina war, had over the years yielded to Vietnamese Communist pressure to grant their forces the facilities that he knew Hanoi would establish with or without his consent. But Cambodia's long-established hostility to Vietnam propelled this agile diplomatic navigator to tell America that he would be glad if it chased the Vietnamese back into Vietnam, as long as such action did not bring the war to populous areas of his country and was kept secret.

Less than two months after taking office, Nixon ordered the bombing of Cambodian border areas. In 1970, when Sihanouk was overthrown and the North Vietnamese, rejecting an ultimatum to clear out by the new regime, which had no means to enforce its threat, penetrated deeply into Cambodia, Nixon used the occasion to stage a major American foray of two months' duration into that country. The stated aim was to eliminate the

Communist headquarters for the war in South Vietnam. What was not stated was that by spreading the North Vietnamese army into another country and thus thinning its strength in South Vietnam, American troop withdrawal, a difficult maneuver, became easier. The headquarters was not found, but the North Vietnamese army, to avoid the American pursuers, established itself even more deeply and firmly in Cambodia, conquering the nation's most hallowed shrine, the temples of Angkor, in June, a most painful blow to Cambodian pride. The extensive Vietnamese presence, which waned only as Pol Pot, the Cambodian Communist leader, built up his own forces with Vietnam's help, made most of that unfortunate country a target of possibly the most intensive American bombing, which continued for seven months in 1973 after it had ceased in Vietnam. Domestically, the invasion of Cambodia was one more large milestone in the rise of public revulsion against the war, which Nixon had widened rather than bringing to an end.

In June 1969 Nixon announced a first withdrawal of American troops; twenty-five thousand men. It was the beginning of the policy that became known as "Vietnamization," later elevated by the president into the "Nixon Doctrine." It meant that more American supplies to indigenous anti-Communist forces in Southeast Asia would increasingly replace the commitment of American troops in their countries. Forty thousand more troops were ordered to return home in September. But the heavy bombing of the South Vietnamese countryside and the extensive use of noxious chemicals to defoliate jungle and plantations that might offer cover to the Communist forces continued unabated. While the fighting and the official peace conference in Paris dragged on, secret negotiations had begun in Paris between Kissinger and Le Duc Tho, a high North Vietnamese party leader and organizer of resistance in the south to France and America. The number of American troops continued to decline and, perhaps more significantly, so did their offensive actions and consequently their casualties. By the end of 1970 there were 280,000 troops in Vietnam. Among them, a feeling of not wanting to become the last American killed in Vietnam understandably took hold. Low morale increasingly found expression in the high use of easily available heroin.

No encouragement for the success of "Vietnamization" was derived from the first and, as it turned out, last major offensive carried out by the South Vietnamese army in February 1971. This was an attack from northernmost South Vietnam into Laos, with the aim of cutting the Ho Chi Minh Trail at a particularly important point, at which several supply routes intersected. Its main target was the village of Tchepone, elevated by American military briefers over the years to the status of a major "marshaling yard" and a steady target of the U.S. Air Force. The outcome was a rout of the invading force, which withdrew in chaos, having suffered heavy losses and left the trail's traffic only marginally and very temporarily reduced. Demoralization grew among the South Vietnamese military and the country at large, and as American troop withdrawals continued — 140,000 remained in the country at the end of the year — people began to worry out loud about an impending defeat. The war that the South Vietnamese had come to consider as America's was indeed becoming Vietnamese, and the Vietnamese had little doubt that the disciplined north, its dictatorship more austere and effective than their own, was bound to win. These fears were deepened by a Communist offensive on several fronts in 1972. It struck at the north, capturing the northernmost provincial capital of Quang Tri and threatening Hue, the Central Highlands, and the rubber plantation region north of Saigon. American ground troops stood largely aside, but American airpower was perhaps the main pillar on which South Vietnam survived.

In retaliation, Nixon, for the first time since Johnson halted bombing of North Vietnam, ordered its resumption on a broad scale. The use of airpower had continued in a limited way in the guise of "protective-reaction" strikes by bombers covering reconnaissance flights. Soon bombing was extended to the Hanoi region and the mining of Haiphong, the main harbor of the north. On the diplomatic front, too, Hanoi was submitted to severe shocks. In February Nixon had paid his astonishing visit to Beijing, achieving a rapprochement between what had been believed to be irreconcilable foes. And in May, while North Vietnam was under heavy air attack, Nixon was greeted as a friend by Leonid I. Brezhnev, the Soviet leader. Hanoi's main allies clearly showed they had national interests superior to their "lofty internationalist duties," as *Nhan Dan,* the official party daily, called their obligations to their beleaguered ally, which were evidently taking second place.

No doubt Hanoi's clearly established military superiority over the south and the international trump cards that Kissinger's diplomacy had procured led both countries to review their negotiating positions, which until then had seemed too far apart for any agreement. But while Kissinger and Le Duc Tho reached a preliminary accord in October, and Kissinger announced "peace is at hand," the Americans found President Nguyen Van Thieu adamantly opposed to the draft agreement. The two negotiators returned to Paris in a mood of mutual suspiciousness, and Tho suspended the talks. With Kissinger declaring the draft "ninety-nine percent completed," Nixon, in what must have been a last paroxysm of fury at a war he could not win, unleashed the most intensive bombing of the conflict, concentrated for eleven days on the heavily populated area between Hanoi and Haiphong. While the attacks were still under way, Hanoi agreed to resume negotiating if the bombing stopped. It continued for four more days. On January 9, 1973, agreement was reached, and Thieu was browbeaten into acquiescence. Kissinger and Le Duc Tho signed what Nixon called "peace with honor" on January 27 and secured their shared Nobel Peace Prize. On March 29 the last American troop units left Vietnam. More than 58,000 Americans had left in body bags.

The war continued without significant interruption.

What proved to be the final northern offensive began late in 1974, with the objective of laying the groundwork for eventual victory in 1976. But as demoralized South Vietnamese forces crumbled and fled, Hanoi realized that total victory was already in its grasp. On April 30, 1975, the first North Vietnamese tank crashed through the gate of the Presidential Palace in Saigon.

Vietnam was at peace. It was not to last for long.

Hanoi did away with the division of the country more quickly than many of the leaders and fighters of the National Liberation Front and its Provisional Revolutionary Government had hoped. In view of the great political, economic, and social differences that had prevailed in the two halves, many of the southern revolutionaries had expected a period of several years of adjustment to prepare for a smooth joining, a period in which, for example, some of the economic advances of the south might be adopted by the north, and the north might lessen some of the restrictions on civil liberties that it had justified by the needs of war. Instead Hanoi imposed upon the more developed southern economy the collectivist system of the north, to the great disadvantage of productivity and popular support in both halves. On July 2, 1976, the country was reunited under the new name of the Socialist Republic of Vietnam and under the un-diluted control of the northern leadership. Le Duan had been the Communist Party's general secretary since 1960 and the country's leader since Ho Chi Minh's death in 1969.

With the United States no longer at the apex of the triangle of the three superpowers within which Vietnam had to operate in war, Hanoi lost its diplomatic ability to remain on good terms with the two mutually antagonistic others. As both the Soviet Union and China sought to draw Vietnam into their camps, Vietnam inevitably chose the more distant one, which it had no reason to suspect of domineering designs, the more so since the Soviet Union and its European allies could be counted on for more ample and technologically more advanced assistance for the rebuilding and economic development of Vietnam. As ten-sion between Vietnam and China increased and Chinese aid declined, Beijing made overtures toward the ethnic Chinese in Vietnam, urging them to take sides in China's dispute with the Soviet Union. Vietnam responded with moves against the Chi-nese minority, particularly their largest and richest community in Cholon, Saigon's Chinese twin city. It closed their businesses, seized gold and dollars that they had stashed away in 1975, and forced many to try to carve out for themselves new lives in so-called New Economic Zones, insalubrious wilderness areas. An exodus of Chinese to the country of their ancestors began, and it remains difficult to tell whether push or pull was the stronger impetus. China claims that it received a quarter million such refugees; tens of thousands of others escaped as boat people.

Cambodia was the other main arena of the Vietnamese-Chinese conflict, one that finally led to a Chinese invasion. Long before the end of the fighting, the brotherhood of arms between the Vietnamese and Cambodian Communists had begun to show the unsurprising rifts that have always existed between these unfriendly neighbors. To Cambodians of all political persuasions, the Vietnamese are above all the conquerors of Cambodian soil and thus a threat to the very survival of the Khmer nation. Modern southern Vietnam was seized from its Khmer population in the steady advance southward of the Vietnamese. A large Cambodian minority still lives under Vietnamese rule on land that has always been theirs, which Vietnam incorporated into its borders. Moreover, in colonial times France, which esteemed Vietnamese competence more highly than Cambodian, imported large numbers of Vietnamese for jobs requiring skills, which heightened Cambodian resentment not of the French but of the Vietnamese. Even while Cambodia still lived at peace, the Vietnamese minority there was always on its guard; Vietnamese women did not often wear their distinctive national dress in public, and parents instructed their children not to speak Vietnamese loudly outside the house. Prince Sihanouk, the head of state, in the last years before his overthrow in 1970 decreed a list of trades and crafts that Vietnamese were no longer allowed to practice.

Within a month after his coup d'état, the regime of General Lon Nol organized a barbaric pogrom against the Vietnamese minority in Cambodia, which killed many, dispossessed virtually all, and drove them to flee to Vietnam. Most of those who could not escape were imprisoned in primitive camps through the five war years and killed at the end by the victorious Khmers Rouges. Even at the height of the war, when the Vietnamese and Cambodian Communists were fighting the same enemy and it was the Vietnamese who organized, equipped, and initially fought in the name of their Cambodian brothers in arms, Sihanouk told me of tensions between them. President Nicolae Ceauşescu had sent the prince, his guest in 1973 on a state visit as nominal leader of the Cambodian resistance to the American-supported regime of Lon Nol, to spend a week in a remote Carpathian mountain resort while he paid a more important state visit to West Germany. Sihanouk, angry at the snub, with nothing to do, and bored, had invited me to come to see him. "The Khmers Rouges have not given me permission to say it," he told me. "Under their discipline it must never be said, never be admitted that the North Vietnamese have helped us." The prince went on to complain repeatedly that the Vietnamese were no longer supplying badly needed arms and ammunition to their Cambodian comrades. Ieng Sary, a top Khmer Rouge leader and later foreign minister, who served as Sihanouk's Communist watchdog during the war years, accompanying him wherever he went, confirmed this, while clearly embarrassed at the garrulous prince's indiscretion.

Border conflicts erupted almost immediately after the Khmer Rouge victory on April 17, 1975, two weeks before the Vietnamese war ended. As Pol Pot installed his regime, Cambodian incursions into border villages grew in scope, and by mid-1977 hundreds of Vietnamese villagers were being murdered by Khmer Rouge raiders. Hanoi began to stage its own offensive actions in October but maintained silence about the border warfare to keep alive the fiction of unity among the victors. On the last day of 1977 Cambodia broke the silence. It accused Vietnam of aggression and "suspended" diplomatic relations. Tension and border warfare continued through 1978, until in December Vietnam announced the formation of a Cambodian "Salvation Front" opposed to the Pol Pot regime and shortly thereafter mounted its full-scale invasion of Cambodia. On January 7, 1979, the Vietnamese army occupied Phnom Penh, the capital, and Pol Pot and the entire Khmer Rouge leadership fled to the Thai border, where they were received as secret allies, established bases, and with the material and diplomatic assistance of China began their continuing campaign for the reconquest of Cambodia.

On February 17 the Chinese army launched a punitive

invasion of northern Vietnam. For sixteen days Chinese troops, absorbing and inflicting heavy losses, set about methodically laying waste to the main cities of five border provinces before withdrawing. Ironically, the invasion brought devastation to a region that the U.S. Air Force had spared; no bombing had taken place so far north, so as to avoid any risk of accidentally targeting Chinese territory.

The painful blow from the north did nothing to deter Vietnam's occupation of Cambodia against the continuing resistance of the Khmers Rouges from their well-supported bases along the Thai border. For most Western countries, indignation over Vietnam's violation of international rules by its drastic violation of Cambodia's sovereignty determined policy. This indignation was stronger than relief at the overthrow of a regime that, in an insane experiment in social engineering that began where Mao Zedong at his most radical left off, had transformed Cambodia into a land of large agricultural communes by emptying cities, towns, and villages overnight and herding a population estimated, on a very weak statistical basis, at seven million people into the empty countryside. The regime had also given free reign to the violent resentment of ignorant peasants, many of them enrolled in its army by force as children, to wreak vengeance not only on their opponents but also on those who had simply lived on the Lon Nol government side. They had suffered so much less. They had experienced only the dangers of arbitrary Khmer Rouge rocket and mortar attacks rather than the destructive horror of carpet bombing by the B-52s of the U.S. Air Force. The Khmers Rouges would make them suffer for the destruction the U.S. Air Force inflicted on the "liberated zones," the regions under communist control during the fighting.

No one will ever know how many hundreds of thousands of Cambodians fell victim to murder, starvation, lack of medical care in a country that virtually abolished all education, banned religion or profession of belief in any idea other than the absurd dogmas of their tyrants, and did away with money along with all other tools of economic order. Numbers are loosely bandied about; they are idly arrived at. But I know that in a country in which I had many friends and acquaintances, acquired in many long visits, I have in subsequent visits found only three or four whom I knew, and none of those who had enjoyed the advantage of more than minimal education.

The international goodwill that Vietnam had gained by its tenacity and triumph over America's interference was dissipated by an action that, while not inspired by humanitarian motives, produced the result of freeing a nation from a murderous and fatally incompetent regime and turning it into a more or less normal Communist dictatorship, in Vietnam's image. Cambodia became to Vietnam what, say, Bulgaria had for decades been to the Soviet Union, a servile dependent. Yet the West shunned neither the Soviet Union nor Bulgaria as it did Vietnam and "its" Cambodia. No one doubted that, had the Vietnamese occupation army, which was in constant combat with the Khmers Rouges, been withdrawn, its client regime in Phnom Penh would have been unable to halt the return of the monstrous Pol Pot. Vietnam became an international outcast, deprived of badly needed aid except for what the Soviet Union and its friends furnished. The international boycott paralleled the vindictive American refusal to make peace.

America found it easy in 1945 to reestablish normality with Germany and Japan — fierce enemies in war, but not only that. These were nations guilty of rapacious conquest and crimes against humanity of rare barbarity, on a scale of magnitude new in history. But they lost the war, which apparently makes forgiveness and moral rehabilitation easy. Not only did the United States refuse to make peace with Vietnam, it also used its potent economic influence to deny Vietnam access to the credits it needed to repair the damage and backwardness for which the United States shared responsibility, and to enter into normal economic relationships with the rest of the world. It was not only because of their ideological affinity that Vietnam became a Soviet client instead of a mere friend and ally of Moscow — and this status was to endure for as long as the Soviet Union did.

10

The Big Neighbor

Deputy Foreign Minister Tran Quang Co saw a bright future ahead. He believed Vietnam was back where it had been in 1945, after the war against Japan had ended and before the French returned to recolonize the country and cut short the brief dream of uncontested independence. "After almost a half century, we can see again clearly a prospect of peace, freedom, and social and economic development," the long-serving diplomat said. "That is why we decided to join the Cambodian peace accord and normalize our relations with China, our big neighbor. Without that, with our big neighbor as an enemy, we can have no security."

Co was forthcoming in a wide-ranging conversation about Vietnam and the world at his ministry in Hanoi in 1992, not long after the general secretary of the Communist party, Do Muoi, and Prime Minister Vo Van Kiet had returned from a visit to Beijing that signaled a resumption of neighborly relations after a long freeze. The hostility was occasioned by Vietnam's siding with the Soviet Union in the schism between the Communist giants, and relations were driven virtually to the breaking point when Vietnam invaded Pol Pot's Cambodia in 1978. (Virtually, because although the two countries were at war from February 17 to March 5, 1979, when China invaded Vietnam to punish it for its action against Cambodia, formal diplomatic relations remained intact.)

In 1978 also, Vietnam expelled tens of thousands of its Chinese ethnic minority. The war that China waged was brief but devastating to large regions of northern Vietnam. Vietnam needed to be taught "an appropriate limited lesson," said Deng Xiaoping, China's supreme leader, in briefing President Jimmy Carter at the White House three weeks before the attack. The Chinese leader emphasized during his American visit that an important link between America and China was both countries' bad experiences with Vietnam.

The deputy foreign minister made no secret of Vietnam's low expectations for good relations with China. "Are you confident normal relations can be restored?" I asked. "I wish I could be, but I can't be sure," Co replied. "We think China, at least for this decade, also needs peace and stability for its development. Their highest priority is the modernization of their country. They have to shelve other ambitions for another time. And we have to use this time to create another balance of power in this region."

All Vietnamese pronouncements on China to a foreign inquirer, whether public or private, include a kind of statute of limitations in time. "For the moment there is no threat from the north," said General Tran Cong Man, the unofficial party spokesman. "For the moment they can't threaten a big war against us." And in the longer term? "I think that for the moment there is a normalization between the two countries," he said, insisting once again on the cautionary clause. "From the ideological point of view there is a similarity. I think China also is concentrating its force on economic development. It doesn't have the necessary conditions to provoke a big war. For the long term we have to be vigilant and take into account the world situation. Today it wouldn't be approved; no act of provocation would be accepted. But there is always the danger of border incidents. That is why we have to be vigilant."

The ideological similarity the general emphasized is both real and undoubtedly vexing to the Vietnamese leadership. The country the Communist leaders fear the most is also the country whose political and economic course they admire and emulate. They see China as their potential enemy, as the only military threat Vietnam faces, and as a country that has never been

Vietnam's friend. (If only America's leaders in the 1960s, when fear of a monolithic Communist bloc led by the Soviet Union and China propelled the United States to make war in Vietnam, had learned that much history!) But despite their security cautions, Vietnam's leaders also look enviously northward at what they regard as their only ideological model.

China is achieving, far more successfully than Vietnam, the goal to which Hanoi's leaders aspire: Beijing has been hugely successful in attracting foreign investment and stimulating growth by stripping its economy of many of the counterproductive restrictions that it imposed when its leaders still believed in communism. But while giving individual and local entrepreneurship its head, the Chinese leaders have guarded against any spillover of liberalism into the political sphere. They maintain stern one-party control, cracking down mercilessly on any stirring of glasnost to accompany their perestroika. They have learned their lesson from Mikhail S. Gorbachev's debacle when the Soviet leader tried to maintain control and preserve the existence of the Soviet Union while loosening the political as well as the economic reins.

The Vietnamese Politburo and its pervasive, snooping supervisors of political correctness at all levels of society, at home and at work, are successfully emulating China in maintaining the party's hold over all citizens in the sphere that counts: allowing no challenge to their absolute power. Vietnam has also made progress in raising production by dismantling agricultural collectivization, encouraging private enterprise and foreign investment, and reducing state controls over trade. But the party has fallen far short of China's success in attracting foreign capital and technology to lift Vietnam's backward, war-blighted economy into the twentieth century before it passes into history.

"They have authorized foreign investment projects totaling nine billion dollars so far," the head of a French bank's Saigon branch said in 1994. "But so far only two billion has actually been invested. In China, Shanghai alone draws two billion dollars of foreign investment every three months. And most of the two billion here is in petroleum exploration equipment. If they don't find enough petroleum, that two billion is unproductive investment." Foreign investment commitments have risen more steeply since 1994. The total commitments for that year amounted to four billion dollars; in the first three months of 1995 agreements in the value of two billion dollars were concluded.

Vietnam lags behind China's success because it was a late starter in economic reform. Only in 1986, when under Gorbachev's perestroika the Soviet Union signaled a sharp reduction in its generous handouts to its main Asian client, did Hanoi's Politburo give the green light to its own reformers. By then, China was already booming as a magnet for foreign capital. Moreover, the U.S. persistence in punishing Vietnam for America's not having won the war, by excluding it as rigorously as possible from international economic life, has greatly delayed and limited Vietnam's access to international lending institutions and discouraged foreign investment.

Emulating China despite enduring distrust is national policy that is only unofficially and implicitly owned up to. "We are part of the chopstick civilization," said Dr. Nguyen Xuan Oanh, a Saigon economist who heads his own financial firm and has served both the pro-American and the Communist governments. By "chopstick civilization" Dr. Oanh, a Harvard Ph.D., described the four nations that are linked by much deeper cultural ties than their use of Chinese eating utensils — China itself, Japan, Korea, and Vietnam. The motherland of Chinese culture and its three offspring, with all their differences, form a cultural family quite distinct from the rest of Asia. Vietnam is its southernmost member.

What Vietnamese like Dr. Oanh mean by the "chopstick civilization" or other proud references to their nation's Chinese heritage is adherence to the strong Confucian culture that China brought to the countries it conquered or placed under its suzerainty. It means a world placed under an established order, with a revered, godlike figure at the top and center of a highly centralized system and a rigorously structured hierarchy devoted to its service. Access to the hierarchy, as it developed gradually in

Vietnam and reached its apogee during the Ming conquest in the fifteenth century, was through competitive examination, which assured a common striving and respect for education. Unquestioned respect is due to the senior figure in each of the concentric circles that make up the nation — the ruler and his ministers, one's ancestors and parents, the elder brothers and sisters, the teacher. The system places responsibility on each individual but does not encourage individualism. Reverence for the ruler or at least unquestioned obedience to him does not foster open societies or the development of a political opposition.

Dr. Oanh was just back in his well-equipped Saigon office, computerized and furnished in Western modern, from a business trip to the United States on behalf of N. X. Oanh Associates (Management, International Finance) and the Vietnam Frontier Fund, of which he is the chairman. In his press release announcing the fund's establishment, Dr. Oanh lists William Colby, former head of the Central Intelligence Agency, as one of those who will join him in managing the enterprise "in close collaboration."

Sipping from a Harvard Club of Boston coffee mug and exuding the assurance that has helped him to the upper reaches of all the hierarchies through which a seventy-four-year-old Vietnamese of our day has had to make his way, the financier described Vietnam as "a major country." But not major enough, he suggested realistically, to cause Beijing to tremble. He seemed at pains to assure Beijing that it need not fear despite an implication of Vietnamese superiority. "The Chinese see us as part of China," he said. "We originate from there but are different. Still, we have no reason to look for a fight with more than one billion people. We will not be able to knock them out, not even twenty years from now."

Dr. Oanh is one of the anomalies that a visitor to the Communist countries of Europe used to come upon — surprising survivors of prerevolutionary days in societies whose revolutionaries tended to make cruelly clean sweeps of all who had done well under the old regimes. These survivors often have thrived inexplicably in what one would have thought to be adversity. Dr. Oanh did remarkably well under all old regimes, from the French years of his youth through the Japanese occupation, the American period, and visibly, today.

Born in the north, he began his studies in the elite French Lycée Albert Sarraut in Hanoi. When the Japanese army occupied French Indochina after France's defeat in Europe in 1940, Oanh was among the young men the Japanese singled out for education under their auspices to prepare him to be a future member of the indigenous elites that would manage their countries in Japan's postwar Greater East Asian Co-Prosperity Sphere. He attended excellent schools in Tokyo and Kyoto. The Japanese sphere failed to materialize, but Oanh remained in American-occupied Kyoto, where he obtained his first university degree in 1949. By the following semester Oanh was at Harvard's graduate school. He received his Ph.D. in 1954 and stayed on as an economics instructor until 1955. Five years at Trinity College, where he reached associate-professor status, were next. His last job in the United States was as a senior economist at the International Monetary Fund in Washington, D.C., from 1959 until 1963.

He returned to his country after twenty-three years abroad as deputy prime minister for economy and finance of the Saigon government in 1963 and served until 1967. On two occasions in 1964–65, during one of the worst of the periodic leadership crises and seasons of coups that marked America's stewardship of South Vietnam, Dr. Oanh served for a few days as acting prime minister.

When his likes fled by the thousands in 1975, with the collapse of the country that he had served, Dr. Oanh remained and found surprising acceptance by the Communist regime. He has served as an adviser to the government, deputy of the National Assembly, and member of the Central Committee of the Fatherland Front, the "mass organization" under Communist party control that in Communist nations is called into service when required to issue statements said to represent the views not of the party but of the entire nation. "We want to be friends with China," Dr. Oanh said.

China does not share the wish. Vietnamese in official positions, speaking privately, say they believe that just as the United States was reluctant to put aside the animosity of the past, China, too, has a long and hostile memory. Beijing has not forgotten that after decades of military, economic, and diplomatic assistance throughout Vietnam's wars against France and the United States, Hanoi threw in its lot with the Soviet Union after its victory in 1975. This should not have come as a surprise to China, in view of the age-old hostility that separates the two neighbors and the eternal natural law that makes a weak country forced to choose between two mighty friends elect the one with whom it shares no common border or history.

A senior official with access to internal party documents finds in them evidence that Beijing, far from eager to see Vietnam emerge from poverty and underdevelopment, is encouraging the orthodox, doctrinaire Communists in the leadership to stonewall against reforming tendencies in all fields. He said Chinese pressures were largely responsible for putting a rapid end to a brief, timid flowering in the late 1980s and early 1990s of realism and candor in public discussion and literature.

A leading official of a government institution in the capital spoke in tones of despair. He is convinced that China is deliberately undercutting Vietnam's economic development. "Relations with China are extremely difficult," he said.

In outward appearance, China has normalized relations. The number of high delegations who visit, here and there, seems to indicate that all is going well. It is not so. All the economic contracts that have been concluded seem to stagnate. On communications, air, rail, sea links, nothing is advancing. A large credit was promised; nothing has been realized. None of the commercial treaties is being lived up to. Yet there is an astonishing illegal but tolerated border trade, just as China is trading all along the old Soviet border. They send cheap goods that are not up to the standards of their regular exports and pump them in at dumping prices. Everything — beer, clothing, toys, etcetera. At our land and sea borders the Chinese put great pressures on us. While Russia is preoccupied with its own problems and the United States not yet ready to normalize, this danger is extraordinarily acute.

The official is convinced that Chinese dumping is aimed at discouraging Vietnam from enhancing domestic production and developing a lively, more varied manufacturing economy of its own.

A senior Russian diplomat with decades of experience in Vietnam said that a compelling motive for Vietnam's eagerness to normalize its relations with the United States had been to throw on the scales a major counterweight to China. He was not alone in saying that Hanoi would be ready to rent the naval base at Cam Ranh Bay in the center of the country, built by the United States and taken over by the Soviet Union after 1975, back to the power that created it. "They don't want the South China Sea to become the Inner Sea of China," he said.

This splendid natural harbor, one of the most important American military bases in South Vietnam, has stood empty since Russia shelved its ambition to rival China and the United States militarily in Southeast Asia. The few Russian sailors who remained after their navy ended operations at Cam Ranh, the diplomat said, were there only "to protect a Vietnamese base against the Vietnamese." Abandoned American bases in 1975 were looted of everything but the foundations and walls of buildings by swarms of Vietnamese, who reached the scene far more quickly than the security forces.

Since the normalization of formal relations between Vietnam and China, the real tensions between them have slipped beneath a surface of outward calm. There is one exception: both countries are at loggerheads over who owns two far-flung chains of mini-islands in the South China Sea. The larger of the two groups is the Spratlys, about five hundred islets and reefs spread out between the Vietnamese coast and the large island of Borneo. Sparsely inhabited by fishermen, the islands are claimed by both countries, as well as by Taiwan, Brunei, Malaysia, and the Philippines. Each, except Brunei, maintains garrisons on separate islands to lend weight to its claim. In 1988, China expelled Vietnamese detachments from some, but not all, of the islands. The situation is less international in the smaller group of the Paracels, which only Vietnam and China lay claim to and China is alone in occupying, having expelled a South Vietnamese detachment based there in 1974. This great interest in barren islands is, of course, due to the likelihood that much petroleum lies beneath them. Without abandoning its claim to sovereignty over both archipelagoes, Beijing unilaterally declared in 1991 its readiness for a peaceful settlement and joint exploration by all claimants. The issue remains alive as a possible flashpoint between two nations that regard each other with profound distrust.

Suspicion of China appears to unite Vietnamese from north to south, Communists and non-Communists. It extends even to the most tolerant Vietnamese, cosmopolitan intellectuals who have transcended all nationalist narrowness.

Duong Tuong, the art critic, is a most broad-minded and internationally oriented man. The sixty-three-year-old critic is also a poet, literary translator from French and English, and founder of a gallery in Hanoi showing the most unacademic and unconventional contemporary painters. "You will find nothing dogmatic on my walls," he said, smiling with evident satisfaction. He volunteered as a thirteen-year-old to serve as a messenger for the liberation forces even before World War II ended and fought as a volunteer against the French. During the American war he served as a translator on the Commission of Inquiry into American War Crimes.

He said he saw no future danger from the United States or any other country and regarded none with suspicion — except China. Why? "For two thousand years of history." But the Chinese could change, could they not? "I'm not sure." Would he receive them as he receives Americans and all foreigners in his gallery, with tea and friendly conversation? "Of course." But quickly he added, "But with the Chinese we like to keep a distance."

11

Living in Truth

I have learned over the years to believe in the truth of dissidents above all others in countries that muzzle critical voices. When the powers that have made them step beyond the narrow confines have collapsed into history, the dissidents' vision stands as the essential, perhaps the only, truth told in the decades of the lie. Muzzling brings forth women and men who can't live-in untruth. They are people whom honesty with themselves compels to step outside the narrow consensus permitted in the societies whose powers grant no legitimacy to critics but persecute them.

I have come not only to prize their friendship, which in countries of the kind that produces dissidents rather than an opposition is the most courageous and generous gift that a citizen can offer to a foreigner. Such friendship is suspect to the authorities and carries the risk of even more determined persecution. I have learned not only to admire the courage that defies such risk and is often exercised at a painful price, always paid by the dissident, not by his friend. Not only that. I have also learned what is essential about their countries from seeing how they lived their lives. My friends offered me their eyes and sensibilities as the prism through which to see their countries less as an outsider, more as I would see it if it were my own. Yet at the same time it is clear to me now that I was mistaken when I believed that I was listening to forlorn voices, hearing those destined never to see their dreams realized. This deepened sympathy, perhaps, but at the expense of credence in the realism of their hopes.

And then, in July 1989, I sat among the spectators in Poland's parliament while Adam Michnik took his freely elected seat, and General Wojciech Jaruzelski, one of the dictators who had put him in prison, looked on before sinking into political oblivion somewhat later, his place taken by Lech Wałesa. And soon Václav Havel became president of Czechoslovakia, Jiri Dienstbier his foreign minister, and Lubos Dobrovsky his defense minister. Gyorgy Konrad suddenly saw his novels and essays in the Hungarian language in which he wrote them on sale in all Budapest bookstores, after all the years of being published only in translation in alien countries. Then one day Lennart Meri, a writer and filmmaker, telephoned and slipped into the conversation, with cunning casualness to heighten the effect, the mention that now he was Estonia's foreign minister, although his country was still part of the Soviet Union. How often, over how many years, had I benefited from their friendship and been wrong about what the future held for them and their countries!

And when the Soviet Union died in 1991, I thought of my dear friend Andrei Amalrik, who asked me in Moscow twenty-two years earlier to take abroad for publication the manuscript of a book he had entitled *Will the Soviet Union Survive Until 1984?* I thought all those years that I had been the first to share with him the wistful joke of a clever title, a self-mockery of his hope, witty, wishful thinking. Sadly, he was no longer alive when a mere seven years past the date of his questioning title Moscow provided its negative answer. I could not ask him whether, when I slipped his manuscript under my shirt, crouching to be out of sight in a rising elevator in the strange Moscow apartment house that he had chosen for the transaction, I had been the only one of us to take his title as only one more of his sardonic barbs against the colonial empire he hated. Did he believe the Soviet Union would perish before the Orwellian date?

So nowadays I listen to the handful of Vietnamese who overcome well-founded fear to speak their independent minds not only with sympathy and wonderment at the rare personal alchemy that has kept their minds free through decades of oppressive isolation and battering by one-sided propaganda but also with the attention merited by intelligent men and women expressing hopes that they have a right to believe capable of realization in their lifetimes.

Dissidents as they were in Communist Europe — men or women who openly challenge the regime, springing from small, close, informal communities united by a determination not to abandon their sense of truth to regimes that make them live a lie — hardly exist in Vietnam. There have been individual actions of great courage: Dr. Nguyen Dan Que, a Saigon physician, was imprisoned for twenty years in 1991 for "collaborating with people who publish periodicals to fight against the government," according to Nguyen Son, a spokesman for the city government. "He called on the people to revolt." In fact, Dr. Que wanted to form an organization for the protection of human rights. Dr. Nguyen Khac Vien, a physician and officially sponsored writer of several books that the government circulated widely in foreign languages for their public-relations value, and Phan Dinh Dieu, mathematician and deputy director of the Hanoi Institute of Sciences, have from their somewhat protected positions as respected members of the establishment issued appeals for greater civil rights and fundamental, liberalizing party reform. Bui Tin, who as a colonel of the North Vietnamese army accepted the surrender of the last South Vietnamese government at Saigon's Presidential Palace in 1975 and was deputy editor in chief of *Nhan Dan,* the Communist party's official daily, broke with the party to which he had belonged for forty-four years during a visit to Paris in 1990 and publicly demanded far-reaching political reforms.

There is also a silent minority of men and women in Hanoi who by their actions in Vietnam's wars proved their commitment to the cause of independence from foreign dominance. They harbored the hope for freedom not only for the nation but also for its citizens, and today, with the slight opening that *doi moi* provides, take the risky liberty of expressing in private and for the first time to outsiders the pain of their disappointment.

They are not dissidents as they were in Europe, because they do not band together to propose political alternatives, or to sign joint appeals against injustice or for civil liberties, or to protest against arrest or discrimination against someone whom they know. They do not act in opposition but step outside their restrictive system only by thinking and speaking to their friends as though they lived in a free, civil society. They live in truth surrounded by many a lie.

Duong Tuong, the man who wants to read Musil, is a slight, self-effacing intellectual, who in quiet tones emphasizes only what he depicts as the ordinariness of his far from ordinary life. He was born in 1932 in Nam Dinh in the Red River Delta south of Hanoi, a son of a public works contractor and grandson of a Confucian mandarin, a scholar. As he sits surrounded by his friends' paintings hanging or leaning on his gallery's walls, it is easy to see in this erudite critic and poet in French of aching verses of love, which betray an acquaintance with surrealism and dada, a modern replica of this learned ancestor. He began studying at the Lycée Louis Pasteur in Hanoi, but the Japanese occupation ruined his father's business, and he had to drop out at the age of twelve. "I never finished secondary school," he said, laughing apologetically to cover a certain embarrassment unsurprising in a traditional society that takes academic titles at least as seriously as the learning that procures them. "I must say that my culture is fragmented. I picked up what I know here and there."

At thirteen Tuong volunteered to carry messages for the anti-French and anti-Japanese resistance in the final months of the occupation. "I knew nothing about politics," he said. "This was simple patriotism." In 1949, at the height of the war against France, he enlisted in the Viet Minh army, fighting in the Red River Delta and central Vietnam and in Laos during the decisive Dien Bien Phu campaign. "Laos is the only foreign country I've ever been in," he said, laughing apologetically once again, his eyes narrowing to slits behind thick glasses. Throughout the fighting, Tuong said he knew nothing about socialism but shared to the full the Viet Minh's determination to make Vietnam independent. Communist indoctrination began in earnest after the victory of 1954, he said, and for a while he felt himself converted to the cause. After his demobilization he continued to work as a journalist, a craft that he began to practice as a soldier.

"It was the Twentieth Congress that awoke me from my dogmatic slumber," he said. At that historic meeting of the Soviet Communist party in 1956, Nikita S. Khrushchev lifted, at least partly, the veil that had covered the true nature of Stalin's rule. The Soviet leader's report was delivered behind closed doors, and news leaked out only gradually. As it did, it sent tremors through Europe's Communist countries and stirred revolts in Poland and Hungary. The news was never published in Vietnam, whose leaders despised the Khrushchevian thaw, but it circulated in bits and pieces among Hanoi's intellectuals. Ferment stirred, largely among writers and artists impatient with the tight reins under which they lived and worked. The party's angry reaction led to the exclusion of many of them and their banishment to the edges of life, with few means to earn a living. Great pressures weighed on their families and friends to disavow them; wives were counseled for the sake of their children to divorce husbands who had fallen into political disgrace for the sin of "revisionism."

Although he had never been invited to join the Communist party, Tuong was accused of revisionist sympathies. "They let me know they were keeping an eye on me," he said. "They let me continue as a journalist but no longer assigned me to important tasks." Through the mid-1960s he was occasionally called in for questioning by police, and he remained under surveillance through the 1970s. For a while his articles and translations, the work to which he had turned to provide for his family, ran into obstacles to publication. He made up for some of his lost income by donating blood. "They drew almost three hundred cubic centimeters each time," Tuong said with the same self-mocking short laugh. "How many times can one do that? But I had no other way of making a living." Relief came in 1970; he was assigned as a translator to the Commission of Inquiry into American War Crimes, a state body associated with the unofficial war crimes tribunals organized by Bertrand Russell, the British philosopher, mathematician, and peace activist.

Since 1979 Tuong has devoted himself to literary translations and freelance articles, mainly on art. He has translated more than forty books and plays from English, which he taught himself and speaks fluently, and French. The range is astonishing and includes many books in languages he does not speak, which he translated at second hand, from French or English versions. They include Shakespeare (*Twelfth Night, Othello, Antony and Cleopatra,* and *Much Ado About Nothing*), *Anna Karenina, Wuthering Heights, Gone With the Wind, Roots,* the novels of Stefan Zweig and Nikos Kazantzakis, and many more.

Tuong takes hope from the fact that pressures on people like himself have sufficiently eased for him to have assembled the gallery of nonconformist art, which his daughter manages, and to receive visitors, now including foreigners whom he could not have met before, around a low table bearing a seemingly bottomless teapot. He or his wife see to it that the small cups never go empty. Like Tuong's wide reading despite the immense difficulty of finding other than a brief, prescribed syllabus in Hanoi's bookstores and libraries, and like his acute awareness of life beyond Vietnam's borders although he has been only to Laos, the gallery's paintings and their dates show that the work of Picasso, Matisse, and Klee had reached the eyes of North Vietnamese artists many years before the socialist realist barriers fell. How did Tuong create the "undogmatic" gallery? "I think I must be grateful for the ignorance that reigns in the seats of power," he replied. "They have come to believe that an abstract or surrealist painting cannot overthrow them. Of course they are right. In the past, everything that strayed from realism was considered weeds. They suppressed everything that deviated from socialist realism. Today, they have to show a more open spirit, for the sake of *doi moi.* Writers are in a more difficult situation, of course. They manage to understand them.

"I must say, a great step forward has been taken. It has become easier to breathe. That is due to the force of events, the global upheavals, the collapse of the Soviet Union and what was called the socialist camp. *Doi moi* is the reaction to perestroika in the Soviet Union."

Tuong believes that *doi moi* carries the same risk for those in power in Vietnam as perestroika did in the Soviet Union. "The political regime here remains almost the same as it was," he said. "They still cling to the dictatorship of the proletariat. But I believe that when the old guard comes to be replaced by younger men, a more open, more clear-sighted new intelligentsia will arise. I believe such an intelligentsia is being formed now." He disagrees with those who believe that this younger generation is oriented only toward economic and technocratic progress. "Not only that," he said. "My friends among the intellectuals, including the young, have wider interests. It's not for nothing that I'm optimistic."

Such high expectations are not shared by Vietnam's closest equivalent to the dissidents of the Soviet Union and Eastern and Central Europe. Duong Thu Huong, a 48-year-old novelist and screenwriter, is, I think, the only person in a nation of seventy-three million who openly and without the protection of a favored status confronts her country's powers with total opposition. She calls herself a dissident, and the utter fearlessness with which she challenges the authorities and speaks her free mind fully justify that designation. A stretch of seven months of imprisonment in 1991 has, if anything, only stiffened her determination. She has many readers at home and abroad, and some friends, but she does not lose sight of the chastening fact that none joins her, as was the custom in the struggles of Europe's dissidents, in shouldering the risks and burdens of confronting publicly and uncompromisingly a dictatorial government. When she was imprisoned, the only appeals for her liberation came from readers and human-rights organizations abroad.

Like so many Vietnamese, this tiny featherweight of a woman, whose eyes twinkle as she speaks and whose frequent peals of laughter punctuate her funny twists in the most serious conversations, does not look the part that life has assigned to her. It is hard to imagine this high-spirited, carefully groomed woman, whose vigorously gesturing hands impress with many rings, as a young girl who spent her twenties during the war against the United States and South Vietnam serving eight perilous years as a volunteer with a front-line auxiliary military unit in the tunnels and bunkers along the heavily bombarded dividing line between North and South Vietnam.

In the first of many long conversations — it took place in the empty office of the director of the film studio in the center of Hanoi for which she officially works, but which refuses to let her make or write a film — she compared her situation with that of European dissidents. She noted that by political history or intellectual tradition the ground of Warsaw or Prague, or any of the European Communist capitals, was more fertile for opposition to dictatorship because of the rooted existence of a political class of many tendencies, however suppressed, and an intellectual tradition emphasizing individual freedom and responsibility.

"In Asian countries there was never true freedom, never a true democracy," she said, speaking of the world that begins at India's eastern frontier. "Those who want freedom and democracy must pay for it. I don't know how many people here are ready to pay the price. I don't think there are many. In my generation I think I am alone. There is no dissident community. The Vietnamese have a tradition of resistance to foreign aggression; they have no tradition of resistance to internal aggression. I have been extremely shocked to see how men who were very courageous in war are extremely cowardly toward this regime. In their daily lives they are quite capable of unworthy and cowardly actions, like denouncing their friends, doing things that hurt their friends, things that totally contradict their personalities in war. My conclusion, in short, is that the Vietnamese has not the capacity to stand up alone, affirm himself alone. In war, one can rush forward, everybody goes, and all are alike. In peacetime such a force doesn't come into being, because we Vietnamese have very little talent for living independently and standing up alone. In Vietnam today there is no social class that one might call the intelligentsia. Only a few are true intellectuals. The rest are government officials or apparatchiks. Do you know the word?"

Huong, who knew the Soviet Union from having accompanied an official delegation of the Vietnamese movie industry on a "brotherly" visit, sees many similarities to that country in the structure and character of Vietnam's ruling *nomenklatura*, or party hierarchy, the apparatchiks and their friends and relatives. She sees them as a feudal class lording over the people. She fears that foreigners are too prone to see in the present opening, which allows them to come to visit and do business, a beginning of democratization.

"The foreigners are only passersby, who see only the surface, the appearance," she said. "They get an impression that is not true to reality. They should see that for Vietnamese now the essential interest is money. The money motivation explains everything. They feel that if you have money you can satisfy all your desires. The party officials and the leaders are not sufficiently cultivated to refuse money, nor to consider that money may not be the only motivation. There are cadres who are poor, but that is because they occupy positions that they can't turn to profit."

Huong believes that democracy in Vietnam is not for tomorrow. "I think Vietnam is very different from Eastern Europe," she said.

> Our people are very strong in times of war. We have what it takes to support deprivation, losses, massacres. These qualities come from our traditions. But to live in a civil society, with a full awareness of individual value, our people is still very young and naive. Notions like democracy, the rights of man, are seen as something very distant, luxuries. Vietnam is not a normal country. Its abnormality is its own; it is not the same as China's, for example. The Vietnamese are more supple than the Chinese, and behind that suppleness there lies a certain pragmatism. You might say that Vietnam is always ready for compromises based on pragmatic considerations. But the Vietnamese and Chinese have much in

common. The essential is the gap between action and word. What they say is one thing, the reality another.

Unlike Tuong, who sees the future of Vietnam as determined by a younger, open-minded class of educated people, Huong foresees a change in name covering an unchanged reality. "There is a class of new capitalists in Vietnam," she said. "When their appetite is largely satisfied — they are not yet sufficiently stuffed, far from it — I think the brand name of 'socialism' will fall quietly by the wayside, all by itself. If this socialism falls and I am truly liberated I will be a very happy person. But I think it won't happen like that. The 'socialism' brand name will fall away, but we still won't be liberated."

Huong sees as the immediate consequence of the dropping of the "socialist" brand name the rise of a savage materialism threatening the traditional values that have preserved stability through the worst of times. "I am a dissident who struggles with determination against this one-party system," she said. "But I am not a woman who clamors for its replacement by the market and capitalism. The free market and capitalism introduce their own form of rottenness — depersonalization. They can depersonalize and corrupt human beings. Material pleasure is not the goal of life. If that is what I wanted I would have left a long time ago. I stayed in my country because I want not only the liberation of its soil, but I also want this country to have a spiritual liberation. Yes, the dignity of man. This country suffers from an amalgam of feudalism and communism."

12

"Pain, but Not Shame"

Duong Thu Huong became what she is today for the simplest and most compelling of reasons — being true to herself. "What I dislike in this regime is that it obliges people to live in lies and shame," she said. "The lie is that we are made to say that this regime is a thousand times more democratic than the 'bourgeois' regimes. I can bear deprivation and pain, but not shame. The lie debases the human being. It is an affront to human dignity, and it is rooted in the ideology of this regime."

Vietnam's present tragedy lies in the reasons that led a woman who throughout her agitated life has been motivated by lofty and patriotic sentiments and spurred by a rare determination to act on her beliefs to take the lonely road of dissidence and pay its heavy toll. How did it come to that?

Huong's life could not have started more conventionally for a North Vietnamese born in the war year 1947. Her mother was a teacher, her father a tailor who during the war against France served General Vo Nguyen Giap, the commander in chief and defense minister, as a communications specialist. He was the only one of a large family who participated in the anticolonial war. His mother, a rich landowner, sternly Confucian in exercising her hierarchical family power, ruled that her son, Duong Dinh Chau, should join the liberation army. "My grandmother had no sympathy for Ho Chi Minh, but she said that in our family there must be one who does his share in the resistance against foreigners," Huong said. After the war he became a communications technician in the postal system.

Huong grew up in Thai Binh, a town in the Red River Delta south of Hanoi. After finishing high school in 1964, the year in which the United States bombed North Vietnam for the first time, she experienced her first rejection: a good student, she was denied admission to a teacher's college because her parents did not belong to the "basic class"; her father's family owned land. In the most doctrinaire years of Vietnamese communism, to be classified as other than "peasant" or "worker" constituted a social stigma. Another disqualifying mark, having close relatives in the south, kept Huong's father from being admitted to the Communist party, despite his important service in war.

Huong took entrance tests for several other colleges and was finally admitted to the Ministry of Culture's College of Cultural and Artistic Theory. She was assigned to a course of study that prepared young people for work as organizers to bring Communist culture to the masses. It was while still a student that Huong said she had the earliest experience that stimulated her social activism. She was assigned with others from her school to prepare a photographic exposition on the early anti-French movement. "Through this exposition I learned what the suffering, pain, and humiliation of a small nation subjected to foreign rule was like," she recalled. "While I was putting up these photos of a peasant rebellion led by scholars, I got the idea of what forms resistance must take. I saw the American intervention in Vietnam in those terms. I saw pictures of resistance fighters forced to their knees before the French, pictures of baskets full of Vietnamese skulls held up by the French. I was not motivated by big theories but by photographs."

As she spoke, Huong's voice hardened from the jaunty tone in which the conversation had begun, her features tensed, and she followed intently the interpreter's rendering of her rapid flow of carefully chosen words. She understands far more French than she speaks.

There was a second event that motivated me, and again it was something I saw, not a theory I heard or read. It was early in 1965, after the steady American bombing had begun, and we had been evacuated to the province of Ha Bac, northeast of Hanoi. Planes were fighting each other above the village, and we and the villagers ran to watch it. There was intense antiaircraft fire, and four planes were shot down. One fell on the farm where we grew grain and raised cattle. Another fell in a field nearby. The villagers and we students ran to the planes to capture the pilots and to admire the proof of our victory. But what we found was two dead Vietnamese pilots, and the planes that crashed were MIGs. In fact, all four planes that had been shot down were MIGs, and the Americans had suffered no loss. That evening the villagers erected an altar for the dead. And for a second time I realized that the aggressors against us, the Americans like the French, were enormous military powers, and that in the face of them we were a small, a very weak people. Those were the strong feelings that impelled me when I finished my studies in 1968 to join the fighting.

Huong volunteered to lead a youth brigade of "singing soldiers," which under the banner of "Sing Louder Than the Bombs" was assigned to North Vietnam's southernmost province, Quang Binh, to serve as auxiliaries. Their mission was not only to gather local people to participate in putting on musical shows for the troops, for which she composed morale-building texts and patriotic skits, but also to help the civilian population, tend the wounded and bury the dead. There was no lack of those; Quang Binh, which lay directly above the demilitarized zone, the cutting edge between the two Vietnams, was under constant bombing and shelling from air, land, and sea. "The shows had only one message — resist the American invasion and save the fatherland," Huong said. "We did what we wanted with that theme. There were patriotic songs, we composed new songs. I often adapted traditional songs and poems and varied the texts."

For eight years, without ever a leave, Huong lived with the soldiers and the sparse remaining civilian population in the underground tunnels that traversed the battered province, where none slept above ground. Being a woman in a world of soldiers carried its own risks, and Huong said she always slept with a knife under her pillow. Famine was a regular guest, and Huong observed that the party officials were the last to suffer from the frequent food shortages. (With the almost ritual importance that food and the presentation of meals occupy in Vietnamese social customs and folkways, the years of deprivation have precipitated in Huong's fiction a remarkable preoccupation with minutely detailed descriptions of meals, meager or opulent.) "I saw the cadres who preferred to flee to the safety of the bomb shelters instead of staying up front to fight," she said. Still, she said, a general perception abroad was not unfounded: in comparison with the social injustices and corruption for which South Vietnam was rightly pilloried, North Vietnam was a place of austerity and egalitarianism. "There is some truth in that," she said. "The differences in the south were big, and they weren't covered over. In the north they were not so big, and they were veiled."

It was in Quang Binh that she married and gave birth to her two children. Her son, Minh, was born in 1970, just before a heavy air raid, in which the midwife who had delivered her baby was killed. Her daughter, Ha, was born two years later. Both are students in Hanoi. Her husband was a violent man, about whom she prefers not to speak. Wartime conditions made a divorce impossible. When peace came and Huong, respectful of strict family tradition and submissiveness toward her elders, asked her parents' permission to seek a divorce, she found that her even more traditional father adamantly refused to let her bring "shame" on the family. He made her "admit" that the problems of her marriage were of her own making. She did not divorce until 1981 and has lived alone since.

During the war, Huong said, Marxism or communism were not part of her motivation or world of ideas. She felt she was following her country's tradition in fighting against a foreign invader. "But the first time I saw prisoners of war, in 1969, I saw they had black hair and yellow skin, like me. They were Vietnamese, like me. I thought it wasn't what we were told, just a war against the Americans. It was the first time I had that feeling. It was so new I didn't dare think it through to the end.

That was the beginning of the mental itinerary that led me to change my views."

Not long after her self-questioning began, the secretary of the military unit to which she was attached invited Huong, then twenty-two years old, to join the party. This occasioned the first instance of her direct resistance. "The reason was quite clear, and all knew it," she recalled. "We lived in a tunnel, and everybody heard and saw everything that went on. I told the party secretary: 'This may be acceptable for the men, but the women are the servants. They prostitute themselves to those who hold power and let themselves be corrupted for small material benefits. So I don't under any circumstances want to join you, because the most important thing in life for me is to preserve my dignity.' "

The discovery that Huong described was one that she shared with many idealists in Communist countries over many years, as they awoke to the fact that the party, tolerating no rivals, corrupts its proclaimed ideals and many of its members by becoming a club of the privileged, of the sole holders of power over others. This did not alter her commitment to war against the Americans, despite her recognition that the combat in which she was participating was also a civil war. Both realizations weighed heavily on Huong throughout the war — the corruptness of those in power and the fact that Vietnamese were not only repelling a foreign intruder, which was the dominant theme of wartime propaganda, but also killing each other. To this day, the official version of the war continues virtually to ignore the South Vietnamese "puppet army" and its hundreds of thousands of war dead and crippled and depicts the United States as the sole enemy against which all of Vietnam fought.

Despite her questions and doubts, Huong soldiered on to the end of the war. "Nothing changed," she said. "I had to do my job because I was part of an enormous machine. I had to do all the machine ordered. I continued to work in the artistic group, to put on skits, to write lyrics for songs, to stage propaganda for the soldiers in the combat zone. It was very dangerous, very difficult. Above all I had to face atrocious scenes of war — wounds, blood, victims. It was not only physical hardship, there was constant emotional pain." The realization that even the northern victory, for which she continued to long ardently, would not realize her hopes for her country dawned only dimly. "You know, changes in the mind do not often come abruptly," she said. "It takes a long time. Only when you arrive at a critical moment a radical change occurs. For me, the period of change was very long. For a long time I didn't think very clearly about these matters. There were too many doubts. Life was very hard. There was solitude, there were fatigue and hunger, I thought about survival. The critical moment didn't come until after liberation."

Victory day, April 30, 1975, remains engraved on Huong's mind as perhaps the happiest of her life. "For three or four days no one slept, and fires lit the sky. It was an unforgettable joy. Everyone felt, 'This is it, it's over and we are alive!' " Her first thought as the celebrations waned and people turned their minds to the homes they had not seen for many years was to visit Saigon, where many of her family had gone in 1954, preferring to uproot themselves and leave their properties behind rather than live under Communist rule. With a friend, a poet, she made her way across the Ben Hai River, which had marked the border, the open wound that split the country, and entered the land that had been so tantalizingly near her for eight years and so forbidden. The two women hiked to the ruins of the provincial capital of Quang Tri, the most northern town of what had been South Vietnam, which had been devastated by fighting in 1972, and from there hitched rides to Saigon.

"From the day I entered Saigon begins another itinerary, which ended with my separation from this state, from this system," Huong said, underscoring by fastidious choice of words that she did not mean that she would ever separate from Vietnam, her country. She went on to describe a wrenching experience that she shared with many Vietnamese — the reuniting of one of the countless families that had been separated by the polarization between North and South Vietnam through the Geneva accords of 1954. This split was intended to be temporary but, with the help of considerable bad faith on both sides, was made to endure for twenty-one years, occasioning appalling bloodletting. Many Vietnamese who could have fled under American auspices in 1975 because of their association with the United States or the Saigon government stayed because, whatever else the Communist victory would bring, it would lift the barriers within their country and make one again a people that, with all its deep regional differences and the artificial divisions of colonialism, never stopped feeling as one indivisible nation. Many paid for this love of the nation with imprisonment in harsh work camps, ostracism from the community, years of enforced unemployment, and finally flight into exile in tiny, unseaworthy boats, many of which never reached shore.

Only Huong's father had remained in the north after 1954; his brothers and sisters had left for the south, some even before the division of the country. Her father's elder brother, the favorite uncle of her youngest years, had become known in Saigon as "the King of the Dikes." Huong explained how throughout the war the comportment of many South Vietnamese, little understood by Americans, was influenced by their obligation to protect their close relatives in the north, knowing that the Communist intelligence machine kept Hanoi remarkably well informed about who was on whose side. "As a contractor, he built many of the agricultural dikes around Saigon," she said. "He was very aware that he had a younger brother in the north, so he avoided working for the Americans but did only agricultural construction. The family had remained in contact through a brother who had gone to live in France. The uncle in Saigon had sent money to my family through the brother in France."

Huong found her uncles and aunts and the many cousins she had never met. "In a very big room the entire family was reunited, and everybody cried," she said, the emotion of that day almost two decades earlier still mirrored on her face. "They said, 'Little Sister, why is it that you look so deprived, so poor? Dressed so poorly, and your fingernails blackened?' I was dressed like all of us who came from the jungle, with black pants and a shirt. They couldn't imagine a woman looking like me.

My cousins gave me many rings with precious stones; I wasn't used to that." The poor country cousin said she felt no resentment toward those who had lived in comfort and grown wealthy while she survived below the ground and took part in the struggle against those who protected the rich way of life. "In family relations there are no victors and no vanquished," she said. "Common blood overcomes all divisions. I wasn't overwhelmed by their luxury, their elegant clothes. I saw in an instant that there is no real difference between the people of north and south. We are simply Vietnamese, and I saw that all Vietnamese were victims. I felt painfully the atrocity of civil war, its stupidity."

Her uncle gave her a considerable sum of money. "A party writer and filmmaker had also come to Saigon and said to me, 'This is capitalist money, if you take it you are betraying the revolution.' I didn't care, so I gave it all to him. And he went to spend it in restaurants and such places. He took all the other Communist writers to have a good time betraying the revolution with that money." She laughed without bitterness, clearly relishing her ironic memory of the hypocrisy that she castigates with savage passion in her novels and stories.

It was not the material wealth of Saigon that brought about Huong's "separation" from what she had known. "All that I could learn in my youth was Communist poetry," she said. "It was only when I arrived in Saigon that I could see, sold on the sidewalks, all the great authors, Russian, American, and so many others. I jumped at the occasion and bought a houseful of books. That was a fundamental experience for me. When I came to Saigon in 1975, what impressed me was not the houses, the goods, all the material riches. It was the riches in books. I could buy Marx in Saigon, but I couldn't buy the authors of different opinion in Hanoi."

Saigon, a city with a well-merited reputation for the crassest kind of greedy commercialism and gross vulgarity and, under all the American-supported regimes, of crude repression of any political opposition, looked different to northerners who found there, in the brief period before the Communist regime took stern hold of its looser ways, marks of an openness that surpassed their expectations. It made many like Huong realize, perhaps for the first time, how much they had been missing. Saigon intellectuals, who now found Hanoi accessible for the first time in two decades, experienced a reverse image of Huong's shock of discovery.

Ly Chanh Trung, a professor of philosophy at the University of Saigon until 1975, is a left-wing Roman Catholic and was a caustic critic of the Saigon governments and the American intervention. As a reward, he was included by the victors in the first delegation of Saigon intellectuals to be taken on an official visit to Hanoi in September 1975. Even today, when his views of the Communist regime have grown far more critical, the voluble professor, who now heads the Francophone Circle of Cultural and Scientific Information of Ho Chi Minh City, recalls this visit with emotion. "In Hanoi, time seemed to move more slowly," said Trung, who until 1992 was a member of Parliament chosen by southern intellectuals.

> They were twenty years behind. I loved its serenity. The north was almost totally destroyed except for Hanoi; one saw no men, only older women in the countryside. I admired the sacrifices that they had made and the serenity they had retained through it all. They were badly dressed, the women wore no makeup, but they were serene and happy with their fate. For us, all we saw was the rottenness America had brought. We would have liked Hanoi's image to exist also in Saigon. I don't know what freedom there was, but they were the Vietnamese who had taken their destiny in their own hands. That freedom they had taken.

It all depends where the newcomer to Hanoi or Saigon came from.

On her return to civilian life, Huong was hired as a screenwriter at the Hanoi Feature Film Studio. In her first try at playwriting she also drew first blood from the censorship. Her satirical play was banned, and, transgressing from established usage, she protested publicly. To no avail. The damage to her standing before the authorities was repaired in 1979, when China invaded northern Vietnam in retaliation for Vietnam's attack on Cambodia and overthrow of Pol Pot's regime. Huong volunteered to join a documentary film unit at the front, where she was the only woman. She wrote the script for a strongly anti-Chinese film. She shuddered in recollection of the brief but savagely destructive war, which laid waste Lang Son, the historic garrison and trading town near the border, where much of the filming took place. As in her novels, she did not shrink from unsparing narrative. "There I experienced the most terrible odor of war," she said. "There, not in the American war. Of course, in the American war I often had to go out to pick up bodies, but there were many of us, and the bodies were strewn over large areas. The stench was diluted; there was not such a concentration of the dead. But in the Chinese war, there were sometimes perhaps as many as one hundred people killed in one bunker. We couldn't see the dead, but we saw the flies that circled. Fat flies, very plump. The stench was terrible."

Huong began publishing stories in 1980. Until the end of that decade, when the authorities decided, without formal announcement, to make her a literary unperson by quietly removing her books from circulation and allowing nothing further to be printed, five novels and six collections of short stories made her a major figure among young Vietnamese authors. Her first novel, a work for children, *Chronicle of a Childhood*, was published in 1985 and received the supreme accolade in the Communist world — publication in Russian for the young of the motherland of socialism.

"I was pampered by the state as a young hopeful among writers," she recalled, laughing today at the recollection that once she enjoyed the favor of the regime with which she is at war. "I received some prizes and state subsidies." At the same time she began to earn a reputation for chafing under censorship and saying so in public, even in speeches at official cultural events. She presumes that this was written off among those who ruled over culture as no more than youthful skittishness, which would abate with maturity and the granting of personal privileges. Ironically, it was her boldness in speaking her mind to the Communist functionaries that made her, in 1984, a member of the Communist party, long after in her own mind she had concluded that the party represented nothing that was important to her. Why she became a Communist, at least in name, and the manner of her exit from the party six years later are the stuff of a whimsical satire on the hollowness of the shining image of the ideological austerity and purity of Vietnam's triumphant communism.

Huong related her career as a party member like a farce in a setting of mordant cynicism. "It was my friends at the studio, those who were not party members, who urged me to join," she said. "They wanted me to fight for them. You know, even in a movie studio it is the party cell that makes all the decisions. They say who gets permission to make a film. To travel abroad, you need a permit from your cell. To get a raise, the same thing. This is part of a totalitarian system. So my friends wanted me to be the voice that defends our honest colleagues." She laughed when asked why they turned to her to be their advocate. "Probably because they noticed that I never go to battle for personal benefit, and they thought I had a sense of justice." She laughed again. "And because they knew I am not in the least afraid of the bosses and talk back to them." As Huong's national and international reputation as a dissident grew, party officials began first to suggest and later, in 1990, to demand that her cell expel her.

"But there are some extremely good people in my profession who supported me," she said, and no action was immediately taken. "My colleagues couldn't understand why. I was a volunteer in the war against America, I volunteered in the war against China, I am in the vanguard for the renewal of the country. Why should I be expelled? It dragged on for two months. I used the cell meetings as a tribune to say what I think. I think my words had influence. I have an ideal, I cling to it and want to express it to people. It was only when the party said it would dissolve the cell and even the Film Institute that they agreed to hold a cell meeting to expel me. The cell secretary came to me and said, 'I did what I could to save you, but they insist from above.' "

What followed, Huong could hardly have turned into a credible comedy script. When the vote for Huong's expulsion was called after the article of accusation had been read, five of the eleven members of the cell voted in favor, but five others, in a display of exceptional courage — inspired, perhaps, by Huong's arguments — voted against. "It was up to me to decide whether I would stay or be expelled," Huong said, reliving the crisis as a comedy. She cast her vote to spare the party secretary further embarrassment. "I expelled myself," she said. "If the choice had been mine alone, I would have quit earlier."

Huong's dissident career, with the ups and downs that in any dictatorship are the barometer of the intellectual climate, began in earnest in 1980, at a congress of the Writers' Union — every Communist country followed the Soviet example of creating a vast organizational structure in which every branch of human activity, from boys' choirs to collecting butterflies, could be integrated under party control — to celebrate thirty-five years of culture in independent Vietnam.

"They wanted me to speak as representative of the young generation," Huong said.

They thought with the prizes and money I had been given I would say things pleasing to their ears. I wasn't thinking of what they had given me. Only later did it dawn on me that if they treated me so nicely it was because they expected other words from me. After the official speeches of the dignitaries, they called on me. I said what I thought. I said we have many great traditions, and there are already too many writings that glorify them. If we continue just to glorify our traditions, this people will get stuck in misery and slavery. Other people don't have as many heroes as we, but our heroes, when at lunchtime at work they open their little boxes of rice, they find only two or three shrimp and a few slices of vegetable. We have too many poets, and they know only how to glorify. A people that spends its time singing praises on an empty stomach will never get ahead.

The young literary hopeful was speaking out of turn at a time when hunger and malnutrition were the ghosts that stalked all of Vietnam but could not be mentioned in public. The collectivization of South Vietnam's once-productive agriculture and the low, artificially fixed prices paid to producers had caused dramatic passive resistance among rice growers, provoking shortfalls that the Soviet Union, itself an importer of basic food grains, could not compensate for. China, then an enemy, had halted its food aid, which had been considerable throughout the wars. Dr. Ton That Tung, surgeon general during the French war and Ho Chi Minh's personal physician, was the only official who felt that his high standing allowed him to speak freely to me during a visit at that time. He wanted me to deliver a message from his isolated country. "A whole generation will bear the stigmata all their lives," Dr. Tung said gravely. "The Vietnamese people do not have enough to eat."

Huong's blunt and impolitic words, at a public meeting of the kind at which words of praise and self-congratulation are the rule, caused an unsurprising stir. The presiding Politburo member, Ha Xuan Trung, rushed to the podium. "There are writers and poets who foment disorder in society," he said, and continued threateningly, "For such people we have to send for the police." Huong continued her account: "After that, a whole gang of people went to the podium to attack me," she said, not hiding how afraid she had been. "At the noon pause, all those who earlier had greeted me with so much warmth turned their backs on me. The young writers, who before had followed me like little dogs, disappeared. I heard one say, 'She's completely crazy.' After two more hours of meeting it was time for lunch. There were five hundred people at that congress, but I found myself all alone at a table. Nobody dared sit with me. That was the first time that I learned what it means to be isolated. The girls who served the food passed around me and gave me looks as if I had the plague.

"I wasn't very hungry," she continued, in what must be a considerable understatement. "But I reacted in my fashion. That is, I put my ration tickets on the table and ordered, and then forced myself to eat everything. If I hadn't eaten they would have known how afraid I was. And I really was afraid, because it was the first time that I had to confront such solitude amid such a mass of people." What might have ended dramatically did not, thanks to a courageous stand by the party secretary of the Film Institute. Huong said that Department 87 of the secret police, an agency more recently known as the Counterespionage Service, demanded that the institute punish the unruly writer. But the director defended her "ardently," Huong said, citing her war record and her anti-Chinese film produced under fire. Having saved her skin, he took Huong aside to warn her, in her paraphrase, "Shut up now, I beg of you, because the next time nobody can save you."

Warning never heeded, as Huong steadily multiplied her calls for greater freedom, not only for artists and writers but for all Vietnamese. She assumed in her country the leading role played by courageous writers and intellectuals throughout the Communist world in a lonely struggle for an open, civil society. Because of Vietnam's isolation from events even in the community of "brotherly countries," she was never fully aware that she had inserted herself into a historic international movement. "I am not a politician," she said, rejecting any comparison with the likes of Václav Havel. "I became a writer despite myself," she wrote to a journalist for the *Wall Street Journal* who had denigrated her person, her politics, and her work in a scurrilous article mirroring the government campaign against her. "I have never harbored literary ambitions. I write because I find no other way to scream the pain of my generation, of my people — a people drowned by their interminable misfortune."

Other writers of her generation — Nguyen Huy Thiep, Bao Ninh, Pham Thi Hoai — have published novels and stories dwelling on similar themes, usually more elliptically than Huong's Zolaesque graphic naturalism. They too have confronted the grim realities of the war and its aftermath. "I am not ashamed to be less talented than Nguyen Huy Thiep or Pham Thi Hoai," Huong wrote to the journalist. "Since Heaven only endowed me with one cent of talent, I have spent the cent." The other writers, too, have been muzzled and hounded. But Huong is alone in going beyond literary expression to issue direct political statements, much in the tradition of Andrei Sakharov, Václav Havel, or Adam Michnik.

Doi moi returned to Huong her literary voice. Her novels *Beyond Illusions* and *Paradise of the Blind* were published and made her a national name during a brief thaw in intellectual life. The warming was brusquely chilled in 1989, as the leadership panicked while the Soviet Union's European dependencies liberated themselves from Russian domination and one-party rule and Chinese students demonstrated on Tian An Men Square. *Paradise of the Blind* was published in 1988 to great public acclaim and official regret, and remains the last of her works to be printed in her own country. Its two main themes are the corrupt power of party hacks and the ruthless brutality of North Vietnam's land reform of the 1950s. Publicly recognized as an "error" and apologized for after the fact by the regime, the land reform was partially undone too late for the thousands of landlords or those arbitrarily classified in that category who were summarily executed, unceremoniously murdered, or driven to suicide in an orgy of vengefulness, settling of long-standing private scores, and lawless personal enrichment. "I wrote *Paradise of the Blind* at a time when I felt that I could no longer find a compromise with the regime," Huong said. "I needed to write a book in which I could settle my debt to those whom I knew, who described for me the historical experience of the agricultural reform."

Huong said she compromised with the censors and deleted four chapters that stood between banning and publication, and still, shortly after publication, Nguyen Van Linh, who was then secretary general of the Communist party and reputed to be a liberal reformer, ordered the publisher to withdraw the book. The publisher said the entire edition had already sold out. In fact, after a first edition of 40,000, a second printing of 20,000 also sold out. Since Huong's expulsion from the party, when word was passed to editors, publishers, and the film studio that she had been blacklisted, all her works have disappeared from display. Nevertheless illegal photocopies, covered to resemble schoolbooks, can be bought under the counter in Hanoi and Saigon bookstores. Her last novel, *Death's Inn*, has been typeset and had a cover design for several years. But the chief of the publishing house has told Huong that he schedules it for publication regularly but cannot go ahead unless the authorities give express permission. The only answer he receives is "tuy," "it depends." Huong said she had not been expelled from the Writers' Union, the official literary organization, despite a furor over a text that she read to its 1989 congress, over the chairman's objections, in which she said that the party should be grateful to the people rather than the reverse. "But I have expelled them from me," she said sarcastically. Her expulsion from the party followed her stormy appearance at the congress.

What Huong had feared for years finally happened on April 14, 1991. She was arrested and imprisoned in solitary confinement in Thanh Liet Prison at Ha Dong, a small town just southwest of Hanoi. Huong is quick to correct those who say she was jailed for seven months; "seven months and seven days," she says. Early in the morning, her mother's house in the center of the capital was surrounded by secret police troops as she slept there, and her mother came to wake her and say that a policeman wanted to speak to her. For the first four months, she was questioned every morning by experienced interrogators, some of whom had honed their techniques on American airmen shot down during the war. The accusation, never formalized as a judicial charge, was that Huong was part of an international conspiracy directed against Vietnam's socialist system and government. She is convinced that she was entrapped by a visiting Vietnamese exile from the United States, who came as a professed admirer of her works, which have a large readership in all the countries where Vietnamese refugees have found new homes. The interrogators accused her of passing to the visitor four appeals for greater democracy that had been circulating hand to hand and which she had gathered to prepare a critical essay that she intended to write and address to the approaching Communist party congress.

Huong is convinced that a trial was being prepared and was aborted only because of the collapse of the Soviet Union, which occurred during her imprisonment and made the regime more dependent on the goodwill of the non-Communist world. The political trial of a woman writer who had begun to make an international name for herself, with two books published in France and English-language editions in preparation, would not have been helpful. Huong's interrogations let up, her guards became friendly to the extent of discussing the news of the downfall of the Soviet Union loudly in the corridor, clearly for her benefit, and her release, thirty pounds lighter, came as no surprise. Perhaps she owes it to an impending visit by Roland Dumas, then France's foreign minister.

Harassment, visible surveillance, and chicaneries continue; so do her political candor and solitude. Her friends stand by her, which takes courage, but they do not join in her protests. That would take Huong's rare order of blazing passion against the lie, and defiance of unjust authority.

In 1994, after a long campaign on her behalf by French intellectuals, who had also organized protests during her imprisonment, Huong was given a passport and the exit and reentry visas that Vietnam requires even of its own citizens granted the rare privilege of a trip abroad. Guest of the Société des Gens de Lettres, the organization protecting the rights of French authors, she was awarded the high honor of Chevalier des Arts et des Lettres by Culture Minister Jacques Toubon. Sadly, on that occasion the respect of governments for governments, even at the expense of the human rights some governments espouse, was made evident. In an incident reminiscent of the frequent disappointment of Soviet and Eastern European dissidents hoping for moral support from foreign governments, French officials showed little backbone when Hanoi protested, "violently," an official told me, against the award. Fearful that Vietnam might withdraw its agreement to serve as host for the 1997 meeting of the leaders of all countries that France considers francophone, a distinction hardly merited by today's rather anglophone Vietnam, high officials attempted, not too subtly, to persuade Huong to decline the honor. Showing more courage than France, she stood by her acceptance, forcing the embarrassed French to go through with the less than gracious honor.

What makes Huong singular in Vietnam? She laughed gleefully. "That's approximately the question I was asked by the man who signed my arrest warrant," she replied.

He said, "I don't understand why you are so strange. You must know that the Vietnamese are ninety percent peasants, and they don't even know who you are. There is only a small minority in the cities who know who you are, and some foreigners. If you were to die, nobody would remember a week later." And I replied, "Your reasoning is very clever, and your investigators have done efficient work. Indeed, those who know me and are interested in what I write live in cities. And some foreign journalists looking for a story know who I am. If I die, it will not be a week; in three days all will have forgotten me. What you don't understand is that I am not like you. I don't do what I do in order to be remembered. I oppose you because I want to, and it pleases me to oppose you. Earlier I volunteered against the Americans, against the Chinese, and now I'm volunteering against you with the same force. My motivation is always the same."

He asked me: "But why? For what reason?" I replied that our people are a people who know only how to die and are ignorant of how it is to want to live. If the Communist power accuses me of betraying the party, of working for foreign agencies, this same people will reject me and lead me to the scaffold. I know very well that this same people will stone me. I know it very well, but my aim is exactly this people, this ignorant people. Because I think one must not only resist foreign aggressors but also unjust masters inside our own house.

13

One, but Not the Same

"I'm a northerner but a southerner in my ideas," said Professor Vu Van Tao, an assistant to the education minister. He had been explaining to me in the reception room of his ministry in Hanoi new approaches to the organization of education, particularly the introduction of "semipublic" schools, where the state provides only the building, while the school is privately run. There are more of these being started in the south, he said, "but we northerners are also intelligent and will adopt them." He continued his outline of "southern" ideas: "We must reexamine dominant ideas that came from European countries that have now collapsed. There was here an overly dogmatic, machinelike application of ideas; it was something obscurantist. In the end we will gain our second independence, the independence of our mentality. The period of isolation from the rest of the world has been too long."

Professor Tao is a voluble man who, unlike most officials, does not appear to submit his rapid flow of ideas to an internal self-censor before giving them voice. (In fact, at our first meeting he apologized for reading to me from a relevant Central Committee decision, exceptional in a state where many officials of his rank unashamedly read answers to questions from prepared scripts and never apologize for mouthing party verbiage.) The professor illuminated not only a major difference between Vietnamese, north and south. He also showed that at least some of those who determine policy are aware of that difference and its implications. The difference is between northern innocence of the ways of the world, intellectual rigidity, and conservatism and southern worldliness, adaptability, and eagerness for the new, not necessarily always the best.

The reasons are manifold; the roots are historic, cultural, and sociological. But perhaps the most important is the legacy of the sharply different political pasts of the two Vietnamese states. Despite America's professions of fighting to defend South Vietnam's democracy and underwriting its government's total budget in the name of upholding liberty, the Republic of Vietnam, as it was called, stumbled from one dictatorship to the next, changing regime by coups. Its governments suppressed political freedom with a will; its jails were full of political prisoners, its elections rigged, its press censored.

And yet . . . In order to uphold the noble pretense, the United States had to insist, with the governments it sponsored, underwrote, sometimes installed, and sometimes brought down, on a minimum of openness, an appearance of democratic institutions, an occasional glimpse of freedom for dissenting voices, if only to be able to offer counterarguments to an increasingly hostile American public opinion. American eagerness to erect a democratic facade went so far as an attempt in 1971 to offer to finance the opposition candidacy of General Duong Van Minh, nicknamed "Big Minh" by Americans, in a presidential election campaign grossly rigged by General Nguyen Van Thieu, the incumbent dictator lavishly supported by the United States. This was patent window dressing, to prevent the undemocratic spectacle of an unopposed victory for Thieu. Minh was, in fact, anathema to the American "war effort." He worked, with not always discreet French support, for an unattainable political compromise with the north to end the bloodshed. Minh declined the American proposal and did not become president until three days before the end.

Then, as the first tanks of the North Vietnamese army crashed through the front gate of Doc Lap — Independence — Palace, he surrendered the government of South Vietnam to Colonel Bui Tin, now ironically a defector and dissident living, like General Minh, in Paris. "I have been waiting since early in the morning to transfer power to you," he said to the North Vietnamese officer, who was actually there as deputy editor of *Quan Doi Nhan Dan,* the army daily, and as a war correspondent. He has retold the scene of humiliation many times. "You have no power left to transfer," said Tin. "Your power has collapsed. You cannot transfer what you do not possess." One wonders whether today, when both are in political asylum in France, the conquering colonel and South Vietnam's last president meet sometimes and reminisce about the scene that unites them forever in history.

The very corruption of the Saigon regime and many of its servants created breaches through which the truth was made visible to the people, and, although foreign travel was controlled through selective issuance of passports, official venality often made it possible for opposition opinion to be heard loudly abroad. Entry visas were generally easily obtained, and foreign journalists had ample access to much of the truth about the workings of the regime and the conduct of the war, not only from Americans in the know but also, and more intimately, from Vietnamese, usually with the help of the local journalists who worked for the foreign press. South Vietnamese opponents of their dictators found help in their brave struggle from Americans who had been sent by their government to help the regime of its ally. South Vietnam remained linked to the open world beyond its borders. The victors found for sale in Saigon immediately after its surrender a wealth of varied literature, reflecting a multiplicity of political and philosophical thought, which they hastened to confiscate. It was a measure of the important difference in degree between two dictatorships. However hard its governments tried, the South Vietnamese could not be isolated in ignorance, informed only by the manipulators of news in the service of the government.

North Vietnam managed most successfully all that the southern regime would have liked to achieve. Its leadership created an almost hermetically closed nation, in which no criticism of its rule or its conduct of the war found an outlet. Even the diplomats, technical-aid specialists, or journalists from the

Soviet Union and other "brotherly" countries were severely restricted in their contacts with the Vietnamese. The only non-Communist foreigners allowed to pay carefully supervised brief visits were chosen from among Westerners who had given proof, at the least, of their strong opposition to the South Vietnamese and American side in the combat and more often than not of their admiration for North Vietnam. I don't believe that, for example, Mary McCarthy's or Susan Sontag's books on their wartime visits to North Vietnam, with their far-reaching suspension of disbelief and the critical faculty, count among their most perceptive work. Thus, foreigners did not help to provide a window to another world.

In the late 1960s I met a friend, a French journalist with long experience in the European Communist world, then stationed in Hanoi. He asked me how it was to work in Saigon. Then he described his own life of virtual isolation from the nation about which he was reporting. He recalled almost wistfully his long years in Communist Poland, where his many Polish friends and office staff provided constant insight into the real Poland and allowed his dispatches to reflect that reality. In Hanoi the only Vietnamese that he could talk with were propaganda officials and his office assistants. "The people in my office speak perfect French," he said. "But they tell me the truth only with their eyes."

The population of what was until reunification in 1976 the Democratic Republic of Vietnam remained largely shielded from the non-Communist world until *doi moi*. Only gradually since then has the curtain risen, and only gradually are the North Vietnamese learning to deal with the influx of outside people and ideas. Many resist what they see. The surface can be deceiving. Young North Vietnamese have taken quickly to universal pop culture, mainly in music and clothing. Their T-shirts proclaim the same inane or vulgar messages as those of Bangkok or New York. The sounds that issue from the tiny, street-level "video cafés," which show remarkably recent video clips of Western pop music and its Vietnamese equivalent — produced by the California boat-people community — are often raucously rap. But the bankers and businessmen, who are second in number only to the largest group among the foreign visitors, the overseas Vietnamese, find that the officials with whom they have to deal often simply do not understand the world of international finance and commerce that Vietnam is so eager to enter. And yet they possess vital powers of decision making.

The same businessmen do not have the same problem in Saigon, still the center of business competence, despite the enormous brain drain of the refugee outflow. But the fundamental decisions are made in Hanoi. The number of northerners who have set foot in the non-Communist world is very small. Those who have traveled are largely men or women of impeccable party loyalty, not the ideal qualification for absorbing ideas that until not long ago were deemed those of the class enemy, even if now they are the essence of the new, acquisitive dogma. The language problem is a much bigger barrier in Hanoi than in Saigon. "It is a pity that the general secretary, the prime minister, the other ministers cannot speak foreign languages," said Hoang Tue, a scholar of the Institute of Linguistics and the father of Bao Ninh, the novelist. "Some ministers, directors, or writers know broken Russian. The intellectuals of the old generation learned Chinese, then French, spoke good Vietnamese, even ancient Chinese. Since the revolution, only the study of Vietnamese has been encouraged. That is not enough, and some generations have grown up like this."

Many Hanoi officials continue to make no secret of their distrust of the non-Communist world and distaste for the new flow of visitors. "A lot of foreign tourists come here now that we practice a policy of opening," said Nghiem Xuan Tue, the hardline deputy department director in the Ministry of Labor, not hiding his wish that this had not happened. "They bring social evils. There are sex tours. There is child labor in private enterprises. Western culture is coming to our country. There are more divorces now. There are drugs; there is prostitution. There were no homeless children in the past." On the other hand, the official was nostalgic for the Soviet Union, where he studied for seven years, in Leningrad, Moscow, and Minsk, and evidently never

walked in the streets of that most alcoholic of countries. "It wa
a good country, with a good culture," he reminisced. "I neve
saw a drunk on the street."

Other reasons for the greater receptivity to change in th
south are imbedded more deeply than in Vietnam's recent his
tory. Southerners are the offspring of those who propelled Viet
nam's steady expansion southward, the pioneers of the conques
of new territories, in their day surely among the most enterpris
ing of Vietnamese. Northerners claim, with a large measure o
justification, that they are the true guardians of traditional Viet
namese culture, the custodians of almost all the surviving monu
ments of Vietnam's early history, the speakers of a purer and
richer language, the "real" Vietnamese, living in the heartland,
the region where the nation was born. Southerners counter with
an equally well-founded contention of a more worldly cosmo
politanism. They take pride in being the offspring of the men
and women who conquered alien territory in Vietnam's steady
expansion southward. They are more at ease with foreigners,
perhaps because they have had the advantage of having added
to the culture that their ancestors carried southward with them
the cultures of the people they subdued and with whom they
founded their families. (But with the sentiment of ethnic pride
equally highly developed north and south, it is doubtful that
southerners would admit to being less "pure" Vietnamese than
northerners.)

But undoubtedly southern Vietnam has been far more open
to foreigners, has received via the vanquished and largely vanished nation of Champa (now central Vietnam) and Cambodia
the enrichment of great cultures with Indian roots and been the
home of the vast majority of the overseas Chinese who settled in
Vietnam and brought with them their close links to Chinese
communities throughout Asia. And the huge emigration of Vietnamese that began in 1975, first by American evacuation planes,
then by the seemingly unending, tragic flotilla of unsafe little
fishing boats heading toward hostile shores, and now as legitimate emigrants, has been overwhelmingly a southern phenome-
non. It has created family ties with America, Canada, Australia,

and France and other Western European countries, which ensure not only a flow of material assistance of enormous importance to the Vietnamese balance of payments but also a stream of family visitors, correspondence, and telephone calls that keeps millions of South Vietnamese intimately abreast of the ways of the non-Communist world.

Southerners concede that, perhaps, the people of the north are more disciplined, organized, and hardworking. They often cite in evidence that the most energetic and efficient people in various fields, official and private, in wartime South Vietnam were refugees from the north. But they feel that their own qualities of knowing how to enjoy themselves and producing a superior cuisine, based on much richer supplies of everything that grazes, crows, or swims in a climate that would put leaves even on a broomstick if left outside for a day or two, are at least equally estimable and more generous. Northerners may be better at turning phrases of exquisite courtesy, they admit, but they contend that there is no way of being sure that they are sincerely meant. "You always know how you stand with a southerner," is a phrase in various tonalities often heard from southerners, with the implication that the contrary is true when dealing with those from the north or center. Other Vietnamese concede to the south in general, Saigon in particular, a reputation for savoir vivre, which they envy. When tailors, dressmakers, or beauty parlors in the north want to give themselves an aura of elegance and sophistication, they choose "Saigon" or "Paris" for their shop's name, two "enemy" capitals that Hanoi brought to their knees.

14

Iron, Not Velvet

The banal generalizations that people of one group make about their equals of another have the same narrow validity in Vietnam as anywhere else. There is enough that is partly true not to reject all out of hand; a common history, traditions, landscape, climate are at work shaping personalities. Yet the commonplaces contain also so much that is false, contradicted by the infinite variety of human character regardless of common influences, as to make nonsense of all such categorization. Still, the generalizations have currency and shape attitudes that influence actions. In Vietnam, where the attitudes of the victors determined the fate of the vanquished, they helped to continue the north-south gulf that once split a country that is rightly one and that the northern victory promised to heal. It did not.

The redundantly named National Council of National Reconciliation and Concord, a structure provided for in the Paris peace agreement of 1973 after protracted negotiation between Henry Kissinger and Le Duc Tho, was never set up. Unsurprisingly; for the very notions of reconciliation and concord were anathema to two governments locked in a civil war in which both were determined to strive for nothing less than the crushing of the "enemy," that is, the other half of their own people. Hence each side, as many expected from the outset, subverted the notions as much as their power permitted and continued the war. Northern determination and power were superior, but not northern wisdom.

The worst fortunately did not happen; some American and

South Vietnamese officials before the fall had predicted doom for the south. Calling up the terrible precedent of the northern capture of the former imperial capital of Hue during the 1968 Tet Offensive, when thousands of people rightly or wrongly believed to be supporters of the Saigon regime and the United States were murdered, the doomsday prophets conjured up the probability of a bloodbath in Saigon following a northern victory. Nothing of the kind occurred, but the victors took their vengeance, nonetheless, and did so only after they had created for the benefit of the vanquished and the outside world the opposite expectation. They conquered Saigon like lambs, not lions, fraternized with the populace, and put on a convincing and tranquilizing show of reconciliation.

The foreign press, including American correspondents who had the courage to decline their embassy's invitation to join the evacuation exodus, were allowed to stay to observe the friendly encounters between the *bo doi,* the North Vietnamese troops, and the population and spread the word of the velvet victory. Reporting accurately what they saw in those first two or three months, they created an image of a gentle conquest, which sadly proved unjustified over the long run. Journalists were aware, for instance, of the general roundup of officers and officials of the fallen regime, as well as senior Buddhist monks and Roman Catholic priests, women accused of prostitution or men of addiction to narcotics, for something called, quite reasonably, "reeducation." Word was informally circulated that the process would last no more than a few weeks, to a world that was understandably eager to learn not only that a terrible war had ended but also that it had come to a relatively happy end.

When only the "prostitutes" and "addicts" came home quickly, the few weeks of reeducation stretched into months and years for most of the others, and it became evident that the roundup had included hundreds of thousands; the foreign journalists had long been expelled. The full misery of long-term imprisonment without trial or appeal, under conditions so cruel and primitive that countless prisoners died, reached the outside world too late to make its full impact, in dribs and drabs and at a time when the travails of Vietnam, which had overstayed their welcome on front pages by so many years, no longer aroused much interest. Moreover, the horrors of Pol Pot's reign in Cambodia, belatedly acknowledged after years of wishful disbelief, made any other reports of woe from Communist Indochina pale in comparison.

The "soft" occupation of Saigon had not only deceived the outside world. More importantly, it had raised the hopes of the ordinary people of South Vietnam that their worst fears of the Communist victory had been groundless. Throughout the war, with two opposing regimes and the ever-present propaganda machine of the United States, the world champion of advertising humbug, clamoring for their support, most of the people of South Vietnam were clearly disengaged from all three of the powers fighting over their destiny. During the major Communist offensive of 1972, when the people of Saigon were confronted with the growing probability of the eventual Communist victory, I spent three weeks going about the popular quarters of the war-swollen city, then thought to have a population of three million, surely a serious underestimate. I was accompanied by a first-rate Vietnamese journalist and interpreter, and we sought to sound the state of mind of ordinary Vietnamese. We engaged men and women, the workers and peasants — many were refugees from the war-torn countryside — whose battle the Communists said they were fighting, in long, discursive conversations in crowded courtyards and humble one-room homes in the teeming back alleys of the city. We tried to penetrate past cut-and-dried answers to reach true feelings. After dozens of such interviews my Vietnamese friend, who had little sympathy for any of the three contestants, and I agreed on a consensus of what we had heard.

Three negative emotions dominated in people's minds: weariness with the unending war; deep dislike and mistrust of the South Vietnamese government, which was virtually unanimously held to be incompetent and corrupt; and perhaps the strongest sentiment — fear of the Communists. To the Saigonese, who had learned through painful experience how to cope with the impositions of their unloved government and the United States, the men from Hanoi represented a threat of something they might not know how to resist: harsh and rigid regimentation of all aspects of life, efficient and, they feared, incorruptible. The general feeling was that southerners would lose even the limited freedom that Saigon had conceded to them; that is, to go their own way, particularly in how they went about earning their living, as long as they did not oppose the government.

The fear proved justified over the long run. The regime that was instituted swept aside all hope of reconciliation and national concord. Soon it was made abundantly clear to the people of the south, including those who had fought in the ranks of the National Liberation Front, the Viet Cong, or helped it in other ways, that the North Vietnamese would rule as conquerors over the conquered. To some, the northern takeover suggested a historic revenge for an earlier defeat, almost two centuries ago. In 1802 the southern Nguyen dynasty, under the rule of Nguyen Anh, captured Hanoi from the northern Trinh dynasty. As monarch of the country thus reunified, the victor assumed the name of Emperor Gia Long and established Vietnam's capital in the central city of Hue. The North Vietnamese capture of Saigon 173 years later reversed Gia Long's victory.

Dr. Duong Quynh Hoa, as health minister of the southern National Liberation Front's Provisional Revolutionary Government, constituted in the name of the Viet Cong in 1969, arrived in Saigon with her husband on the first plane from Hanoi after its "liberation." It was clear from the beginning, she said, that it was not the Provisional Government that was in charge, now that its time had come to govern the South Vietnam that it represented. The Military Management Committee, whose orders came only from Hanoi, held all power in the southern capital. The following year, with no regard for the will of the southern Communists and others of the National Liberation Front, Hanoi decreed the unification of the country and the elimination of all institutions through which the southern revolutionaries intended to achieve gradual reconciliation after twenty-one years of war and prepare a smooth joining of the two disparate entities.

There was nothing smooth about what followed. Northern officials, major and petty, descended in great number to take over everything, from the principal political posts to the running of branch post offices, clinics, schools, food supply, transport — everything official in a system in which the state left nearly nothing to private initiative. Men and women from the north, whose devotion to the party over many years of bitter war and deprivation was being rewarded by assignment to the richest place in Vietnam, took the place of qualified southerners eager to serve now that peace had finally been restored. Physicians with postgraduate degrees from European or American universities were replaced by doctors who because of the urgent needs of North Vietnam after the defeat of the French and the subsequent departure of many qualified Vietnamese professionals for the south had to be sent into practice after only the most rudimentary professional training. Experienced specialists who had proved their patriotism and will for reconciliation by declining to join the American-sponsored exodus in the final days of the old regime were replaced by imported, incompetent party hacks. Northerners with no experience of the more sophisticated technology that the United States had brought to its client took the places of qualified engineers, while those whom they replaced, if they were not being "reeducated," had to try to make a living for themselves and their families pedaling "cyclos," bicycle taxis. And for many of them there was simply no work.

Economic and social marginalization by exclusion from any job was a form of punishment devised for many who were spared reeducation or who had been released from these concentration camps. Many families stayed afloat selling their possessions — their houses, electric appliances, clothing, furniture, heirlooms — until they were down to what they would need to sell to buy places on a refugee boat, and only then made the painful decision to flee. Dr. Ton That Tung, Ho Chi Minh's comrade and personal physician, told me in Hanoi in 1979, at the height of the boat-people exodus, that he understood the decision of so many southern doctors to accept for themselves and their families the high risks of fleeing toward an uncertain future, because their willingness to serve at home had been "so stupidly" spurned.

Professor Ly Chanh Trung, the leftist Catholic philosopher from Saigon University and member of Parliament until 1992, described the vital problem of food distribution in Saigon after the Communist victory, which he said had filled him with joy. "The Chinese community had controlled the market and prices. The Vietnamese never knew how to break into this Chinese monopoly. But the Communists introduced another monopoly — the state's. They bought rice at a low price, which did not encourage the farmers to produce it, and sold it cheaply to state employees, and somewhat more expensively to the public. Production declined, of course, and the very bureaucratic distribution system made matters worse. The situation grew Kafkaesque." Not that it was normal in the past, he said; then everything depended on American aid. In the early period of the new regime, he continued, "We had to go once a month to buy our ration of rice. And it wasn't only rice, there was not enough of it. Part of the ration consisted of cassava and sweet potatoes. There were long lines, and we had to wait long times for our names to be called out. We had to bring a sack and then carry it home. Imagine, fifty kilograms." The small, elderly professor went through the motions of trying to shoulder a 110-pound sack. "They treated us like beggars, these very haughty women in charge. It was a dehumanized, sclerotic bureaucracy. This was not socialism but an idiocy invented by Stalin."

Many shops in what had been one of Asia's most feverishly bustling, twenty-four-hours-a-day commercial cities closed, as their stocks ran out or their owners fled. Boys played football on empty Nguyen Hue Boulevard, the once-busy shopping street that descends from the pompous nineteenth-century City Hall, a French architectural wedding cake, to the Saigon River. The Central Market turned into a place of echoing footsteps where once the cries and haggling of sellers and buyers made an earsplitting din. The ambulant kitchens on pushcarts of the sellers of noodle soup, dried fish, fruit, and the many sticky sweets of a city that eats on the run as much as seated grew rare, and the soup watery and expensive. The women of Saigon scaled down their habitual and varied elegance, which had endured through the war, by adopting the uniform dress code introduced by the northerners: loose black trousers and white or blue shirts hanging over them. The distinctive national costume, the graceful *ao dai*, a swallow-tailed, high-collared, tightly fitted tunic, was put away in closets, a museum piece of the past. No makeup, stern hairdos. What had happened thirty years earlier to Budapest, Warsaw, and Prague, cities once admired for an individual and lively style, happened to Saigon. It was forced to wear its poverty unadorned.

The Saigonese resented the northern "cadres," the *can bo*, more deeply than the soldiers, whom they often found touchingly innocent and naive. They were astonished at the young men's evidently sincere belief that they had come to "liberate" them, and in turn, their astonishment came as a surprise to the soldiers, who had expected a liberator's welcome. The Saigonese found nothing innocent about the *can bo*. They considered them crude and commandeering profiteers, eager to take everything that they had been missing or never known with a conqueror's greed. Villas, not only of former officials who had fled or been imprisoned to be "reeducated" but also of people who had chosen to remain, as well as their cars, refrigerators, or television sets, were prized booty of victory. Their former owners were often banished to what were called New Economic Zones, inhospitable, malaria-ridden jungle or mountain areas. Here, city people with no rural experience, equipped with the most primitive of tools and some seed, were told to carve out new lives, beginning with felling trees to build shelters and planting food crops on infertile ground. The zones were not much different from the places on which reeducation camps were installed, and the policy of creating them was eventually largely abandoned. It was no wonder that many of the banished made their way back to Saigon, sleeping wherever they could find a relative or friend who would take the risk of sheltering them, or in the street, and looking for the opportunity of finding — that is, buying — for themselves and their families a place on a fishing boat for the dangerous voyage into exile.

Through the early years of their new lives as citizens of Ho Chi Minh City, the population grew used to frequent calls over loudspeakers or megaphones in their neighborhoods to gather that evening for mandatory sessions of "political education." At the same time they worried about a real educational problem, the schools that their children went to. The new curriculum and teachers put all subjects into the changed political context; everything was designed to wean the children of Ho Chi Minh City away from their Saigon past and parents. Uncle Ho's words were the basic text, whether the subject was geography or mathematics. And sons and daughters of men of objectionable political past, officials or officers of the South Vietnamese government or of the "wrong" social origins, the bourgeoisie, were often rejected for the higher education for which their report cards qualified them. Many of the traditions of Confucianism had certainly waned over the years of modernization, which was speeded by the presence, if not the intentions, of the French colonial power and the American patrons, but the earnest belief of Vietnamese in the vital importance of education had not. In years of interviewing boat people in the refugee camps of Southeast Asia, concern over the impoverished education of their children was a theme constantly struck when I asked those who fled about what had motivated them.

A sentiment that ordinary people were being punished for being southerners took hold quickly in Saigon and other towns, and so did fear of being constantly under surveillance. In every quarter of the city, in every office or enterprise, school or clinic, informers and petty party officials became persons to be suspected, feared, and before too long, bribed. Arrests for reeducation continued through the early years, keeping alive an atmosphere of fear. The danger of arbitrary punishment for being falsely denounced was always present. And many did have

something that was punishable, something to hide — their projects of escape. This was the period of the greatest population
drain in Vietnamese history, the exodus of the boat people and
the subsequent flow of legal emigrés, which is still under way.

This exodus constitutes the severest judgment the Vietnamese people have ever expressed against those who govern
them. Unlike China and Japan, Vietnam until 1975 had never
been a land of mass emigration. On the contrary, when the
French conscripted thousands of Vietnamese as laborers,
mainly from the north, for their other colonies — most were
sent to work on the plantations of New Caledonia in the South
Pacific — or for France itself during World War I, to replace
men in military service, the great majority eventually returned.
And I know of no exile group in this century, surely the century
of the refugee, that remains so deeply emotionally linked to the
country from which it fled. Many Vietnamese refugees keep
nostalgically alive a hope of returning someday to live on
native soil, near the family grave sites, perhaps even now, when
the Communists from whom they fled are still in power but
have eased their ways. At least one-half of today's foreign
tourists are Viet Kieu, overseas Vietnamese, many of them
former boat people or even reeducation camp prisoners. But
there are also great numbers of Viet Kieu so embittered by their
experiences after 1975 that they are firm in insisting that they
will never return.

The authorities maintained an intentionally ambiguous
policy on the flight of the boat people. Leaving the country
without official permission is against the law, and yet it is a
reasonable estimate that about two million people escaped
without passports or entry visas for other countries. This clearly
could not have happened without at least the connivance of a
regime that has proved throughout its existence its sure hand in
controlling the population. In the case of the mass outflow of
ethnic Chinese in 1978–79, at the height of the hostility between the two countries, the Vietnamese authorities went so far
as to charter large, almost derelict freighters and force thousands of unwilling refugees aboard. But first they made them

pay in gold or dollars for their involuntary voyage to nowhere, in inhumanly overcrowded conditions. To nowhere, because there was no destination that was willing to receive them. For weeks the ships were shunted from port to port and back onto the open sea while the United Nations High Commissioner for Refugees, supported by some Western countries, tried to persuade unwilling Southeast Asian countries to accept their passengers for at least temporary asylum.

The total number of those who set out to become refugees will never be known. One cannot count how many fell victim to the perils of passage. There were the natural hazards of the South China Sea for unseaworthy fishing boats navigated by inexperienced seafarers. Fishermen in considerable number, mainly Thai, turned into murderous pirates. Boats crowded with exhausted people bearing all they owned — converted into gold before they left — as well as women to be raped or sold into prostitution were an easy prey, more attractive than fish, that they could not resist. Many perished because of the indifference of ship captains of various nationalities, who refused to cause their owners financial loss by stopping to rescue the desperate. And there was the frequent cruelty of local officials and ordinary people of other Southeast Asian countries, who pushed the boats away from their shores or towed them back out to abandon them to the hostile sea. The quality of asylum is strained in Asia, not least in Japan, its richest nation. All these dangers were known to the refugees before they set out; many women even prepared themselves for the high risk of rape by contraceptive measures. And yet they continued to flee. This is a measure of the despair about the present and fear for their future and their children's that the new regime inspired.

Many refugees set out in flight only to be caught and frequently jailed for usually brief periods by Vietnamese authorities. Five, six, or seven failed attempts before eventual success were not unusual. Yet at the same time local officials throughout the former South Vietnam proved eminently bribable, and few who were willing to take the risk seem to have been permanently prevented from setting out on their dangerous voyages. By the early 1980s even northerners found it not too difficult to set sail for stop-and-go voyages along the Chinese coast, where authorities did nothing to hinder them, and reach the safety of Hong Kong's camps. This outflow stopped only after the Hong Kong authorities turned the camps into harsh prisons and began the forcible repatriation of those who could not find a country willing to accept them as immigrants.

One can only speculate about what motivated the Hanoi government to permit, or even to further, the exodus. Was it to rid an overpopulated country critically short of food, jobs, and housing of a mass of questionable loyalty, which it had done everything to make discontent? Or did a very poor country wish to draw into circulation, or put into private pockets, the wealth that it knew was hidden in 1975? Even today, when it is more or less officially admitted that Vietnam could ill afford the loss of so much expertise, depriving the country of those best qualified to make a market economy work for the benefit of national development, there are no answers to those questions. General Tran Cong Man, the unofficial but fully authorized party spokesman in Hanoi, offered a limp reply: "We committed certain errors after 1975. We put people in reeducation camps. They were not in favor of socialist economics. Their advice was not always appropriated. The refugees? There were economic errors. We could not pay them enough, and their standard of living declined. Naturally there was a certain discrimination against some people. We did not give them very good jobs, and we allotted no university places to their children." Enigmatic smiles, weak denials, and accusations against corrupt low-level officials in the provinces are Hanoi's only answer to the question of official collusion with the boat-people exodus.

But there is no embarrassment in Hanoi or elsewhere about other major measures of gross discrimination against those of their own whom Vietnam's turbulence cast on the losing side. That is the attitude toward the men of the defeated South Vietnamese army, its crippled and even its dead. The absence of a spirit of reconciliation toward the veterans of the "wrong" army has left painful open wounds on millions of bodies and souls. The vast National Cemetery at the edge of Saigon, a burial place for thousands of war dead of the former capital, has been razed. The same has happened to smaller cemeteries in towns and cities throughout the former South Vietnam. In some cases relatives were given a chance to remove remains, but many cemeteries were desecrated without such acts of minimal respect for the dead, an offense of particular gravity in a civilization that considers family graves as places of worship. Archeologists who dug in Vietnam before World War II reported considerable local opposition even to the opening of tombs dating to the period before the beginning of the current era. To have removed immediately after the fall of Saigon the vulgarly bellicose Monument to the Unknown Soldier that faced the Parliament was understandable and justified; the vendetta against soldiers' graves was indecent. The memorials to the war dead all over the country are pointedly one-sided, as though the nation mourns only some of those who died. Hanoi says that two million civilians and more than one million of its soldiers and those of the National Liberation Front were killed from 1954 until 1975. The United States has estimated at 200,000 the number of South Vietnamese soldiers killed. The two million figure for civilian dead presumably includes victims on both sides.

"The families of men who were killed in the war are treated without charge," said Dr. Tran Quoc Do, the deputy director of Bach Mai Hospital in Hanoi. Pensions are given, of course, to wounded veterans, but only those of the North Vietnamese army and the National Liberation Front. Do was taken aback when asked the reason for the exclusion. "The work of liberation was mainly the work of the people of the north," he replied. "Some in the south also took part. The Saigon army people are considered like ordinary people. They get free care only if they are too poor to pay." That proviso must cover a great number of veterans. Those whom the war has left permanently handicapped are many; their chances of employment are poor, and they receive no pensions. Neither do the widows and orphans of the southern war dead. But so great is Vietnam's poverty that even the pensions that it pays to North Vietnam's war wounded are very small. "It's not even enough to buy tea," said Bao Ninh, the author of *The Sorrows of War.* "How can they give something to the wounded of the south!"

The disdain for the soldiers of what is generally called "the puppet army" continues widespread in the north twenty years after the end of the war. "They do not deserve to be considered as the opponent of the Vietnamese army," said Duong Quoc Thuan, a regular officer who retired as a captain after twenty-two years of service in 1992 and returned to farming in the village of Xuan Dang, north of Hanoi. "Our opponent was the American army." Thuan, forty-six years old, served for many years on the breathtakingly beautiful, much-bloodied Plain of Jars in Laos, a constant mountain battleground between the North Vietnamese army and the secret army of Hmong mountain tribesmen, surreptitiously organized, armed, supplied, and guided in battle by the Central Intelligence Agency, as well as heavily backed by steady, devastating bombing by the U.S. Air Force. Thuan laughed when reminded that he had given away a major diplomatic secret, since Hanoi, just like Washington, has consistently denied that it was involved in fighting in Laos. North Vietnam even refused to acknowledge and accept family letters from its soldiers who were captured in Laos.

Ly Van Cu, another former captain, is the caretaker of a hallowed shrine, the house in the countryside near the central city of Vinh where Ho Chi Minh is said to have been born in 1890 and named Nguyen Sinh Cung. Ho Chi Minh is the last of a series of noms de guerre that the founder of the country adopted in his extraordinary life. Cu spoke with warmth of meetings he had had with American veterans of the war. "Before, I fought against them," he said. "I saw them as the enemy. If I didn't shoot them, they would shoot me. But now is a time for reconciliation. Now they come here as friends. We want to cooperate with them and receive aid from them. I have no hard feelings toward Americans. I think in war soldiers must listen to their government's orders." Cu even showed some indulgence for the American bombers, who devastated Vinh more than any other city. "There were no bombs here," he said. "Maybe the

Americans respected the place where Uncle Ho was born. Perhaps they regarded him as the leader not only of Vietnam but also of the Third World." Yet Cu had no indulgence for his former Vietnamese enemy. "Many southerners who come here cry," he said. "Of course they were forced to fight. But I am afraid I cannot consider them my comrades. That is only natural. Since we were an army of volunteers who fought for noble causes like independence and freedom, we received no pay. They received money to feed their families. We had to share everything we had with one another. But our attitude and policy are very simple. We do not rely on the past to judge a person, even a former puppet soldier. But we fought for a country called Vietnam. They fought for a country called South Vietnam. Now we have one capital, Hanoi."

The caretaker of Ho Chi Minh's official birthplace — it is said that he was really born in a nearby village, but the house where his birth is celebrated is a more dignified place — is clearly a man who must present the full party line with conviction as a condition of employment. But the belief that only North Vietnam fought for reunification has general acceptance in the north. Dr. Pham Van Dien, the hospital director in Vinh and a man of balance, voiced the same belief, adding that only "Uncle Ho" stood for national unity. He went no further toward reconciliation than to say that former southern soldiers were accepted back into the society after they had received reeducation, "even those who committed crimes against the nation."

Bao Ninh, the novelist and former combat soldier, a corporal, was more conciliatory. "If I met a corporal from the Saigon army, I would feel closer to him than a captain from our side," he said. "There is no problem between ordinary people. But in the late stages of the war there was bitterness toward one another. Because after the Americans left, the war took on the dark color of a civil war. To tell the truth, the victory of the north, by any accurate description, was an attack by the north on the south. Later there came the slogans of national reconciliation. The leaders brought a model, the wrong model, to the south, and that created bitterness. We soldiers from the north feel sad today. We struggled for the liberation of the whole nation, but after fifteen years, what we achieved was the poverty of the whole nation. We feel sorry for the southerners who had to become boat people, and for the nation that became tattered, and the soldiers of the south who could find no work. We feel sorry for those who spent years in reeducation camps. That is why there is bitterness in the hearts of both sides. The situation is totally different since the time of Gorbachev. I hope time will heal the spiritual wounds."

Much of the bitterness over "reeducation" has left Vietnam as many former prisoners departed first as clandestine refugees and later legally, under an agreement with the United States, which accepted as immigrants a great number of those released and their families. But many did not take advantage of the American offer, usually for painful family reasons. They remain, and with them their stored-up anger, which they do not hide. A haggard man of middle years, who had served as official interpreter for a Saigon interview with a group of dogmatic minor functionaries, drew me aside on the way out to whisper hastily his story, so as to set himself apart from those whose words he had put into fluent English. He had spent two years in the United States on an American government scholarship to obtain a master's degree in a technical, most unmilitary field of study and been drafted on his return to serve as a lieutenant in an office job. This had cost him two years of his life for "reeducation." A higher price was paid by his wife, whose depression over his arrest degenerated into lasting mental illness. "That's why I am still here," he said, as if his staying in his country and translating for uninspiring hard-liners called for an apology.

A former South Vietnamese political figure of minor significance or influence, who also served as a senior technical official in a provincial town and was a wealthy businessman to boot, paid a higher ransom for his successful career until 1975. His "reeducation" lasted fourteen years, in twenty-two camps, from the Chinese border in the north to the deep south, as well as in Saigon's main prison. Responsibility for his very old mother, unable to travel, has kept him from emigrating to the United

States. He recounted his history soberly, often laughing dryly at the depth of squalor to which he had been condemned without trial. His narrative was reminiscent of the tales from the Soviet gulag or the milder German concentration, not extermination, camps, Dachau, not Auschwitz. At the beginning he was chained for many weeks in a dark cell. He lifted his trouser legs in evidence; the scars the chains left are deep and indelible. In the camps, with only minor variations over the fourteen years and the twenty-two different locations, the typical day began at 4:30, with a meal of boiled cassava, about one hundred grams per prisoner. At five o'clock the prisoners, always under armed guard, were marched to work, clearing the forest and planting their food crops — mainly rice, cassava, and sweet potatoes. At ten o'clock they were marched back to camp and usually had to wait for about an hour at the locked main gate until it was opened at noon. "A sun bath," he called that minor form of mass torture. A repetition of the morning meal, and back to work until four o'clock. The march back to camp, another repetition of the meal, and at 5:30 the gate was locked. From seven until nine o'clock in the evening was the Marxism-Leninism and self-criticism period. Each prisoner had to judge his own work and was then judged by the others and the wardens. "If your work was bad you got a bad mark, like in school," he said. "Sometimes I was beaten, but the main punishment was hunger."

For the first five years he could not be punished by withholding mail or packages, he said, because none were allowed. Starting in 1980, the prisoners could receive a package of three kilograms, which is 6.6 pounds, every three months. Medicines and sugar were the usual contents. The medicines particularly were badly needed. Chronic diarrhea and malaria were rampant, and the death rate was high. No reliable figures about the total number of prisoners or how many died in the camps are available; estimates by former prisoners, which one hopes are greatly exaggerated, speak of as many as 1.5 million prisoners and 800,000 who died. It is impossible to tell how such figures are arrived at. The first five years were the hardest, the former inmate said, an observation repeated by most former prisoners. The political courses and self-accusation sessions were daily events in the early years, and reduced to three times a week subsequently. He received his first family visit six years after his arrest. Starting in 1983 he was allowed two such visits a year, and three beginning in 1985. Today, the multilingual former prisoner, showing no intellectual effects after fourteen years of reeducational effort, is looking for a place for himself in private business. So are his sons, who until the liberalization of the late 1980s were unable to find work because they were their father's children.

15

The Wages of the Just

It was not only those who served the old regime who were made to suffer the victor's vengeance. It was enough to have been a free-thinking participant on the Saigon scene, so independent as to have been one of the most critical of observers of all South Vietnamese governments and their American ally, independent enough to have left North Vietnam in 1954, elated over the Communists' victory over France but knowing them well enough — having collaborated with them until then — to know that he could not live under their rule. This was Cao Giao, a friend to whom I owe a fundamental introductory lesson on Vietnam, one that continues to stand me in good stead. It was delivered in his favorite lecture hall, Givral's, once the closest equivalent in Asia to a Central European coffeehouse.

Givral's was situated at Saigon's central crossroads, facing onto the Continental Palace Hotel, a colonial leftover occupied by the foreign press; the French Opera House, which the South Vietnamese government converted to another kind of theater, its powerless Parliament; and the hall of half-truths in which American and South Vietnamese military briefers put on daily performances staged to demonstrate how they were winning the war. This politically vibrant junction served as the seat of a vital, sometimes reliable source of information informally called Radio Catinat, of which Cao Giao was a leading tenor. Rue Catinat was the colonial name of the tree-lined main street onto which Givral fronts. It was renamed Tu Do, "liberty," by the Saigon government, and Dong Khoi, "general uprising," under the present dispensation. Givral's continues to offer coffee, beer, ice cream, and classic French pastries, now in poor imitation, but no longer anything of interest. Radio Catinat broadcast without microphones, more often than not in whispered French, to a limited audience interested in what neither the South Vietnamese nor the American authorities would say in public. Its broadcasters were, like Cao Giao, a regular if informal round of Vietnamese journalists and others, of the kind that the press used quite appropriately to call "political observers" or "informed sources." Many, like Cao Giao, worked for foreign news organizations; he was *Newsweek's* political reporter.

Cao Giao's lesson to a newly arrived colleague, whom he favored with attention because he had come to Saigon from the Soviet Union, a country that fascinated him, was, in paraphrase: "Moscow is easy. You know that whatever the Russians say, the opposite is likely to be true. Here, nothing is what it seems, including myself, but the opposite is also not the truth." He was mocking himself; in fact, except for his physical image — which, in what I always assumed to be an intentional provocation to the authorities, he had fashioned to resemble, of all people, Ho Chi Minh — he was entirely what he seemed. Cao Giao was the acutely intelligent and erudite son of generations of North Vietnamese mandarins; he covered profound anguish over his country's enduring tragedy with bitingly iconoclastic wit, his mordancy rising proportionately with the power that his target held over the lives of others, particularly the Vietnamese people. The principal objects of his savagery, delivered as he gesticulated with his pipe in a soft voice, with maliciously sparkling eyes and a seemingly innocent smile, were the governments and military leaders of South Vietnam and the United States; the minor butts of his scathing sarcasm were many of the leading figures of the foreign press in Saigon and their editors in New York or Washington. As early as six years before the fact, he left me in no doubt that he believed the Communists would eventually win and, because of their consistent defense of Vietnam's independence and national unity and their refusal to allow themselves to be taken over by the foreign powers that supported their cause, deserved to win.

Nothing illustrates the current of the Vietnamese tragedy better than the sad life of Cao Giao. He fell victim to the paranoia of those who possessed the vision and boldness to force an end to the ignominy of alien rule over an ancient, civilized nation, yet who failed to seize the opportunity that their victory created to restore peace and unity through reconciliation among the Vietnamese. This is Cao Giao's story, told to me in bits and pieces over the years at Givral's and brought up to date in a long telephone conversation after his release from the last prison of his life and his departure into exile in 1985, and in an article he wrote not long before his death for the German magazine *Der Spiegel*, the last foreign news organization whose readers he enlightened about the complex truths of his country.

He had been imprisoned twenty-one times, the first time by the French, as a fourteen-year-old student of the Lycée du Protectorat in Hanoi, an excellent French high school. He and some classmates had published an underground anti-French newspaper. But no imprisonment caused him as much pain as the last, because it was undeserved even if one accepted the jailer's view. He was loyal to Vietnam and had been sympathetic to the new regime. He had never given thought to leaving in 1975, as he could have done with the rest of his *Newsweek* colleagues, because he hoped that the new rulers would not persecute Vietnamese nationalists, even if they were not Communists. He had admired the Communists and collaborated with them under the French regime and the Japanese occupation. He did not believe in their doctrine but thought he knew that they, unlike the various Saigon governments, wanted reunification and reconciliation. After the victory at Dien Bien Phu in 1954, when he told his Communist friends that he rejoiced in their defeat of the French and the restoration of Vietnam's independence but would leave for the newly independent but non-Communist south, they accepted his decision and posed only one condition. They wanted him to stay true to nationalism and put behind him all that remained of French rule. "They said as they let me go,

'D'accord, mais fini café-croissants!' " he told me at Givral's, laughing as he disobeyed the letter, if never the spirit, of this parting injunction. And he continued until that last arrest, in 1978, to trust that the Communists would accept his loyalty to Vietnam as a patriotic non-Communist.

Cao Giao needed no reminder of what nation he was a part. He was brought up in the highest Vietnamese mandarin traditions from his birth in 1917 in a village thirty miles south of Hanoi to a family that through the generations participated in opposition to French rule. Cao Giao's father was an exception: as an only son, his father forbade him to join that struggle, in order to assure the continuance of the family name. Out of respect for tradition, Cao Giao's father obeyed and became a mandarin, or civil servant, in the French judicial system. But he also sympathized with the revolutionaries whom the system prosecuted. In one of the paradoxes that would defy credibility almost anywhere but in Vietnam, Cao Giao's fascination with communism began through his reading of basic Communist texts, ranging from Trotsky on the left via Lenin to Stalin on the right, in the piles of forbidden books seized from Communists and put under his father's control. What he read did not convince him that communism was the future and that it would work, but he was convinced that the Vietnamese Communists would always place the struggle for national independence above any commitment to an international cause. A further paradox: Cao Giao's first private tutor was Nguyen Luong Bac, a Communist who fifty years later was named president of the Socialist Republic of Vietnam. However, he did not serve; he died on the day of his nomination. The French had placed Bac under house arrest, supervised by his pupil's father.

Cao Giao, confirmed in his nationalism for having been briefly jailed by the French, took his first journalistic job after graduating from the lycée on a newspaper that was published in French but critical of colonialism. When the Japanese occupied the French possessions in 1941, Cao Giao was one of many young Asian nationalists in the French, British, and Dutch colonies to follow their invitation to collaborate with the country that was driving out the Western colonialists and promised to create an Asia ruled by Asians. "My first lost cause," he said. He became an aide of the Japanese Cultural Mission in Hanoi, a cover name for the organization that coordinated pro-Japanese movements in the region, and editor of a Roman Catholic, pro-Japanese newspaper.

Because of that experience and his knowledge of where the Japanese had hidden the equipment and paper for their newspaper, Cao Giao was co-opted by the Communists after Japan's capitulation and before the return of the French to direct the first daily of the newly proclaimed Democratic Republic of Vietnam. He worked under the direct supervision of Pham Van Dong, later the longtime prime minister. But after a few months, when his professional skills were no longer needed, Cao Giao had his first experience in a Communist jail. He was arrested for his earlier collaboration with the Japanese, and had his first exposure to torture by electric shock. At the end of 1946 France returned to Hanoi, driving Ho Chi Minh and his supporters into the armed insurrection that defeated France eight years later. The French Sûreté arrested Cao Giao for having collaborated with the Communists.

His first arrest after his flight to South Vietnam took place in 1958, under the government of President Ngo Dinh Diem. Cao Giao had first met the Roman Catholic, nationalist mandarin from central Vietnam while both collaborated with the Japanese. He had incurred the authoritarian president's anger by opposing his policy of making the 1954 north-south partition under the Geneva agreement a permanent division into two states. "Reunification," to the minds of Diem and his even more authoritarian brother and security chief, Ngo Dinh Nhu, was a Communist goal. Once more Cao Giao was tortured by electric shock to make him confess that he was a Communist agent. He refused for seven months and was finally released. Several arrests later, in 1963, he collaborated with the generals who, with the backing of the United States, which had lost confidence in Diem and Nhu, overthrew their regime and had the brothers murdered. In the following years, when coup followed coup in

Saigon, Cao Giao was taken into custody repeatedly. The jails were always the same, and sometimes even the wardens; only the regimes that arrested him changed.

After 1975 Cao Giao shared the fate of many Vietnamese who had worked for private Western organizations, particularly the press. He lived in fear of being arrested for "reeducation" because of his Western connections. It did not happen, but like so many others, he was left without a possibility of earning his living. Arrest finally came in 1978, when many non-Communist Saigon intellectuals were rounded up as "agents of the CIA." "They arrested myself and my books and papers," he said. At dawn on June 18, police surrounded his house in a populous quarter, and a small truck was loaded with all the documents and manuscripts from his desk and shelves. "No crying," the chief of the arresting squad ordered his wife. "We are used to this," she replied. "No one will cry." She handed him a last package of tobacco for his pipe.

For thirteen months Cao Giao, sixty-one years old at his last arrest, vegetated in total darkness, solitary in a tiny cell at the headquarters of the state security police. His only company were rats and ants, swarms of them, all day and all night. A small hole in the door, which was opened only when he was led out for interrogation, served to hand in his food in a plastic bowl; opposite, in the floor, a hole served as toilet and conduit for the rats. The daily siren at noon was his calendar and clock; when the pause between its howls was very long, he knew that it was Sunday, the day the siren remained silent. The temperature in the cell varied from very hot to very cold; the darkness was permanent. The interrogations were repetitive; they always centered on his relations with foreigners and the accusation that he had worked for the Central Intelligence Agency. He denied all accusations and signed nothing, not even when he was ordered to sign only the protocol of the interrogation. After nine months of frequent questioning there followed a period of four months when his cell door was never opened.

And then, thirteen months after his arrest, Cao Giao was transferred to Chi Hoa Prison, a traditional, rude home for political prisoners in Saigon under all regimes. He had been there often before. Instead of being placed in solitary confinement, Cao Giao became one of seventy-two political prisoners in a single cell. They included a full spectrum of those the government distrusted — a Jesuit provincial, a former Viet Cong colonel, old-regime politicians whom Cao Giao had often interviewed and later mocked at Givral's, members of suspected resistance groups, and men from Cholon, Saigon's large Chinatown, accused of being agents of Beijing. A single straw mat was the only bed. As the oldest, a position that merits respect, he was given the best sleeping time, from midnight until three in the morning. One day he was taken to the prison's administrative office and introduced to a group of three foreigners, including a woman from Sri Lanka. They were a delegation from Amnesty International, which had "adopted" Cao Giao as a "prisoner of conscience." (About a year after his arrest, in Hanoi, I asked Nguyen Co Thach, then the foreign minister, why my friend had been arrested. He professed to know nothing about it but promised to inquire and let me know. He never did, but as a probable result of my question, his office canceled the following day my visit to Saigon, which Thach had authorized.) A few weeks after the Amnesty International visit, Cao Giao's daily meals of rice soup began to be supplemented by vitamin pills, and he realized that his emaciated frame was being made presentable for release. It was three and one-half years after his arrest when he was called to the warden's office, told to forget what he had experienced, and freed. He had admitted nothing, nor forgotten anything.

It was 1982, and for three more years Cao Giao lived in his Saigon home, under close surveillance, unemployed and abandoned by hope, he said. Several times his wife and he, who had always felt that they would never leave Vietnam, negotiated places on refugee boats and paid for them, but they were too closely watched to make good their escape. Their two oldest sons had lived in Belgium, where they had gone to study, since well before 1975. Their youngest son escaped by boat while his father was in prison. Finally, in 1985, Cao Giao and his wife were allowed to rejoin their children. This is how he described in *Der Spiegel* his feelings on reaching France:

> I am glad to be free. For the first time in my life I stepped on French soil. Despite the earlier struggle against the French, I am finding my own self again, now that I am here, and feel myself almost at home. But I cannot accept the thought that I have to end my life as a refugee.
>
> Too much links a man with the landscape and the history of his country. One cannot simply leave it without dreaming of returning one day.
>
> How else could I survive, after I got to know so many prisons from the inside and sacrificed a lifetime in the struggle for this unfortunate Vietnam?

Cao Giao never saw his country again. He died in exile shortly after he wrote this.

In the final years of the war Trinh Cong Son also knew the Communists would eventually win, and that he, too, would stay to live that further adventure in his country's history. After all, Vietnam would be at peace and would once again be one, and he had directed all his creative impulse, his poems and songs, to that cause. In a land of poets, Trinh Cong Son was one of the finest. He was also South Vietnam's troubadour of peace. He was immensely popular among the people but persecuted by the Saigon government, which paid tribute to his considerable art by banning his most telling songs. The censors said the songs undermined the nation's determination to pursue the war to victory. Son was a subversive defeatist in the eyes of the Saigon regime, but for much of the nation, and particularly its youth, his poems and music, through his voice and guitar, expressed a people's profound grief over the unending bloodshed and its yearning for peace — forbidden sentiments. Son's songs traversed the artificial border between the two warring halves of the nation and spoke to and for the hearts of the young of both armies.

Here is one of his most moving and popular songs of the mid-1960s, whose place names are a catalog of the great sites of battle of the ground and air war of those years:

The Love Song of a Madwoman

The one I loved is dead at Plei Me;
The one I loved, somewhere in Zone D, is dead at Dong Xoai;
Dead in Hanoi, quite suddenly at Chu Prong;
The one I loved is dead, his body carried off by swift currents;
Dead in the rice paddies, in the fields;
Dead in the dark forest;
Dead, cold, burned,
Vietnam, how I would love you!

On stormy days I wander, bearing your name on my lips,
Vietnam, so close to me by the voice of your yellow skin,
Vietnam, how I would love you!

Since my youngest days my ears know the sound of bullets
        and bombs,
My arms that know not what to do, my lips useless,
I have forgotten the language of humans.

The one I loved is dead at A Shau;
The one I loved lies dead at the bottom of a valley,
Dead under a bridge, dead without a word on his lips,
        without flesh on his body;
Dead at Ba Gia;
Dead last night,
Of a blind death, of a death unplanned, dead without hatred,
        dead as if in a dream;
Vietnam, how I would love you . . .

This and many poems like it were the voice of Vietnam's youth and the bane of its intolerant government. The more the regime banned Son's songs, the more the pirated cassettes seemed to multiply throughout South Vietnam. Vietnamese, and not only the young, felt that Son sang what they could not say. The songs were heard in coffee shops everywhere, and many a shop was fined or temporarily closed because the owner did not turn off the cassette player quickly enough when the wrong person, a policeman or informer, entered. Son's popularity was huge — Saigon's most popular singer, Khanh Ly, made her career interpreting his songs and continues to do so in Californian exile — but Son did not live the life of a star. Official disapproval pushed him to the edge of society in Saigon, where he lived most of the time, and in his native Hue. Vietnam was not a land for pacifists.

Our last conversation before the end of the war took place in a modest Saigon apartment in 1973, Son's gentle voice competing with the raucous traffic of the street below. Vietnam's hope, he said, was that after the Communists had reunited the country their nationalist sentiments would steer them to carve out an Asian version of the Yugoslav path. In 1973 the dismemberment of Yugoslavia was unthought of; it was still one country, a Communist country that rejected both the Soviet and the Chinese ways, maintaining open borders for its citizens and fewer restrictions on personal freedom than any other Communist nation. He is a nonpolitical man, Son said, and he will find his place in such a society. (Two years later, as Laos was being taken over by the pro-Vietnamese Communists, a friend in Vientiane, the capital, expressed the same hope for an "Asian Yugoslavia" as he explained why he would not join the exodus to Thailand then under way. A day or two later, he was sent to the Laotian version of a reeducation camp, there called "seminar," and did not reemerge until six years later.)

I did not meet Son again until twenty years later, in 1993. A stairway lined with his paintings leads to his studio in his pleasant, quiet villa at the dead end of an alley in a prosperous section of Saigon. His paintings, strong in color, vaguely figurative, a new form of self-expression for him, are selling well, to foreigners and the nouveaux riches, he said. His guitar is leaning against his armchair; a whiskey and soda is in his hand on a sultry midmorning. My friend is fifty-six years old now, his face still young, his smile still gentle, and his voice soft. He is still widely popular; in national polls conducted by the newspaper of the Communist youth organization he regularly places first as the most popular artist, he said. His cassettes are on sale everywhere, and Hong Nhung, a popular twenty-five-year-old singer, from Hanoi this time, is building her career with his new repertory. He has been allowed to take several trips abroad. "I was in

Canada for four and a half months," he said. "I was constantly homesick. I couldn't live there." His five sisters and two brothers do. All has gone well for Trinh Cong Son, with the exception of the twelve years preceding the opening, *doi moi,* he said. He described his life over the two decades.

When Saigon fell, Son retreated to Hue, the city to which he had repaired through the years of the old regime whenever he felt it advisable to stay out of harm's way for a while. But the following year, he said — his customary poetic delicacy tinged perhaps with a capacity of more recent date for creating ambiguity that is certainly not due to any decline in the expressiveness of his French — he was ordered to a village at the northern limit of what had been South Vietnam, "to learn what peasant's work is like and understand its value." It was more than simple field labor, but highly dangerous work of clearly punitive nature. "The fields were full of everyone's mines, American mines, Viet Cong mines," he said. For four years the poet planted and reaped rice, sweet potatoes, and cassava on this perilous ground and came to no physical harm. During 1977 and 1978 Son was the target of a campaign of criticism in press, television, and radio and, because of his enduring popularity among the young, also in the schools and universities. The main theme was his attitude toward the war, which in one of his songs of the period he had called a civil war. This violated a basic tenet of the Communist version of history: the war was one of "the Vietnamese people" against the United States and its "puppets."

One day during this campaign, in 1978, he was taken unexpectedly to the Hue television studio and told to deliver his self-criticism. Instead, "I sang a song about a woman going to market," he recalled. In the next stage of his gradual rehabilitation, he was asked to submit a self-critical article. He navigated around that shoal by writing instead an open letter addressed to no one in particular in which he told of his sincere joy at national reunification. That seemed to satisfy the authorities. The open letter was widely printed and broadcast, and at the end of 1979 he was told that he was free to return to Saigon.

"In 1980 I began to compose songs again," Son said. "My

themes are love, the human condition, and nature." What happened to the *poète engagé* of the war years? I asked. He refilled his glass before replying. "I am conserving myself," he said. "I must above all exist, under all circumstances. I am marginal, and I protect myself." Is it difficult? "I am another now. I have become wise with age, if you will. I hide my treasure. I faced a painful choice. I chose tranquillity and peace of soul. It was not an easy choice; I had to abandon so many things. I must put aside everything that brings discomfort to my life. I am fifty-four years old; I am aged." Son said, yes, there are "forbidden zones," but what he writes is in keeping with the mood of his public, which is still largely the young, and he emphasized that it was now the young of all of Vietnam for whom he writes and sings and who sing his songs. More than one-half of today's Vietnamese were born after 1975. "They still need me, the young people, like before."

And Nhung, his favorite interpreter — "perhaps my new Khanh Ly," he said when Nhung, even smaller and slighter than her author and composer, was out of earshot — said enthusiastically that her generation loved Son's songs. "They feel they themselves are in those songs." But she said they did not respond to them in the same way the young did during the war, and she could not identify with the way Khanh Ly sang them.

Son said he felt attuned to his public and had no wish to return to earlier themes. The fact that even Vietnamese musicians in exile are singing and recording his new songs is proof for him that he continues to express what is important to Vietnamese — north or south, in San Francisco or Sydney. "I compose love songs," he said. "After thirty years of war, all wanted peace, and what is peace? It is love. Whatever I do, it is all for love. The Vietnamese want to live like everybody else. When peace came, they forgot everything else." Son feels that the reputation of the Vietnamese, based on the long years of war in our time, as a warlike people is false. "The people always had to be on guard," he said. "They were always under attack, even from the forces of nature. To survive, they had to fight. It is geopolitics. The Vietnamese people are romantic. There is a poet in every family, and they are poets of pacifism."

Today, Son said, the wish for peace has been realized. "Today, Vietnam is better than Yugoslavia then. There was a dictatorship. Today, the dictatorship is imperceptible. It is open today, all doors are open. Life is more breathable. It is the same as it was before 1975." He compared the old regime's version of democracy to the present facade of socialism. No one has asked him to join the Communist party. "My only party is my homeland," he said.

Son said he had no regrets about the choices he had made. "I have made the right choice," he said. "I feel at ease only here. It's like sleeping in my own bed."

One of Son's recent songs contains these lines of lost love and survival:

> I have two eyes, one mourns for you,
> For you one mourns;
> The other eye serves to see my life.

16

A Festival of Hope

Tet, the lunar new year, is the high point in the Vietnamese calendar. The festival means more to Vietnamese, wherever they are, than any single holiday does in Western cultures. Tet, which fall most years in February, unites the entire family, including the departed ancestors, whose ghosts return to earth to be honored and feted among their own. To celebrate Tet, whose official three days stretch for at least a week of holiday from all kinds of work, Vietnamese families pull out all stops to show themselves generous in honoring the family, in remembering friends, in sparing no expense. There is no better measure of the degree of well-being of the nation than how poorly or sumptuously it celebrates the festival. Tet 1994 was by all accounts the best in memory.

The measure is, of course, Vietnamese, and Vietnam remains one of the world's poorest nations. Its well-being expresses itself more in being carefree than in luxurious excess. The orgies of holiday spending are not of the measure of what piles up under a Western Christmas tree. But the Vietnamese do not lag behind Western holiday custom in conspicuous consumption on this occasion, even if it isn't all that much by absolute standards. In Hanoi, by far the poorer of Vietnam's two great cities, the ultimate Tet luxury is branches of Chinese peach trees, which burst into white and orange splendor at Tet time. The capital, still dismally wintry in February, dousing its people with the steady, chill drizzle that is the worst that northern Vietnam's weather offers, suddenly springs into incongruous bloom at almost any of its gray and busy street corners. Men and women of all ages come in from the countryside to peddle their branches. Like Birnam Wood coming to Dunsinane bringing death and bane to Macbeth, bicycles, their riders hidden by the profusion of flowering branches that they carry, glide, seemingly of their own power along Hanoi's sodden streets to deliver the most tenderly colorful Tet cheer to the capital.

Ducks and cocks await their end in the many markets that spring up just for Tet alongside the usual places of trade; fish have their final flings in tubs; more meat is bought than is customary for Vietnamese tables, and varied sticky, garishly colored confections special for the occasion are offered. Rice alcohol and beer, even Scotch of doubtful authenticity, for the men; cosmetics and frills of finery for the women; and plastic toys for children fill the shelves of shops and the cardboard boxes of street vendors. An entire alley in the city's bustling trading quarter is crowded with sellers of bundles of fake dollar bills, brilliantly colored mock jewelry, models of television sets, motorcycles, and other highly desirable acquisitions, all made of paper — rich objects incredibly cheap that can be offered to the ancestors on their altars and burned when they return to the other world at the end of Tet. So provided, they will not need to be ashamed of their families, who have equipped them with the best of everything for their journey.

Also on sale in 1994 were figures of dogs, of all breeds, in all sizes, and of all cheap materials, to mark the coming of the Year of the Dog. Kind friends and acquaintances presented me with many a little dog, gifts in which the generosity of the thought that prompted them more than made up for the questionable beauty of the objects. And endless strings of firecrackers, whose machine-gun bursts of bangs, punctuated by the single booms of larger-caliber charges, are intended to chase away evil spirits, are set off at all hours of day and evening and, unfortunately, all through the Tet nights, as well as a couple of days before the festival and a few more afterward. One would have thought that Vietnam more than most other countries has had its fill of explosions; perhaps the Tet pyrotechnics are the clearest evidence that most Vietnamese alive today were born after the big war on their country's soil was over and connect no painful memories with the martial sounds.

Tet 1994, in Hanoi and in Saigon, was the festival of a nation that feels that the worst is over. That is indeed the feeling that makes Vietnam today a nation buoyant despite its poverty, confident that it is finally on the way to becoming a country like the others of Southeast Asia. The Vietnamese have no illusion about how great is the present gap that separates them from the countries against which they measure themselves. They are mainly those of ASEAN, the Association of Southeast Asian Nations, which finally admitted Vietnam to membership in July 1995, the eventful month that also saw America's opening of full diplomatic relations with its former enemy. Vietnam's partners in ASEAN are countries with which it shares the Southeast Asian mainland—Thailand, Malaysia, and Singapore—and the three island countries—vast Indonesia, the Philippines, and tiny, oil-rich Brunei. But after decades of war followed by more war, of isolation from all their neighbors — except for reclusive Laos and, for the years of their military occupation, Cambodia — and from all of the non-Communist world beyond, of scarcity of just about everything, Vietnamese now feel that they have become a part of the whole. Their horizons have grown wider, although still far from open.

For the vast majority, there seems to be no political goal still to be attained — their country is reunited and at peace. Those goals were vital for Vietnamese throughout the war, north and south. However fatuous the slogans that Communist governments feel, more than others, to be the required background music of daily life, there is one that rings true in Vietnam. It is inscribed on a grandiosely minor monument that stands on the northern bank of the Ben Hai River, North Vietnam's edge of the DMZ, the nominally demilitarized zone that divided the warring halves from 1954 until 1975. Beneath a bas-relief of the author, it recalls the grandiloquent words of Ho Chi Minh: "Vietnam is one. The Vietnamese people are one. Rivers may dry up, mountains crumble, but that truth will remain forever."

In Ho Chi Minh's one and indivisible country, there reig today an implicit belief that Vietnam is living the end of Communist era. The Vietnamese have seen the great Sov Union, the motherland of communism, collapse into impo erished particles, humbled and beggared, and they see the fo eigners who are coming to invest and do business as emissari of the victorious forces in a worldwide ideological struggle th the side to which they had been consigned has lost. They loo with equanimity toward the impending passing of communism yet it is hardly something that they passionately long for. For th overwhelming majority of Vietnamese there seem to be no poli ical goals. As they see today's Vietnam, they believe its leader have grown wiser and have recanted the errors that made Vie nam so poor and, anyway, the leaders are old and will soon hav to yield their places to men, far more likely than women, o more modern spirit, attuned to the present ways of the worl rather than stalwarts of the struggle against France's colonialist and America's imperialists.

For a nation that has fought so ardently for political goals a people who engaged in a revolutionary struggle, which man of them resisted with as much conviction as those who carried i forward, the great majority of Vietnamese, north and south, ar remarkably nonpolitical. This is a boon to those in power however big or small their share of it, because it insures thei jobs. It is a sadness to the handful who are not nonpolitical, the few who, astonishingly, cherish in a setting so unaccustomed to it hopes for democracy, a civil society tolerant of all civil views.

What matters most to most Vietnamese — and who can blame them? — is the reality of a brighter outlook for a life richer in such modest gains as decent earnings, a full stomach, a better roof over their heads, safe water to drink and electricity to light their houses, nice clothes, perhaps a motor scooter and someday a color television with video, and above all, the hope for a better life for their children. That is surely not all they wish for: it goes without saying that, despite current trends toward decline, they believe that health care and educational opportunities will improve as part of a rising standard of living. And they know that this standard is on the way up now that the government has had the wisdom to trust the Vietnamese, much more than before, to use their own heads and hands to make their way out of the poorhouse. Optimism is broadly based because the farmers, Vietnam's largest population group, were the first major beneficiaries of the liberalizing reforms when they went fully into effect in 1989. From being an importer of 700,000 to 800,000 tons of rice in the 1986 to 1988 period, Vietnam has since 1989, following the breakup of most collective farms and the liberalizing of pricing, grown enough of the staple grain to export an average of two million tons a year. It ranks after the leader, Thailand, and close to the United States in third place as a source of rice exports. With remarkable candor, the government reported to a conference of aid donors in 1993 that the exports were not a sign of food sufficiency but necessary to earn foreign currency for the purchase of essential agricultural inputs. Rice production remains "still far short of what is achievable and needed to eliminate malnutrition," the government said.

Despite the official socialist label, Vietnam today is to all intents and purposes a country restructuring its economy to fit into a region of fast-growing free-market countries. The market has largely replaced central planning as the place where fundamental economic decisions are made. Much of agriculture has been privatized. Trade and foreign investment have been extensively liberalized. Subsidies to state enterprises have been greatly reduced, about one-half of their total of twelve thousand liquidated or merged with others, and the number of persons on the payroll reduced by one-third. Prices, as well as the exchange rate of the *dong,* have been left to be determined by the market. The result has been annual economic growth averaging, according to the International Monetary Fund, about 7 percent from 1990 to 1994. Growth in 1994 was 8.5 percent. Over the same period, inflation, which had been brought down to below 70 percent in 1990 after having soared to the hyperinflationary rate of 774 percent in 1986, dropped to 5.1 percent in 1993, although it rose again in 1994 to 14.5 percent. By June 1995, the annual rate had climbed to 19.5 percent.

It adds to an appreciation of the magnitude of this achievement to note that it took place in a period in which Vietnam lost the substantial economic support of the Soviet Union, as well as its guaranteed export markets in that country and the other members of Comecon, the Soviet-dominated trading bloc. Vietnam managed the difficult transition from Communist to market economics far more successfully than the European Communist states. "The Soviet Union was not ready; Vietnam is," said Nguyen Xuan Oanh, the Harvard-educated former acting South Vietnamese prime minister. "A mouse can turn around more quickly than an elephant can."

Vietnam's marked economic upturn took place also in a period in which America's unforgiving opposition to a country that it failed to defeat kept it from access to development loans on easy terms from international nonprofit lending institutions like the World Bank, the International Monetary Fund, and the Asian Development Bank. That barrier was not lifted until 1993. The following year, just in time for Tet, the United States finally removed its long-standing embargo on trade with Vietnam. But, although the United States established diplomatic relations in 1995, commerce between the two countries remains minimal because America has not granted Vietnam most-favored-nation tariff status, which makes imports from Vietnam uncompetitive in the American market. This limits Vietnam's ability to buy American goods.

Such progress in a country that not much earlier had seemed economically moribund has raised high expectations, perhaps too high. Raymond Mallon, a knowledgeable economist assigned as a "resident adviser" to the Vietnamese State Planning Committee's State Enterprise Reform Program by the World Bank and the United Nations Development Program, offered prudent cautions in a paper he presented in his private capacity to an investors' conference in Hong Kong in 1994. "The Vietnamese economy remains relatively small," he wrote.

> Despite strong economic growth, it will be some decades before national income begins to approach the levels of

other rapidly growing economies in Southeast Asia. Thus, investors need to be cautious about references to Viet Nam as a new tiger. There is tremendous potential for Viet Nam to start 'catching-up' to other countries in the region — but this is partly because Viet Nam is starting from a relatively small base. . . . Despite recent impressive economic performance, the Vietnamese economy remains small relative to other ASEAN economies. Even at the targeted annual growth rate of 8 per cent, it would take more than a decade for the economy to reach current levels of G.D.P. in the Philippines, and two decades to reach that of Thailand.

The smallness of the Vietnamese economy is made graphic by comparisons with population figures and gross domestic products of the larger ASEAN nations. The closest in population to Vietnam is the Philippines, whose official population in 1992 was 65.2 million, when the Vietnamese total was 69.5 million. Its GDP for 1993 was 53 billion dollars, Vietnam's 12 billion dollars. Thailand, with 56.1 million people, produced at the rate of 124 billion dollars, and Malaysia, with only 18.8 million inhabitants, had a GDP of 63 billion dollars. With about one-quarter of Vietnam's population, Malaysia created values more than five times as great as Vietnam.

Senior Vietnamese economists are painfully aware of how long a road they will have to travel to catch up with the rest of their region. "There is growing evidence of the economic gap between Vietnam and its neighbors, ASEAN and China," said Le Dang Doanh, deputy director of the Central Institute for Economic Management in Hanoi. "That gap is growing, not shrinking." In Saigon, Pham Xuan Ai, deputy director of the Institute for Economic Research, mused pensively. "Look how low our government budget is," he said, knitting his brow. "Malaysia, with about twenty million people, has an annual budget of sixteen or seventeen billion dollars. Vietnam, with seventy-three million, has a budget of three billion dollars." A French banker in Saigon offered a discouraging calculation. "The Vietnamese gross national product is about equal to the annual increase in the Thai GNP. To draw even with Thailand today, the Vietnamese GNP will have to grow 8 percent a year for twenty-five years without any population growth. But at the present birthrate, there will be 168 million Vietnamese in 2025. In fifteen years this country will have to import food."

The obstacles Vietnam must overcome are physical, institutional, and human. Vietnam's agricultural land is extremely densely inhabited. According to the World Bank, its more than nine hundred persons per square kilometer of arable land compare with a density of less than three hundred in Vietnam's neighbors, China and Thailand. In its 1993 report, *Viet Nam: Transition to the Market,* the bank notes that Vietnam's nonagricultural resources are "not overwhelming" given the size of its population, which is growing at a rate of 2.2 percent each year. The government places much hope on offshore petroleum resources, but the report states, "The most optimistic projections show oil reserves at about the same magnitude as those of Malaysia, a country with one-fourth of Viet Nam's population." The World Bank report reaches a dual conclusion: "First, the country will have to develop on the basis of human resources rather than natural resources. Second, it will be a major challenge to preserve the fragile resource base in the face of population pressures." It is this necessary reliance on human resources that makes the present decline in education so worrisome.

But it is not only the resource base that is fragile. After the decades of destructive war, which monopolized all of the country's energies, Vietnam, particularly in the north, is a grossly underdeveloped country. Communications, complicated by Vietnam's impractical geography — an enormously elongated shape that makes for disproportionate interior distances — depend on a destitute road system. It was never highly developed in the north, and in the south, where the U.S. war effort included considerable road building, it has suffered from lack of maintenance and repair since the American withdrawal in 1973. The main national road, Route 1, which links Hanoi with Saigon and then turns westward to end in Phnom Penh, the Cambodian capital, was called "la route des mandarins" by the French, who built it. It was intended to facilitate the movements of civil servants in pursuit of their duties.

A twelve-day drive from Hanoi to Saigon in 1994 was marvelously interesting; the slow speeds imposed by the grandiosely named road's narrowness and state of disrepair, particularly in the north, permitted an almost intimate look at the ever-moving life on the road and in the towns and villages through which it passes. Engrossing for the inquisitive traveler, but extraordinarily cumbersome for the transport of goods and services. As for the lesser roads, the World Bank reports that those of the highest quality, "national" roads, cover twelve thousand kilometers, or 7,500 miles, of which only 60 percent is paved. The Ministry of Transport classifies 45 percent of the length of that network as "poor to very poor." "The other networks are much worse, with about 60–70% poor to bad," according to the World Bank. In the lower category of "provincial" or "district" roads, measuring 40,000 kilometers, or 25,000 miles, only 8 percent is paved. The government reported to the aid donors conference in 1993 that 58 percent of the roads in the north and 18 percent in the south were in "poor or very poor condition." "Some 87 percent of the road system is dirt, including one third of the national road system," the report concluded. During the rainy season most of Vietnam's roads become impassable.

Similarly, a train ride on the main line from Hue to Da Nang, the principal cities of the center, no more than seventy-five miles apart, took more than four hours. This was useful for allowing me to get to know my fellow travelers and have an extensive conversation with a family heading in the opposite direction, whose train was stuck alongside mine sufficiently long to provide a rather full insight into their lives and travels and to sample the homemade snacks they kindly offered, but no doubt frustrating for a traveler in the line of work or a businessman at the other end awaiting his freight.

At the height of a working day in 1992, the port of Haiphong, the largest in the north and the point of entry for everything the Soviet Union and its allies used to supply to their Vietnamese client, was a still and lonely place. I could hear our footsteps in the ambient silence as Truong Van Thai, the secretary of the harbor administration, showed me around, reminiscing about his years of training in Poland and Belgium. Ten years earlier, Thai said, the port fined shippers for not removing their cargoes promptly. "Now we give them ten days storage for free for imports and twenty for exports, and our warehouses are still empty," he said with a shrug. The port has a handling capacity of five million tons, said Nguyen Van Nha, the deputy harbormaster, but never came near handling that much, even in the years when aid-bearing ships and those carrying the tools of war that Vietnam employed in Cambodia stood at anchor outside the port waiting to unload. He explained that the delays then had been due mainly to the cumbersome ways of the centrally directed, over-staffed, and inefficient bureaucracy. So long were the waiting times that sometimes aid donors threatened to turn around and leave without delivering their gifts. The main problem that keeps the port so far below its capacity today is physical. The twenty-two-mile channel that links Haiphong's harbor to the sea is so heavily silted over from years of inadequate mainte-nance that ships of more than six thousand tons now need to reduce their cargoes before entering the channel. At the height of port activity, during the invasion of Cambodia from 1978 until 1980, Haiphong could handle no more than 3.2 million tons, well below its rated capacity. Its rate of utilization has continued to drop since then.

"We employ more than five thousand persons, but at the moment we require a limited number of workers," Nha said, in a gross understatement. At two o'clock on a weekday afternoon there was nobody on the dock except a cleaning crew of cheerful women and a burly North Korean, wearing the obligatory lapel button with the image of Kim Il Sung, the late leader then still alive, and a fierce scowl, guarding a freighter from his country. Coastal shipping, which could take much of the strain off the inadequate road and rail systems, is equally undeveloped. De-spite Vietnam's long shoreline, coastal shipping moves only 2 percent of internal freight traffic, the World Bank reports.

The energy sector is another obstacle to rapid development. Power shortages are a serious problem in the south, placing a ceiling on present prospects in Vietnam's most dynamic region. "They talk a lot about major industrial projects here," said another French banker in Saigon. "Where will they find the energy? Where I live, every Wednesday from seven in the morning until seven in the evening they cut off the electricity. That is the scheduled cut, to save energy, but there are also a lot of unscheduled cuts." While international telephone links have been greatly improved, the government reported to aid donors that 90 percent of villages in the overwhelmingly rural country had no telephones.

The backwardness of most of the existing technology — either from Communist countries, who did not give their best and most up-to-date to their poor Asian cousin, or leftovers from the American period — embarrasses many Vietnamese officials as they seek to attract foreign investment to their provinces or cities. Nguyen Dinh An is vice president of the People's Committee of Quang Nam Province, the equivalent of a deputy governor. In his office in Da Nang, Vietnam's fourth-largest city, lying midway between Hanoi and Saigon, he told me of a visit in 1993 by a Chinese trade delegation. He showed them through the port and other installations, many of which were built for the American military. Then he recalled his moment of anguish. "The head of the delegation said, 'Only my grandfather would know this technology,'" the vice president said ruefully, his embarrassment clearly heightened because the unkind cut came from a Chinese. An, a former teacher of literature in Hanoi, spent the war years doing psychological warfare at Viet Cong headquarters in the much bombed mountains near Da Nang. He visited the United States in 1994 to try to persuade the American companies who built the extensive military facilities in the Da Nang area to return to convert them for civilian use.

A number of institutional and human problems recur in the comments of Vietnamese specialists, experts from international organizations, and foreign businessmen and bankers. These are the principal ones: wide gaps between announced policies and their implementation, as well as frequent and confusing swings of the policy pendulum; jurisdictional contradictions arising from hazy divisions of authority between ministries in Hanoi and between central and provincial or local governments; extensive uncharted areas in the laws governing private business, investment, and the right to use land; unfair competitive advantages that the government continues to confer on state enterprises; and corruption on every level of dealings with authorities. Vietnamese economists and bankers, who talk as though the postsocialist era were already under way in the Socialist Republic, are frank in acknowledging the failings that international officials, bankers, and businessmen discuss only after requesting that their anonymity be respected. Perhaps their candor is a symptom of their relative inexperience in the ways of the world of capitalist business.

Pham Xuan Ai of the Saigon Institute for Economic Research, who has profited from recent study at Harvard, said that changing to a market economy did not come naturally to many officials:

> In reality, things are still done wrongly because people still have to change their mentality. We have to improve almost everything, the legal system, the trade policies. It is a problem for many people on the middle level. Maybe they don't know how to make the situation better, or maybe they want to remain in the past. The policies get better and better, but in the execution people create difficulties. The central government promulgates a policy, but some provinces don't carry it out. We will have to retrain thousands of people — top-level, medium-level, even ordinary workers. We have to make our management system more efficient. Government management, for instance. They have to learn how to govern in a free-market economy. Right now they are confused about it. The ministries in Hanoi, for instance, have dual functions: they govern the country's macro-economy, but at the same time they are the bosses of state enterprises. Sometimes there is a conflict of interests there. The Ministry of Trade, for instance, has lots of enterprises, but at the same time it manages the trade policies of the whole country. This is a very big problem in my opinion.

Huynh Buu Son, deputy managing director of the Saigon Bank for Industry and Trade, a private enterprise in which, ironically, the Communist party City Committee is the major shareholder, was equally critical. "There is a lot of bureaucracy, and this gives rise to a lot of corruption," he said. "It should be the major task of the government to fight bureaucracy and corruption. Administrative reform is under way, but we face a lot of difficulties. We have no professional administrators. Most of them are there mainly because they are good party members. It is very difficult to dismiss such high officials. We must build a state of laws, not of party resolutions. If we cannot fight the bureaucracy and corruption, we will never catch up with our neighbors. This is vital not only for our country but also for the party."

Son, who began his banking career with the National Bank under the old Saigon regime, is more than most aware of the difficulties that Communist-trained officials who hold powers of making economic decisions experience in adjusting to the universe of international banking and business. It is still new to them, and after a lifetime of indoctrination about its evils they regard it with distrust. "It is a matter of education," he said. "They started in another, in a closed, world. People were educated only in a certain way. They all speak the same language, they share the same thinking, and they don't realize how the rest of the world functions. They look at it with critical eyes and don't have the knowledge to analyze it correctly." He spoke of the artificially cocooned, centrally controlled business environment within the Communist world that shaped the officials and of the very different ways of the "new" world of Vietnam's geographic region.

Vietnam is making its entry there after many years of very limited economic relations outside the Communist sphere. "We realize we have to concern ourselves more with protecting our own national interest," he continued. "The world now is different. It is formed by nations that care about their own interests. We live on a continent now where we must cooperate and compete. We must learn to survive by our own means." To this Saigon banker, the direct, highly focused ways of the overseas

Chinese business community represent the efficient antithesis to the cumbersome fashion in which Vietnam conducted its affairs. Their pragmatism makes the Chinese from Taiwan and the Southeast Asian countries the most successful operators in this initial stage of Vietnamese market economics. "The Chinese community has relations abroad and money," he said. "The Chinese traditionally help each other to form productive communities. They see the opportunities in Vietnam and channel their money to their relatives here. This avoids the complicated procedures for foreign investors. They can invest fast."

Total official foreign investment — that is, not through ethnic Chinese relatives and friends in Vietnam — approved by mid-1994 stood at more than nine billion dollars, of which about 2.5 billion had actually been disbursed, according to Pham Xuan Ai of the Institute for Economic Research. Chinese countries held a strong lead — the two largest sources were Taiwan and Hong Kong, and Singapore was in fifth place, after South Korea and Australia. An international official placed heavy responsibility for corruption on the overseas Chinese predominance and found it running counter to the interests of potential major investors, who are holding back their entry into Vietnam until legislation to protect investment is adopted. "The overseas Chinese encourage corruption at the lower levels," he said. "The West wants legality established here, and the Chinese couldn't care less." The Chinese role is prominent enough to cause some grumbling among Vietnamese that China may be in the process of buying dominance in Vietnam after failing over so many centuries to achieve it by force. This is no doubt greatly exaggerated, but an Asian banker said that investment proposals from Hong Kong were being treated gingerly because of a suspicion that Beijing may hold the controlling interests in the "no-name trusts" that do the bidding from Hong Kong.

The bulk of foreign investment is in petroleum exploration and the service sector, with only a small part in production. "Our economy to this day is largely the exploitation of natural resources," said Le Dang Doanh of the Central Institute for Economic Management. "There is not enough labor-intensive production and no capital-intensive or high-technology-intensive activity. We are still at the first stage of development. It is hard to accumulate capital like that." In Saigon, the economic center of gravity, Pham Xuan Ai of the Institute for Economic Research shared his Hanoi colleague's worry. "There are very few new factories," he said. "Unemployment is a very big problem. Officially it is 10 to 12 percent; in reality it is 20 to 25 percent." That, of course, does not include the massive underemployment in the countryside.

To a visitor's eye Vietnam's cities, Saigon in particular, offer an image of burgeoning prosperity, because retail shops present a variety of wares, particularly blaring and flashing consumer electronics and clothing, that were absent for so long. The remarkable increase in cars and motorcycles reinforces the impression. However, this is a superficial prosperity, based largely on smuggling and of little benefit to the overwhelming majority of the population or to a government hard pressed to raise revenues for its budget through taxation and customs receipts. The borders with China and Cambodia, smugglers' El Dorados under all governments, are main transit points for contraband goods; corruption in ports makes for many points of entry. What the World Bank delicately called "unofficial imports" amounted to perhaps one-fifth of the level of official imports, the bank estimated in 1993. It added, "With the country's long, porous borders and thriving informal sector, it will be very difficult to enforce restrictions on this trade."

Vietnam is a country of imbalances, with enormous regional and local differences that detract from the indicative value of statistics and averages. The poverty, underdevelopment, malnutrition, and low state of health in the extensive mountainous areas and the long, narrow strip of the central coast are far greater than the national averages indicate, and the cities and more fertile rural areas, sheltered from typhoons and flooding, are much better off. But perhaps the greatest imbalance is the disparity between Saigon and its surrounding region of the Mekong Delta and all the rest of the country. "This is a partitioned country," said Nguyen Xuan Oanh, the former

South Vietnamese deputy prime minister, in the office of his Saigon investment fund. "The north was a Maoist, badly planned economy; here we have a strictly private-enterprise economy. This is not a north-south imbalance but a huge gap, the legacy of wars. It will take thirty years to close the gap. This is a two-country nation. The tail wags the dog." The World Bank, in less partisan terms, puts it this way: "Compared to the north, the south has more agricultural land per capita, more of the capital stock in light manufacturing, greater entrepreneurial tradition, easier access to capital from overseas Vietnamese, and better infrastructure (except in the power sector)."

The difference begins at the natural-resource base: of the two main rice-growing regions, the Mekong Delta south of Saigon outproduces the Red River Delta around Hanoi. "Viet Nam's exports have come from huge marketable surpluses in the Mekong Delta and modest surpluses . . . in the Red River Delta," the World Bank reports. Oanh, a native northerner but an outspoken advocate of the south, went further. "We produce twenty-four, twenty-five million tons, and two or three million of that is surplus; all the surplus comes from the south," he insisted. "Not a grain comes from the north. In textiles, in shirts, Vietnam produces seventy-five million pieces a year; the south produces fifty million of them. All the marine products come from the south." Shrimp is a major export, mainly to Japan. In 1993 Vietnam's exports amounted to three billion dollars; crude oil, rice, coal, and coffee are the principal other commodities sold abroad.

North Vietnam, less favored by nature, with only about one-half the arable land of the south, compounded its economic weakness by following a thoroughly Stalinist development model from its inception in 1954. Following the heroic Communist tradition, it received from its allies help in creating heavy industry — iron and steel, chemicals, cement. Its agriculture was completely collectivized and the entire economy placed under a strict, centrally dictated production plan. This makes conversion to a market economy a far more intimidating task than returning the south to where it had been after little more than a decade of adapting to the Communist model. Nor does it produce significant quantities of exportable goods other than coal. Moreover, the farmers of the Mekong Delta had so cunningly dragged their feet in accepting collectivization that the process was far from complete when the signal to reverse it came from Hanoi. The result is that most of the declared foreign investment, as well as virtually all the unofficial capital inflow from its two main sources, the overseas Chinese and the overseas Vietnamese, goes to the south in general and Saigon in particular. As a fair estimate, it is assumed that the economic growth rate of the Saigon area averages around 12 to 14 percent a year, compared with the national average of 7 percent, and the disproportion is thought to be widening.

"The south is the locomotive of the market reform," said a Russian diplomat, perhaps the most experienced and knowledgeable foreign observer. "The pressure for more liberalization comes from there, but in the north they are still afraid of repealing some old principles. The party intellectuals, especially in the south, know that at the present rate Vietnam is not catching up with its neighbors, that its development should be more open. But here in Hanoi there are even some who fear that behind this lie southern separatist sentiments." Paranoia clearly comes readily to men who late in their lives witness the reversal of so much that they devoted their careers to.

However great the head start the south enjoys, all of Vietnam, including Saigon, remains leagues behind the other ASEAN countries, even Indonesia and the Philippines, the least developed. Jakarta and Manila, with all their huge urban problems of excessive and unequal growth, make Saigon look like a backwater. "The economic growth at this stage is still superficial," a diplomat said in Saigon. "Where else would you see what I saw the other day?" What he saw was a massive long tree trunk, transported by two men pushing it along the road with the trunk's ends tied each to a bicycle.

17

Socialism in the Socialist Republic

Most of what Dr. Duong Quynh Hoa sees of the effects of
Vietnam's economic liberalization fills her with bitterness. "We
fought for freedom, independence, and social justice," she said.
"Now all is money."

Dr. Hoa, a pediatrician and gynecologist, criticizes from the
inside. She is a founder of the National Liberation Front — the
Viet Cong — and from 1969 until 1976 she was minister of
health in the Provisional Revolutionary Government of South
Vietnam. For seven years she risked her life for the revolution on
the constantly shifting battlefronts of the jungles of the south.
Her eight-month-old son, born in the jungle, died of encepha-
litis, which she could diagnose but had not the means to treat.
She sent another woman to try to carry the baby to Saigon,
where her sister, also a doctor, might have been able to save him.
But the child died a few miles before reaching the city and was
buried where he died.

Dr. Hoa's service to the Vietnamese Communists did not
begin when she went into what she calls, in her thoroughly
Parisian French and World War II terminology, "le maquis," the
armed resistance to the Saigon government and the United
States. She began to work for the French Communist party in
1948, when, eighteen years old, she arrived in Paris for her
medical studies. She became a party member in 1954 before
returning to her home in Saigon, where her father was a professor of Vietnamese and Chinese at the Lycée Chasseloup-
Laubat, the French elite school that was the breeding ground of

Indochinese leaders on all sides of the conflicts of Vietnam, Cambodia, and Laos. Hoa, a brilliant student and one of only a few women at the lycée, obtained her baccalaureate there at the unusually early age of fifteen, but at that age her father thought her too young to study in Paris.

On her return she opened a private practice in Saigon and continued to work for the revolution. Her mission was to organize political support and obtain useful information among the men and women of her social class, doctors and intellectuals. She was at home in the upper reaches of Saigon society and met the Vietnamese elite, as well as top American officials and military officers, on the dinner-party circuit. She was known as a woman of the left, but she said no one took her seriously, because she was a woman and because it was thought that her "progressive" ideas represented more radical chic than the passionate convictions on which she founded her life of action. But she was arrested in May 1960, imprisoned for several months, and tortured by the secret police of Ngo Dinh Nhu, the sinister brother of President Ngo Dinh Diem, when the Communist ring that she had helped to form was betrayed. Undaunted, she was among the handful of revolutionaries who in December of the same year slipped in from the jungle or out from Saigon to gather in a vital center of the armed resistance, the audacious, extensive network of tunnels around the market town of Cu Chi, only about twenty miles northwest of Saigon on the road that leads to Phnom Penh, the Cambodian capital. It was the founding meeting of the National Liberation Front, formed by Hanoi as its southern representative in the battle for Vietnam, and known by its enemies as the Viet Cong.

Dr. Hoa remained in Saigon until the bloody battles of the Communist Tet Offensive in 1968, which brought the war not only to the southern capital but even into the heavily fortified American embassy compound. A few days after the fighting ended, she was ordered into the maquis. "I left on the backseat of a motorcycle," she said with the engaging smile and contagiously melodious laugh that punctuate her conversation. It is easy to forget that this petite, even by Vietnamese measure, and

unquenchably lively woman has led a life of death-defying courage and determination. She continues to this day, at sixty-five, to
reject the facile compromises that would make life easy, in favor
of living, as Václav Havel says, in truth. She still relishes the
memory of how she hoodwinked the forbidding Saigon security
machinery and managed to cross the lines disguised as a peasant. "Three suitcases of clothes followed by other means, a few
days later." Hoa said she kept three outfits and gave the rest of
her city wardrobe to other women of the resistance movement.
Even today, she favors black pants topped by a black blouse,
well-tailored now but reminiscent of the black pajamalike peasant garb that was the Viet Cong's informal uniform, and wears
her gray, wavy hair close-cropped.

Shortly after taking to the maquis, Hoa married Huynh
Van Nghi, a mathematician from the Sorbonne, in a jungle
ceremony. Like herself, Nghi joined the French Communist
party in his student days — for nationalist and anticolonialist
reasons, he emphasizes — but unlike his wife he never became a
member of the Vietnamese party. "When one thinks that one is
the holder of the one truth, one has already fallen into error," the
taciturn mathematician said. "It will end badly." Dr. Hoa, not
the sort of woman who seeks outside approval for her private
affairs, said the party's Central Committee gave its blessing to
their marriage, but her cell never did. She had offended its
leaders by failing to ask prior permission. "There was caviar but
no champagne," she recalled of the ceremony, which took place
near the town of Tay Ninh at the Cambodian border.

They spent most of the war years in that region, where the
command center for the southern campaign was deeply dug in
somewhat to the north on the Cambodian side, remaining even
while President Nixon launched the U.S. Army into Cambodia
for two months in 1970 to try to root it out, without success.
American bombers and helicopter gunships kept the area under
constant pounding; chemical defoliation deprived it of much of
its vegetation. Their child was born and died in 1970. Dr. Hoa
refuses to grant herself pity; the child was one of so many, she
says, struggling and succeeding to keep her voice steady. With

some regret, she says that her orders during the war years forced her to spend more time doing "political work" than treating the wounded and the sick.

When the Provisional Revolutionary Government was founded in 1969, she was named minister of health and remained in that position until Hanoi did away with the separate government for the south by reunifying the nation in 1976. She said she had been offered the position of health minister for all of Vietnam instead but refused because she preferred to stay in Saigon. "I was for reunification, but more slowly," Dr. Hoa said. "I thought it would take four or five years. But they were afraid of their incompetence, which could not stand up against the competence of the south." Dr. Hoa recalled her first visit to Hanoi, which took place in 1974. "I was shocked by the incompetence I saw, including in the hospitals."

Hoa and Nghi told of their lives, the ideals that inspired them, and the abandonment of those ideals by those in power while we sat overlooking the green hill country from the terrace of a Spartan wooden cottage that they built near a cluster of mountain tribe villages between Saigon and the hill town of Dalat. Dr. Hoa heads the Center for Pediatrics, Development and Health, a nominally governmental institution that is financed by a large group of Western, including American, voluntary agencies. The center is housed in a small, modern building in the confines of what was France's largest hospital in Saigon in colonial days, the Hôpital Grall. One of Dr. Hoa's first actions when she began exercising ministerial authority in the newly conquered city was to turn the large complex into a children's hospital. The couple — Nghi prefers not to work in the present academic atmosphere and does not publish his continuing mathematical research — spend most of their weekends working in the poor villages, in which the center carries out public health and development projects and where Hoa and the enthusiastic young doctors who work with her conduct nutritional research among the largely malnourished population.

Their daily work in Saigon and in the villages constantly fuels their criticism of the insufficiencies and injustices of a regime that calls itself socialist but fails to give to its people the benefits of social care that would make it live up to the name, and arrogates to itself the intolerant dictatorial powers that in other countries gave socialism a bad name, making it synonymous with police states. They are confronted with the painful effects of the Vietnamese version of economic liberalism on the human services that should be the essence of socialism. The losers under the new economic policies are above all free medical care and education, fields in which the Communist government once was rightly proud of having established and, until *doi moi,* expanded high standards. Hoa and Nghi and many other former fighters for a socialist Vietnam believe that a government that does away with such fundamental rights, its early accomplishments, loses the right to call itself socialist.

Nothing more clearly illustrates what has so deeply disillusioned idealistic old revolutionaries than this astonishingly frank comment in a major policy statement by the Ministry of Health, entitled *Strategy for Health for All by the Year 2000,* published in 1992: "The shifting from a subsidized to a socialist market economy has more negative than positive influences on health in Vietnam. The increasing cost of medical care and drugs makes them less affordable to the users. The differentiation between the rich and the poor is becoming more accentuated, increasing levels of poverty and exacerbating ill health and quality of services. Disregarding the needs of the poor, private physicians and private pharmacies compete only for the services to the rich." Despite this clear and public condemnation, the statement is at least as true today as it was in 1992. Reporting in 1995 in *Viet Nam: Poverty Assessment and Strategy,* the World Bank stated, in discussing declining health services: "According to Ministry of Health service statistics, the number of outpatient consultations has fallen by half since the late 1980s. . . . The inpatient admission rate also dropped sharply during this period . . . they certainly suggest a picture of reversal in Viet Nam's past gains in delivering health services." The bank notes among possible causes the introduction of fees but also a lowering of quality in public health services. "A large proportion of health facilities have become dilapidated to the point of being unusable for want of equipment and medical supplies," the report states.

In a comparison of government expenditures for health in eleven Asian countries published in another World Bank report, Vietnam is by far the lowest in per capita spending, tied at the bottom of the list with the Philippines in the percentage of total government spending that is devoted to health and also tied at the bottom, with Bangladesh, in the percentage of the gross national product spent on government health services. The Ministry of Health reported that in 1990 the government spent only fifty cents per capita on health. In its 1993 report, entitled *Viet Nam: Transition to the Market,* the World Bank concluded: "The quality of health services is extremely poor and the productivity of health workers (in terms of numbers of patients examined) is very low because of low health worker salaries, poor or nonfunctional medical equipment, and inadequate (and, in many cases, nonexistent) medical supplies and drugs."

An international official with long experience in Vietnam's public health sector made these general terms specific:

> The staff is there, underpaid but motivated. But the equipment is obsolete, the hospitals are in shambles, there is no budget. To continue to function, most rural hospitals grow vegetables and fruit to sell. They cook soup for the midday meal and sell it to the patients and their families. Some even plant tobacco and sell cigarettes. They sell traditional medicines; they even raise pigs. They have to do these things, because outside the cities they are months behind in their pay. In rural health centers, the instruments are only a microscope, a scale, and a stethoscope. The ambulance is a hammock and two bikes. The doctors' midday meal is a bowl of pho [noodle soup with slices of meat, a national dish]; it's not enough. A surgeon can work maybe five hours a day on that. They don't have the strength.

Still, with a doctor's monthly pay about forty dollars, most work at second jobs or conduct small private practices at home, which *doi moi* has legalized. "A survey of health facilities in three provinces found that only 49.3% of rural commune health centers had a functioning sterilizer and only 58.4% had a usable weighing scale for infants," the World Bank reported in a 1992 study, *Vietnam: Population, Health and Nutrition.*

In many conversations, Dr. Hoa drew up a catalog of problems to which she said the government was paying insufficient attention or that were being rapidly aggravated by a policy that makes victims of the great majority of Vietnamese. "You see something that looks like normality being restored," she said. "It is not real. An opening must be kept under minimal control. It is not. We are being overrun. We never built real socialism; we have replaced one social injustice with another. Look at Ho Chi Minh City. I participated in a struggle for thirty years, and what I find now looks like the old regime. What I see is the consumer society in all its splendor. And what Hanoi took from the south is what is negative, not its knowledge, its management skills, only its consumer habits."

Dr. Hoa is particularly concerned over malnutrition. "The health of Vietnamese is declining in monumental fashion," she said. "We are feeling the effects of years of malnutrition. Food is unevenly divided, and the gravest problem is malnutrition that has become chronic. We made a malnutrition study ten years ago in the mountain villages and found that 37 to 40 percent of the children from six to eighteen were undernourished. We were extremely worried. On repeating the study recently, I found the percentage over fifty. This is the case in many regions of the south." The south is by far the most food-rich part of Vietnam.

"Malnutrition is more dangerous now because it is invisible. People are no longer hungry, but they are undernourished. The children seem well nourished, but often I find a ten-year-old who is the size of a six-year-old. I can see it in my own daughter." Hoa and Nghi adopted a child from one of the mountain ethnic groups among whom they work. "She was malnourished when we adopted her. Now she is eleven, and she is considerably taller than her village friend, who is twelve. This is not exceptional. This should not be in a socialist country. I tell the leaders that. The results are not only physical but also intellectual. An entire people is living in low gear. Our study shows the children learn much more slowly. They are deficient in power of memory and concentration, but not in intelligence. They cannot concentrate for more than two or three hours." Sarcastically she added, alluding to another problem: "Fortunately there are not enough classes. The maximum they get is four hours of school."

Dr. Hoa's findings are confirmed by the World Bank. "Malnutrition rates in Viet Nam are significantly higher than those to be expected," it reported in 1992. "Viet Nam had a higher proportion of underweight (25%) and stunted children (56.5%) from 1987 to 1989 than almost any other low-income country in South and Southeast Asia, excepting Bangladesh and possibly Myanmar [Burma]." The study found that despite considerable improvement in food production, a poor system of transport, storage, and distribution produces a situation in which the population "in some parts of the country continues to be prone to chronic undernutrition." Dr. Hoa cited two additional factors: the allocation of food between domestic consumption and export and pricing. "There is a lot of food in the market, but when a dozen mangoes costs seventy thousand *dong,* that means the monthly wage of a lot of people," she said. It represents about seven dollars; in its latest report the World Bank puts the annual per capita gross domestic product of Vietnam at less than two hundred dollars, that is, about sixteen dollars a month per person on average. This, as Dr. Hoa said, leaves a lot of Vietnamese well below that mark. "I have said publicly that when a country like this exports food, it is exporting the health of its people. We export rice, soybeans, meat, fish, shrimp — what is going to be left for the Vietnamese people will be the blood, the heads of the shrimp, and the skins of the pigs. I say this everywhere, on all occasions, to the Politburo, the Central Committee. They say, 'Yes, we will act to change this.' But it is the whole system, a whole apparatus that must change. Democratization begins with primary health care." Despite her critical views, which she has always expressed openly to all who would listen, Dr. Hoa, because of her active involvement in the resistance and long acquaintance with its leaders north and south, remains on candid, even cordial, terms with many of the older generation of revolutionaries.

Although the political leadership, as Dr. Hoa says, has done little to redress the precarious health and nutrition situation, the competent authorities, mainly the Ministry of Health and the National Institute of Nutrition, acknowledge the gravity of the problem and discuss it candidly with such international agencies as the World Health Organization and the World Bank. However, because of the reluctance on the part of the party and the government to make a public issue of such deficiencies at a time when they counsel the poor to get rich rather than striving to meet the basic needs of the bulk of the population, it is left to individual citizens with an exceptionally highly developed civic conscience, like Dr. Hoa or the late Dr. Ton That Tung, who urged me to publicize the malnutrition crisis in 1979, to ring alarm bells.

A 1992 report by the Institute of Nutrition gave extremely glum specifics of Vietnam's state of nutrition. It reported an average daily intake of 1,932 calories, which, the report said, is 16 percent below the minimum requirement of 2,300 calories recommended by the United Nations Food and Agriculture Organization and the World Health Organization. In its latest study the World Bank reported in 1995 that daily consumption stood at an average of 2,075, but that this figure was skewed because of the disproportionately higher standard of living of the one-fifth of urban Vietnamese compared with the four-fifths living in villages. The wealthiest fifth enjoy almost double the calorie intake of the poorest fifth, the study found. The World Bank report also fixed a food poverty line at 2,100 calories a day.

What is worse, according to the Nutrition Institute, in 8.5 percent of households the consumption is below 1,500 calories per member, which must be classified "as suffering from chronic starvation." Most of these households are thought to be in the areas of the mountain tribes. In other poor regions, like the northern parts of the central Vietnamese coast, whose population is ethnic Vietnamese, the report said the average daily food intake amounted to only 1,820 calories, and one-third of the households "frequently suffer from food shortage between harvest times." This is a polite way of describing periods of famine. Studying children below five years in some of the poorest coastal areas between harvests in 1989, for instance, the Nutrition Institute found that their daily intake amounted to only 1,316 calories. Further, the report stated, about one-third of women of childbearing age in rural areas, where 80 percent of the population lives, suffered from chronic energy deficiency resulting from malnutrition.

Statistics on the state of nutrition of young children are discouraging. The report noted that Vietnamese children suffer from malnutrition even before they reach one year, reflecting abnormally low birth weights due to undernourished mothers. One-half of children under the age of three suffer from protein-energy malnutrition, according to the Nutrition Institute. Anemia is a serious problem both among young children and women of childbearing age. The institute pointed out grave vitamin and mineral deficiencies and linked them to the one-sided reliance on rice as not only the staple but also often the virtually unique component of meals. It stated: "Eighty-five percent of energy was provided by rice, which meant that other foodstuffs such as meat, fish, egg, milk, peanuts, legumes, vegetables, tubers and fruits, which could provide a variety of nutrients, play a very little role in the diet."

In a rare implied criticism of government policy, the Nutrition Institute confirmed Dr. Hoa's charge of ill-advised food exports: "Despite dietary intake inadequacies, the State has exported locally needed food and foodstuffs such as rice, peanuts, eggs, shrimps, fish and vegetables in order to earn hard currencies to pay debts and to purchase essential raw materials for production, including agriculture." In its *Strategy for Health* statement, the Ministry of Health put the national percentage of persons suffering from malnutrition at 44.62 percent and said this was one of the ten leading causes of mortality. Dr. Tu Giay, the founder of the Nutrition Institute, is worried by the fact that since before World War II the average height of Vietnamese has not increased, as has been the case for most nations. "Before the war we were taller than the Japanese," he said. "Now the average height of a Japanese man is one meter seventy. We Vietnamese have stayed at one meter sixty."

The damage inflicted on health care by a regime that still professes to be socialist is paralleled in education. The great progress achieved under the Communist government since 1954 in the north and 1975 in the south in providing free, universal education at all levels has suffered considerable reverses under the new economics. Professor Vu Van Tao, the assistant to the education minister who takes pride in his "southern" way of thinking, acknowledged the damage inflicted by what he called "the negative aspects of adopting market mechanisms" and offered a remarkably candid insight into the moral quandaries posed by *doi moi* for men and women to whom socialism is more than a noble word employed to justify a dictatorship. His long discourse also indicated the intellectual disarray among well-intentioned officials who must carry out a policy that puts into question the very fundaments of what they had been taught to believe as the incontrovertible truth, without having been allowed the privilege of skepticism. It is a problem particular to those who have spent all their lives in North Vietnam, with no other possibility of drawing a breath of different air but periods of study in other Communist countries. Professor Tao's attempt to explain a policy toward which his feelings are clearly ambiguous is a curious combination of honest views clearly expressed and wooden party language employed by a Communist functionary to disguise his doubts.

> Now people must pay. Free education was the rule in the past; today it would be utopian. Our former policy was very humanitarian, but it led to a very poor education budget. The former policy was ultraleftist. We see now that many things in the socialist model were utopian. We have to adjust and modify things that are not in accord with reality. Things are not black and white in life. The official policy affirms that a socialist system and a market economy can exist at the same time. Or can they not? We do not yet have a ready model, and we have to experiment in the knowledge that in any case we have to defend the rights of the poor

people. At the same time, we encourage everybody to get rich. It is a very big challenge. Everybody with common sense and belief in the socialist ideology has a feeling now, more or less, of fear that we may be drifting away from this good ideology. This is becoming a serious problem. The label is socialist, but the contents of the bottle are capitalist. This is a subject of major concern for our leaders and the people.

We do not fully understand capitalism, but we understand very well our socialism in Vietnam. Socialism was originally formulated in Germany and Russia. We accepted this ideology in practice, and we have scored major triumphs with it — Dien Bien Phu, the war in South Vietnam. But the problem began with the application of this socialism to the whole country after 1975. We had a single form of property — the state and collectives; a single mechanism of functioning — central planning and state subsidies. The economy was totally subsidized by the state. We extended the formula to the south, which had been a market economy, but we found that it did not work. We find that peacetime does not produce the same readiness to make many sacrifices as did wartime. We thought that the central power could arrange everything for seventy million people. Under the old system we applied a heavy brake to all individual activity. Now the policy is to change this environment. But the market has two sides, positive and negative. We do not say we have achieved socialism, because our system is not yet ripe, not yet tested by life.

Socialism is a means, not an end. The goal is the well-being of the people. The people should be rich, the state poor. Society should assure respect for legality and a civilized life. There are many good things in Marx's theories, but if something is bad we should not impose it on the masses. We were too dogmatic, not sufficiently intelligent in the application. Now everything has been put on the table. There were great insufficiencies, because we did not want to apply policies we thought too bourgeois, too capitalist. Now we think many of these things are to be considered as achievements of civilization. The government must facilitate the functioning of the economy, not direct it. We must

send our students abroad, we must bring foreign specialists here. The problem of how to apply this experience is
ours. Our problem is how to listen, how to receive sugges-
tions that are sometimes contradictory. In education, we
are still traversing a trial period. The party is responsible
for formulating the main directions, but two sides exist in
life. The leaders know their responsibility for the destiny
of the people.

Clearly, Professor Tao is of two minds but one loyalty. His
colleague, Professor Do Van Chung, director of student affairs
at the Ministry of Education, who spent twelve years in the
Soviet Union, proved to be an even better Communist. He
regards the new policy as a political necessity, which to a good
revolutionary sets aside all doubts, the end justifying the means.
"The need and the demand for education are very big, but the
financial capacity of the government is not big enough," he said.
"So the government decided to allow us to collect fees. On the
one hand, the fees are very small in comparison with what the
government spends on education, but they are very big for some
target groups, especially the peasants." So much in recognition
of the existence of a problem. But he went on to reject any other
solution but the one the center of power had imposed because he
said political necessity demanded it. "Stability is the most important goal," he said. "That is the goal of our policy of renewal.
If we do not stabilize, confusion here may become worse than in
the former Soviet Union."

The cost of that stability in terms of a decline in education is
sharply stated by the World Bank in its 1995 report on poverty
in Vietnam. After acknowledging the great gains in access to
education and high levels of literacy and school enrollment,
notable for a poor country, the report continued: "There is
evidence that the impressive gains achieved during the last 30
years are under serious threat. A major deterioration in both
schooling quantity and quality indicators has taken place during
the last decade. This is evident in the marked decline in school
enrollment which has occurred, most dramatically in secondary
schools, since the late 1980s." Tuition fees were introduced in

1989. Parents must also pay for books, which used to be sup
plied free of charge, and school uniforms, as well as the virtuall
mandatory "voluntary" contributions for parent-teacher orga
nizations, a way of augmenting the teachers' low salaries. Ex
cept for primary education (ages six to eleven), which ha
remained tuition-free, all enrollment dropped sharply startin
in 1990. Junior high school (twelve to fifteen) enrollment de
clined from its 1987 peak of 3.29 million in 1987 to 2.71 millio
in 1990, a 20-percent drop. The shrinkage was most dramatic i
senior high schools (sixteen to eighteen), where the number o
students sank from 930,000 in 1987 to 520,000 in 1990, nearl
50 percent. In higher education, the World Bank reports, th
total drop was about 20 percent.

The World Bank's study of why children in rural areas
where the vast majority of Vietnamese live, are not attending
school showed that the mere fact of having to pay for books was
enough to explain why more than 44 percent of those not
attending are staying home. At the junior high school level that
figure rises to 53 percent.

The bank also faulted Vietnam for not making its system,
particularly in higher education, responsive to the new needs of
a market economy. It found "a glaring discrepancy" between
what is required in a modernizing economy and the training
with which university graduates are being equipped. "Few edu
cational institutions currently provide training in skills neces
sary to the manufacturing and service industries of the future,
such as banking and finance, travel and tourism, and data pro
cessing and software development, among others," the report
said. It noted that, on the other hand, there was high unemploy
ment among teachers of Russian, no longer a required subject,
and economists specializing in central planning.

The decline in education is particularly harmful because for
Vietnam, with a natural-resource base that is not rich in relation
to its large and rapidly growing population, the principal asset
in its race to catch up in material well-being with the rest of its
region is its labor force. In the period of transition to a market
economy, relatively cheap and easily trainable, because well-

educated, workers are Vietnam's most attractive offering to draw in badly needed foreign investment. And in the longer term Vietnam, with its unusually high literacy rate of 88 percent, stands an excellent chance of rising more rapidly than most above the status of being a supplier of cheap labor.

Southern Communists or socialists like Dr. Hoa are less interested in the ideological reasoning that preoccupies the two Ministry of Education professors. They see grievous social problems, familiar from the pre-Communist past, coming back with *doi moi* and undoing changes that they fought for. Dr. Hoa is horrified by the startling rise in prostitution that has accompanied the new economic liberalism. She encounters it in her work at the pediatric center in its most recent and repulsive species — the selling of children. The sharp rise in prostitution of very young girls, children still, is the one subject on which Dr. Hoa, who normally manages to compress her outrage into sarcasm, explodes in unvarnished anger. She views it as the single greatest degeneration of what she considers revolutionary ideals and, in an even deeper sense, traditional Vietnamese values.

Within a brief period in 1993, four girls aged between eleven and thirteen years were brought to her clinic bearing gross injuries suffered in sexual maltreatment. They were terrorized, clearly having been threatened by the men who delivered them into the arms of their abusers and later, frightened by the children's injuries, to Dr. Hoa's center. The men described themselves as the girls' fathers, left them in the clinic, and vanished. The addresses they gave proved false. Three of the girls were too terrorized to tell their full stories; the fourth said her "father" had taken her to visit "a grandfather," who raped her. All of the rapists, Dr. Hoa said, were Asians, probably tourists of ethnic Chinese origin; she assumes the girls were street children. Some Asian customers of prostitutes are known to pay high prices for the privilege of deflowering virgins, Dr. Hoa said, and the virginity premium has probably risen with the spread of AIDS.

"Girls of all ages, not just the poor, interpret freedom as the right to sell themselves for fast money," Dr. Hoa said. "Parents now worry whether their children will turn to prostitution. It is becoming a trade like all others. We are losing our human dignity — north, center, and south. People have lost their ideals; our values have become reversed in the last years." The party's injunction to Vietnamese to strive for riches, reversing communism's basic doctrine that personal riches are acquired only through the exploitation of man by man and therefore reprehensible, is to Dr. Hoa the root of the present evil and the very negation of the socialism in which she continues to believe. "I am a socialist," she said, reversing the doctrinaire view that communism is the be-all and end-all of the revolutionary struggle. "Communism was a way station. What we have now is a savage capitalism. They don't even preach socialism anymore. Only, 'Get rich.'"

"The party has lost the confidence of the people," she continued.

> The Communist party no longer exists. This is so visible now, from top to bottom. They have given the people confidence only in the dollar. The young people believe in nothing; what they hear is only words to them. All they want is to get rich. There are no more lines waiting to visit Ho Chi Minh's Tomb. ["We no longer have to," said a young woman from a government agency, smiling meaningfully, when, while passing by the tomb, I noted that fewer people seemed to be waiting in line.] The older leaders were perhaps unschooled and incompetent, but they were honest and loved their country. But the technocrats formed under socialism are very dangerous. They have learned no lesson from the errors of socialism. For them it is all a question of power. You can count on your fingers the revolutionaries who still believe in ideals.

Dr. Hoa resigned from the Communist party, a rare act of daring, when it decreed reunification in 1976, because, she said, it made no effort at national reconciliation. "They had stronger feelings against the south than against the Americans," she said. "I told them I no longer felt at one with them." In view of her high public profile, not only in Vietnam but also in the West, particularly France, the leadership took three years to let her separate from the party. As a condition, she was told to keep her resignation secret for ten years. She did, without diminishing her open criticisms. "I did not agree with the party discipline that kept me from speaking my mind," she said. "I have always been a revolutionary. This country is not their monopoly. I was a Communist when the party was not in power. But then I found that its ultimate goal was power, not the happiness of mankind." Dr. Hoa also resigned her seat in the National Assembly in 1979. She told the party leaders, "I cannot say what the people think of your policies, and they elected me to do that."

Much of Dr. Hoa's thinking reflects the disillusionment of many southern fighters on the Communist side, although she is virtually alone in saying so aloud. They view the rapid reunification, during which most southern Communist activists were elbowed aside, as not only a personal repudiation but also as the greatest error contributing to Vietnam's economic and social disarray. "The failure to create national concord is a disaster for me," she said. "We could have kept all the gray matter that left with the boat people. We could have become a neutral and socialist country." Dr. Hoa is harshly critical also of the "reeducation" process. "Everyone thought it would be for two weeks, and then they did not come back. That was not honest.

"I'll continue the fight in my work," said Dr. Hoa.

We chose revolution, and instead we see today's developments. We must have a revolution within the revolution. What we need is liberty, but true liberty. Not liberty to do anything we want, but within the bounds of dignity. We need democracy, which does not exist; social justice, which assuredly does not exist. These are the goals we must achieve. The young are receptive to that. They must be free to act according to their moral conscience; they cannot compromise their intellectual honesty. Socialism is an ideal that includes more liberty, democracy, and social justice. The sense of social justice was lost here when peace came. This country went from feudalism to colonialism to imperialism to socialism between quotation marks — not the real socialism. It never knew liberty and democracy under any system.

Dr. Hoa retains the optimism that carried her through the years of war against the world's mightiest power. "I am hopeful for Vietnam because it didn't suffer from socialism as long as the European countries," she said, her eyes gleaming with sarcasm. "It will recover faster."

Dr. Hoa's views are shared by many southern intellectuals — some who went into active, open resistance, as she and her husband did, and others who remained in Saigon hoping for their victory. Professor Ly Chanh Trung, the left-wing Catholic philosopher, expressed disappointment in his own terms. "The Vietnamese revolution!" He laughed briefly, bitterly.

> We will have to do it over again. We never had a revolution. We received independence and then reunification — nothing revolutionary. They have proved that you cannot build socialism in a semifeudal country. It is madness. It became state capitalism, a market economy under state direction. We lost all the boat people because they gave them too much crap. The people of Cochin China are very mobile. A village can melt in your hands. If you make them unhappy they leave. I counted on the Communists to establish justice, of which the bourgeoisie proved itself incapable. I hoped for a more egalitarian, participatory democracy.

He laughed the same short laugh to express what happened to his hopes.

Although the exodus of boat people has come to its end, many disappointed revolutionaries say that this is so only because the countries that granted the refugees asylum have largely stopped doing so. Many ordinary people still ask foreigners hopefully when the doors might open again. "Here there is no way out, no hope," a former Viet Cong officer, still a party member, said. "People say: 'The best way to commit suicide is to take a boat. Either you go to the bottom of the ocean or to paradise — California.' "

This is not Dr. Hoa's view. "We are on a volcano," she said. "You can walk all over people for years. But as we told France and the United States — we can wait for twenty or thirty years; in the end we will win."

18

Transition in the Provinces

Nghe An, where the north blends into the center, is one of
Vietnam's largest provinces, one of the poorest, and one of the
most battered by the anticolonial revolution. It is also the place
of Ho Chi Minh's birth. Its capital, Vinh, has suffered more
destruction than any other Vietnamese city. In 1946 Vinh, then a
city of 160,000, was leveled by the revolutionaries, who carried
out a scorched-earth policy intended to leave only ruins to the
French, who were fighting their way back to colonial possession. (It is politically correct in Vietnam but a gross overstate-
ment to identify all Vietnamese with the uprising and the
insurgents' tactics and say that the city was destroyed "by its
population.") Rebuilt after the French defeat with Soviet and
Chinese assistance, Vinh, a victim even in the interlude of truce
between the French and American wars, was laid waste by a
huge fire in 1957.

Between 1964 and 1973 there was no Vietnamese city that
suffered more frequent and intensive pounding by American
bombs than Vinh. In the language of the American military
briefers, Vinh was "the main marshaling yard of the Ho Chi
Minh Trail," or "the northern railhead" of that network of
mountain and jungle paths and roads over which North Vietnam dispatched its men, arms, and supplies to the battle-
grounds of the south. The city is situated on Vietnam's only
north-south highway, at the junction of two roads into the
mountains of Laos to the west. That most inoffensive and
peace-loving of countries, its manifest neutrality blatantly

abused by all combatants, served unwillingly as the main conduit of infiltration southward of the North Vietnamese war machine and the principal target of the pitiless American riposte. Vinh was a focal point for violent attack by the U.S. Air Force from the first raids in 1964 until the last in 1973.

"On 5 August 1964, at 12:30 P.M., the United States under the pretext of the Tonkin Gulf incident launched massive air attacks, of which Vinh was a target," recited Nguyen Duc Que, deputy director of the city's Department of Culture. Que had been assigned, as he clearly had many times before, to meet a visitor who wanted to ask a city official some questions on Vinh's past and present. The result was a gathering of a squad of minor officials around a conference table in a room decorated with many framed honors for the long-suffering city and a lengthy, hypnotically monotone reading by Que from an official local history. Vietnamese officials have a way of masking the genuine interest and drama of what they tell, and sometimes stifling the sympathy that is due to the immense tragedy of their nation, by the stodgy stiffness and wooden language of their discourse.

The deputy director read on. Between 1964 and 1968, the year of President Lyndon B. Johnson's "bombing halt," 4,131 air raids struck Vinh. Four of Que's colleagues scribbled as if taking dictation, ballpoint pens scratching across their school notebooks. Four handwritten copies of the propaganda booklet from which Que was reading were being produced, to uncertain purpose. The planes dropped 77,649 bombs, weighing a total of 234,271 tons. This amounted to 1,860 kilograms of explosive per inhabitant, ninety tons on each square kilometer of the urban area. When Nixon resumed the bombing in 1972 as a cynical incentive to peacemaking at the Paris conference between Henry A. Kissinger and Le Duc Tho, Vinh was struck by 587 further raids, which unleashed 7,964 more bombs. Que provided the corresponding statistics for kilograms per capita and square kilometer but declined to give the human measure of this appalling assault. The casualties were heavy, he said, but no numbers were available.

Whole sections of the town, which then had 180,000 inhabitants, were reduced to rubble, said Tran Minh Sieu, director of the local historical museum and the only one of the functionaries present to have spent the war years in the city. His mission was to keep an account of the city's fate. Almost the entire population was evacuated, and all industrial activity — a railroad rolling-stock factory and repair yard, woodworking, and food processing — halted with the beginning of the air war. The only productive activity that continued was the region's main power plant, which used to generate 10,000 kilowatts. Its equipment was dispersed and reassembled in mountain caves within a radius of ten to sixty kilometers around the city, from where it continued to generate 4,000 kilowatts through the war.

Those who remained behind, mainly military, tried to maintain "normal life," said Sieu. And, he added, "underground." The museum director described as the most memorable product of his record keeping a photo he took of the three-hundredth American plane shot down over Vietnam. "I photographed the burning plane and the dead pilot," he said, and removed the airman's dog tags. "His watch stopped at 8:17 in the morning." Que said reconstruction was begun immediately after the 1973 Paris agreement, and General Secretary Do Muoi, then a deputy prime minister, laid the first brick. "Any other question?" he concluded his recital.

Vinh, now home to 220,000 people, bears all the marks of understandably hasty reconstruction in a poor country, short of all necessities. Even by the indifferent standards of Southeast Asian cities, whose authorities see little merit in urban planning, Vinh is an unattractive place, a chaotic sprawl of low structures built to serve their purpose but no more than that. Builders have dispensed with such finishing touches as plaster to cover over the raw construction blocks or a coat of paint. The only decorations in its dusty, bustling streets or open places, which cannot qualify as squares, are garish commercial posters or shop signs, which under *doi moi* have come greatly to outnumber the political messages, slogans, and icons that once were the main urban touches of color. Nor have a growing preponderance of plastic

packaging, a symptom perhaps of a rising standard of livir
and a common Southeast Asian tendency to litter reckles
combined to enhance Vinh's outward aspect.

The finishing touch to the uninspiring cityscape was pr
vided by the "brotherly" nation that took the leading role
rebuilding Vinh in 1974, even before the north's final victory b
after the Paris agreement had removed the menace of renewe
American bombing. The German Democratic Republic, know
throughout Eastern Europe as the champion in the mass co
struction of prefabricated tenements in a style that has also bec
called "predilapidated" — looking decrepit before they are eve
finished — was Vinh's master builder of housing projects. The
is no overestimating the utility of the massive East German ai
it filled the urgent need created by American destructivenes
But what was passable in Leipzig or Rostock, also largely de
stroyed by bombing from the air, fits into the scenery of
Vietnamese city and its people's style of life like a jackboot on
bamboo floor. The projects are Vinh's equivalent of the de
pressively heavy, squat stone hulk of the embalmed Ho Ch
Minh's tomb in the graceful French colonial, Vietnamese, an
Chinese architectural environment of Hanoi. What may resis
the temperate central European climate — although since re
unification the German government has invested heavily in th
restoration and beautification of Walter Ulbricht's and Eric
Honecker's architectural vision — has not withstood the ex
treme heat of Vinh's summers and the ravages of its autumr
typhoons. Corrosive mildew has covered the multistoried apart
ment blocks with cancerous eruptions in many shades of black
and the winds and rains have opened wounds that lengthen and
widen and do not heal over. Still, the acute housing shortag
caused by the uncontrollable growth of Vietnam's cities make:
the apartments a precious gift, reserved mainly for deserving
public servants like Que. He expressed his gratitude to "tho
friends from the German Democratic Republic."

"To tell the truth, we were really happy to see them grow,"
he said. "We went from nothing to high-rise buildings. That was
twenty years ago. True, now they look rather backward. There

are twenty-two buildings where I live, with seventy apartments in each. They are designed to stand up to the winds from the sea and give relief from the heat. Their appearance may not be artistic, but they are useful." The present German government could show how fully it has taken over not only its five new eastern provinces but also the implicit obligations from their past by extending its housing restoration program to those who received East German foreign aid in that form.

Other European Communist countries also went to Vinh's assistance. Poland's major gift was the Poland-Vietnam Friendship Hospital, built, equipped, and initially stocked with supplies from Poland. It replaced the main provincial hospital rebuilt after the war against France, which in turn was destroyed by American bombs. It opened in 1986, at the edge of the city. "Right after the inauguration the Poles went home," said Dr. Pham Van Dien, the director. "They considered their work done." The five-hundred-bed hospital, the principal medical center of a far-flung province of 2.7 million people, is a place of desolation today, kept running for its six hundred patients only by the dedication of its staff and Vietnamese inventiveness, but kept running at an abysmal level. It lacks everything, its leading doctors said, and a tour of its buildings amply confirmed this. They were teeming with patients and their families, on whom they depend for their meals, but bare of almost everything that makes a hospital. The equipment Poland installed was not the latest, Dr. Dien said; now it is no longer produced, and even if the provincial authorities had the money for them, spare parts are not available. "It was good equipment, but now it is run down," the director said, as if he felt a need to apologize for the woeful poverty the tour of the complex had disclosed.

"The intensive-care unit has become unusable," Dr. Dien said. "We have four X-ray machines, but all the monitors are unusable for lack of parts. The laboratory centrifuge is broken; the scanner is not working. In any other country, all of our equipment would be on the refuse dump." The pharmacy's shelves were nearly bare, and so were the jars and boxes in the laboratory that should have contained the customary chemicals.

Dr. Dien, visibly pained, offered a long and reluctant answer to whether patients were dying for lack of equipment and the chronic shortage of medicines. Both the director and his deputy, Dr. Hoang Dinh Huong, have studied in East Germany and feel keenly what the Poland-Vietnam Friendship Hospital is missing. "If we had better equipment we would have better diagnoses," Dr. Dien said. "Now we have to send many patients to Hanoi for conclusive diagnoses, which is a dangerous journey for a sick person and very costly. Here a diagnosis can sometimes not be precise. That can lead to fatalities. Diagnosis is the most important factor in health care." The question was repeated; do patients die for lack of equipment? "Yes, people die here for that reason," the doctor finally answered. "If for instance a patient has breathing problems. We don't have the necessary respiratory equipment. What can we do? If we had a monitor to check the pulse we can save lives. We don't know when the pressure has dropped, and when we know it, it is too late.

"The big problem now is that everything is out of order at the same time," the director continued. "We need help from the government. The Ministry of Health gave us one billion *dong*. That was just enough for one X-ray machine." The sum is the equivalent of about one hundred thousand dollars.

The director raised what he clearly considered a delicate subject to an American visitor. He said American veterans' organizations had sent some help, "secondhand equipment, but good." There was an ultrasound machine, which he said was valued at ninety-six thousand dollars but has never worked. Almost two years earlier the organization, which he thought was called Horizons, promised to send a replacement, but that is the last he heard from it. A mobile X-ray unit arrived but has never worked. "We appreciate this assistance, but the equipment should have been repaired before they sent it," Dr. Dien said. Similarly, the provincial health director, Dr. Nguyen Tien Hoan, said an American veterans' group had promised to provide an operating theater and surgery ward for the Nghe An Pediatric Hospital and presented an initial gift of forty thousand dollars in 1989. They said they would raise the rest, and the forty thousand dollars was spent to begin construction. The operating theater and four rooms were built, but the money to equip them never arrived. Now the empty rooms serve as wards.

Dr. Dien said he had sent a report to the Polish embassy in Hanoi, and the consul general had paid a visit to the hospital. "He saw the deterioration," the doctor said. "But he said because of the change in government in Poland he could only offer replacement equipment for sale, not as aid." So much for Poland-Vietnam friendship. "We are asking the Foreign Ministry to let us change the name of the hospital to General Hospital of Nghe An Province," Dr. Dien said laconically.

Dr. Hoan described Nghe An's health problems with unsparing candor. Such frankness is as common among Vietnamese officials who deal with practical problems as it is rare among political leaders and senior bureaucrats. He said 53 percent of the province's children under three years of age suffered from malnutrition, and only about 40 percent of the population had access to safe drinking water. He said polio had spread to fifty-five communes — villages or groups of hamlets — by mid-1994, and 15 children of the more than 200 affected had died by then. "The vaccine is too expensive," he said. "The people can't afford it, and the province can't afford it." Of the province's eighteen districts, ten are in the mountainous areas of the west, where the more remote of the 2,031 villages are as much as five days' walk from the district center and the only hospital. "In the mountain districts health facilities are very poor," Dr. Hoan said. "Equipment is very poor in all the district hospitals in the province. We lack most diagnostic and treatment equipment. We want to make things better, but we have no money."

Doi moi has produced an important benefit to health in Nghe An, Dr. Hoan said. Freeing the farmers from the old restrictions, which in this northern province had prevailed for nearly a half century, has greatly improved food production and has begun to raise the nutritional state of the population, except in the mountains. "We were never self-sufficient in rice before;

now we have a surplus," he said. A less positive aspect of *doi moi* has been the introduction of fees for medical care, but he said they were low, and the poorest still received free treatment. It is a measure of rural poverty that only 30 percent of the population of the province pay fees, according to Dr. Hoan. An ordinary consultation in a clinic costs 3,000 *dong,* about thirty cents; an abdominal operation would cost no more than twenty dollars. That is not as negligible as it sounds; a doctor's monthly pay, said Dr. Hoan, was from twenty-five to thirty dollars. They can add to their earnings now by running a private practice in addition to their jobs. Did they not, as was the custom in all Communist countries, receive "gifts" of money or other advantages from their patients even under the old system? They did, he said, but it was less widespread in Nghe An than elsewhere. "We are very strict," he said.

With the introduction of independent agriculture, the right to open a private business, and the obligation to pay for health and education, what is left of socialism? I asked the doctor. He laughed while seeking a graceful way to avoid a reply to so loaded a question. He found it. "That's a difficult question," he said. "It's more for a specialist, not a general practitioner."

Le Man Hai and his sister, Le Thi Tuyet Nga, are among the minority who can afford to pay for doctor visits. They are members of the new class of private entrepreneurs, men and women who were bold enough and quick enough to seize the opportunities offered by the economic liberalization, although nothing in their experience seemed especially to qualify them for their midlife career switch. Each owns a jewelry shop in Vinh, and so do three more of their brothers and sisters. The five Phu Nguyen ("the Rich One") stores — the first opened its doors in 1989 — continue a family tradition that was interrupted only when the city was evacuated during the American bombing. Their father kept the shop that he had founded in 1928 under a rule that allowed the continuation of some small commerce even in the strictest Communist years. With *doi moi,* five of his ten children, those living in Vinh, dropped one after the other what they had been doing and, with loans from their father and a government bank, and their own skimpy savings, combined to corner the jewelry market of Vinh. Hai quit his job as a mechanic in a tin mine; Nga, one year after her brother, walked out of the kindergarten where she was teaching and opened her store only about two hundred yards from her brother's. Together, the five Les employ about one hundred goldsmiths and saleswomen.

"The government gives us favorable conditions," said Hai, a former soldier in the famous 320th Division, which in the final weeks of the war stormed through the Central Highlands and on to capture Saigon. "My business is doing well. The law on private business protects me, and a favorable tax policy will waive my taxes if my business gets into trouble." That does not seem to be near; Hai's midrange Japanese car, parked in front of the store in the center of town, is a mark of big money and rare status in Vietnam. All five of the Vinh shop owners have acquired new houses and cars, Hai said, and the five other brothers and sisters, who live elsewhere, have shared in the family's new riches by acquiring houses while keeping their low-paid government jobs.

Buying jewelry is to ordinary Vietnamese, as it is to many in China and Southeast Asia, the most common way of saving money. Gold is held to be more trustworthy than currency under pillows or in banks. "Our jewelry is not so expensive," said Nga, groomed, dressed, and bejeweled as she would not have been in her kindergarten-teaching years, pointing to her showcases. They were crammed with rings, bracelets, and necklaces and, in the custom of Southeast Asia, brightly lighted with strings of small bulbs to make the gold glisten. "It's mostly gold, no diamonds. About fifty dollars is the average price. And anyway, women need some kind of jewelry on their bodies to make them more beautiful."

The five Phu Nguyen shops pay their goldsmiths varying wages, said Hai. "The better they work, the better I pay," he continued, proclaiming with pleasure a distinctly non-Communist thesis. The saleswomen earn commissions in addition to the minimum wage, 350,000 *dong* a month, or about thirty-five dollars. There is more protection of workers' rights than is common in a region noted for its sweatshops — an eight-hour working day, four or five free days a month, sick pay, and twenty to thirty days' vacation a year.

At the provincial government headquarters, the new policies were explained by those who used to explain their antitheses with equal conviction, and attempts made to square the circle. Ho Xuan Hung is vice-chairman of the People's Committee. In party parlance, local government at all levels is by committees representing the people; Hung is Nghe An's deputy governor.

"Before land reform in 1958 we set up village and commune cooperatives," he explained, outlining the reversal of everything he would have outlined not much earlier. He explained the new position in terms that would bring joy to Margaret Thatcher, with arguments used in the past by hard-line anti-Communists.

This policy was reinforced in 1960. All production equipment was collectivized. In effect, it belonged to no one. In extreme cases, the peasants went to the fields when a bell was struck, then came the lunch bell, then the bell to return to work — you understand. It was close to the Chinese model. We have fundamentally changed this. We have genuine cooperatives now. When the farmers object, the cooperatives are dissolved. Everything is voluntary now. This has motivated production. The farmers feel like real owners. They choose their cooperatives. Government organizations are responsible for irrigation, providing seed, pesticides, and disease control. They also guide the farmers in technological matters. Marketing their produce is in the farmers' own hands. We need to learn the management of the market mechanisms.

Reminded that the farmers as well as the rice merchants of South Vietnam, mainly ethnic Chinese, had mastered and practiced that skill over many decades but had been forcibly collectivized and the merchants condemned as exploiters after 1975 and in large numbers driven from their country as involuntary boat people, the vice-chairman conceded, "Many methods of the south are applicable, not all. What we should learn from farmers in the south is marketing." Hung measured the results of liberalization with pride. "Production is on the rise," he said, his eyes bright with a sense of having discovered a magic formula previously unknown. "Before, the state had to provide as a subsidy to the province 120,000 tons of rice and wheat flour a year. Last year we reached self-sufficiency and were able to put ten thousand tons on the market. This year Nghe An will market fifty thousand tons of milled rice."

His song of praise for the benefits of the free market prompted a question on whether the Socialist Republic was not turning to capitalism. Hung fudged it, with what is apparently the prescribed and fatuous formula for coping with that embarrassment. "I think we have inherited the essence of mankind's civilization," he said. Asked the same question later that day, Nguyen Thanh Tien, the editor of the provincial party daily *Nghe An* and a longtime functionary of the party propaganda apparatus, replied, "We are just using the achievements of mankind." The inspiration of the party's central Agitation and Propaganda Department is ever discernible not only in the empty and evasive replies to embarrassing questions but also in the sameness of their vapid wording.

The deputy governor, asked about negative effects of the turn to liberal economics, conceded that it had put an end to the full employment that had been guaranteed under the total central planning and control of the past. "Under the system of subsidization by the state, all workers had jobs and a guaranteed income," Hung said. "Now, as we change the system of management, some cannot find jobs. We have to accept this in the beginning. We have opened job training centers, aimed particularly at young people. We must find ways of absorbing the labor surplus in the countryside." He put the number of the officially unemployed at sixty thousand in a work force of 1.3 million. This does not cover the considerable male underemployment that results from a reality visible to any traveler:

other than the heavy work of plowing with buffaloes in Vietnam's largely unmechanized agriculture, the tilling of the land is left mainly to women. A black-clad figure, topped by a traditional conical straw hat, bent over the green seedlings in a waterlogged paddy field and painstakingly replanting them one by one, is the very image of Vietnamese agriculture, and far more often than not the bent figures are women.

Is Vietnamese socialism in crisis in the country that officially designates itself the Socialist Republic? The deputy governor had an answer that left all questions open and reflected the leadership's ideological quandary: how to go back on so much of what since 1945 it has postulated as the only, the ultimate truth, yet continue to proclaim it as the truth and not shake the foundations of its dictatorial powers.

"We are in a transition period to socialism," Hung said, ignoring his country's proud name, which proclaims socialism as if it were already achieved. Not long ago Vietnam maintained that it had realized socialism and was heading toward its most perfect form, communism.

> Something of the past still exists; maybe some new things will appear. The people have reconfirmed the objective we have pursued for so many years. Our government explained clearly why we face unemployment, why we have to pay for education and health care. Even in the 1960s, 1970s and 1980s we could not afford with our own economic strength free education, health care and full employment. We were able to do it because of the assistance of friendly countries — the Soviet Union, China, what we called the socialist camp. Now we have to cope for ourselves. We get much less aid. The people have understood this. But we will go back to full employment and free health care and education.

At that point the deputy governor grew vague and uncertain, indicating that the line has not yet been fixed. "Whether we will go back to collective farming and centralized planning will depend on developments," he said. "Whatever we adopt will correspond to the natural laws of development. We have not abandoned central planning. We still use what is good in it." What kind of return to agricultural collectivization did he envisage? The same as before? "No, this is clearly pointed out in our laws. Not the same kind of collectivization. It was a mistake in the past. But collectivization is something that mankind will go to in the end." Hung worked himself up to a peroration that was clearly the fruit of a lifetime of study of the Marxist "science" of dialectical materialism. "Socialism remains the answer, but the question is how to carry it out in practice," he said. "There is no smooth path to socialism. It is a science. You should rule out any idea that the relationship between man and man is not a science."

Meeting the men who carry out at the ground level without benefit of opposition the policies determined in Hanoi reveals time and again that they consider the turn toward the market as a tactical response imposed by the economic crisis into which Vietnam was plunged by the collapse of the socialist camp. They have neither changed their doctrinaire view of the world nor lost their power to strive for its realization and curb all tendencies to extend openness beyond limited application to economics. Throughout Vietnam, such conversations confirm the gloomy view of the Hanoi academic who despairs of his country's future as long as the men of narrow mind and wide ambition remain unopposed in seats of power from north to south. "Although we allow this, it doesn't mean we are deviating from our path," said Tien, the editor, speaking of economic liberalization. "Socialism is the objective. If we want to achieve it, we need to take steps forward, but we need to adjust our steps to the capacities of the country."

Vietnam is indeed in a period of adjustment. The party leaders and their local deputies are gearing the advance toward their unchanged Communist vision to new economic realities; that is, enforced reliance on the capacities of Vietnam unaided by a camp of like-minded nations. The outlook is uncertain. How much of acutely needed economic reform can be achieved despite the evident political misgivings on the part of the leadership and the instinct of self-preservation of the entrenched bureaucracy? Can the geriatric leadership manage a transition to men of similar mind? The party's hierarchy is full of them. But the opening of *doi moi,* however incomplete, has aroused new hopes and appetites, and not only that. It has created and attracted more display of wealth than most Vietnamese have ever seen, and with it resentment over unfair advantages enjoyed by a privileged caste of holders of power. It has created also a widespread belief, perhaps exaggerated, that the combination of wealth and unopposed power has produced unprecedented corruption and favoritism. This is unlikely to be enough to overcome the Vietnamese tradition of bowing to the regime in power, as long as it is Vietnamese. But it may strengthen, in the constant undercover jockeying for power that is customary in closed societies, the hand of those who represent, in addition to party loyalty, a knowledge of the modern world and the techniques that would make Vietnam a part of it.

19

A Day in the Country

Xuan Dang got electricity in 1993, but few of the houses of the village are plugged in. "Too expensive," said Nguyen Khac Truong. Xuan Dang lies only forty miles northwest of Hanoi, but it is not easy to reach. The car leaves the main road to bump along for a long trek on unpaved dirt paths, which are likely to be impassable when the long rainy season turns them to mud. It stops short near an unbridged river. A strong cord spans its width of about forty yards. It serves to provide motive power for a small motorless and oarless boat. Two teenage boys, standing at each end of the leaky craft, propel the boat by pulling it across the Cong River with firm, alternating grips along the rope. The boat docks at the foot of a wide stretch of rice fields, whose limits are marked by a network of low dikes that serve the dual purpose of providing footpaths. A ten-minute walk under a glaring sun leads to the first houses of Xuan Dang.

Nguyen Khac Truong was my guide to his native village in 1994, delivering on a promise that he had made two years earlier to show me an example of his main preoccupation, the poverty of Vietnam's overwhelmingly rural population. Truong is far from being a dissident; forty-nine years old, he retired in 1991 as a lieutenant colonel after twenty-seven years of army service and has been a Communist party member for a quarter century. He is the author of a prizewinning popular novel, which depicts the poverty and social tensions of village life and the virtually feudal powers, often corruptly exercised, of clan elders and party bosses.

It took courage to write the novel, *The Plot of Land That Has a Lot of People and Many Ghosts,* and it was daring of the Writers' Union to award it its second prize for fiction in 1991. To describe the hardships of village life is virtually heretical in a country whose rulers glorify "peasants" and "workers" as the flesh and bones of the nation and the true victors of the years of revolutionary struggle. The award for the best novel went to Bao Ninh for his unheroic, harrowing story of combat from the soldier's point of view, *The Sorrow of War.* Attacked for its choices by the party's ideological supervisors, the union has abstained from awarding prizes since then and remains under constant pressure to produce resolutions renouncing the ideas that prompted the books and the awards. Before Truong's novel could be published, he had to overcome demands to change his title. Its "ghosts," he said, were considered "a remnant of superstition, incompatible with materialism, that is, Marxism-Leninism." Bao Ninh could not prevent the title of his book from being changed. It was published as *The Fate of Love.* The glorious, victorious war against South Vietnam and the United States cannot be admitted to have occasioned sorrow as well.

This is how Truong explained his choice of subject at our first meeting: "I want to remind everybody that 80 percent of the Vietnamese people are peasants. If our country is built on a model that is not suitable to peasants, they will be poor forever. Why are our peasants still living in tatters? Every time I see my native land I am sad."

It was easy to see why. The first house we visited, and most proved like it, consisted of two buildings at right angles — two rooms serving as living and sleeping quarters in the larger building, kitchen and storage in the smaller one. The floors were of dirt, the lower halves of the walls mud, the upper parts bamboo, the roof thatch. What furniture there was — low chairs, bedsteads — was roughly hewn from coarse wood, clearly homemade. Only the small court between the buildings was paved with brick, to provide a surface for the threshing and drying of paddy. An oil lamp was the only source of light. This was the home of Nguyen Nhat Ly, a fifty-one-year-old retired high-school teacher of literature and a former classmate of Truong, and his wife, Tran Thi Thai. "I no longer felt strong enough to teach," said Ly, a wan and worn man. After twenty-five years of teaching, he receives a monthly pension of 180,000 *dong*, about eighteen dollars. His wife's pension of 30,000 *dong* adds three more dollars to their income. She has retired as village chairwoman of the Vietnamese Women's Organization. The couple and their two children, who do most of the work, live from farming their four thousand square meters of land — rice, sweet potatoes, and cassava, as well as their only cash crop, a little tea. The soil is not good for rice, Ly explained, so they produce only the minimum of the staple food to meet their family's needs.

"We don't have a road, so it's hard to market anything," Ly said. "In fact, we are very poor. Life is very hard in this region. We depend so heavily on nature. The weather changes very fast. It rained a lot this morning before you came; now it's very hot. We don't need the water at this time; when we need it, maybe there will be no rain. Before we also raised some pigs, but prices are too low now, so we stopped."

Ly's plaint is one that can be heard throughout Vietnam, except for its two great fertile regions — the Red River Delta in the north and, even more fertile, the Mekong Delta of the south. The country is often likened to a familiar image of Vietnamese rural life: a man, or more likely a woman, carrying two heavy baskets suspended from a flexible bamboo pole that lies on her shoulders. The two deltas are the baskets; the slender, elongated waist of Vietnam the pole. Outside the two rice baskets of the deltas, the farmers' life is a constant struggle to make poor soil, worked with hand tools, yield its harvest against the annual assault of typhoons and flooding. "They are dying for tools," said Truong. Indeed, on a drive of almost the full length of the country, signs of agricultural mechanization were virtually absent. "The majority don't even have money for some better hand tools," Truong said.

Vietnam is a preponderantly agrarian country, of late the world's third-largest exporter of rice, but a tractor to pull a plow is a rarity. It is the muscles of men, women, children, and buffaloes that make Vietnam's soil yield its treasure. Along most of the length of Route 1, the old colonial highway linking Hanoi and Saigon, the edges of the badly rutted and potholed road serve as a drying and threshing floor for newly harvested rice. Farmers flay their spread paddy unperturbed by the constant flow and din of the most motley, least disciplined traffic imaginable — ancient trucks belching bilious exhaust fumes, speeding, horn-tooting cars, oxcarts, honking motor scooters and cycles, hordes of bicycles, and swarms of men, women, and children on foot, often bearing heavy burdens of the most varied kinds. Some lead their buffalo; others are preceded by flocks of ducks. Dogs trot along or sleep on the road while the traffic flows around them. In the south they are pets; the farther north one sees dogs, the more likely they are to be bred for the pot.

"The people of this village are not lazy," said Ly, as if he felt a need to offer an excuse for the village's poverty to the only foreigner whom he had seen, except for a Soviet technical-aid expert and Chinese military advisers during the war. But that was in Hanoi, he added; he remembered no foreigner ever in Xuan Dang. "They are doing their best to improve life here. It is already much better than before. The most important thing is to overcome nature, but we can't change the village's location. What we need most is machinery to work our fields. Still, it would be hard to use because the land is not flat. It would be hard for tractors."

But Ly said there was no reason to complain; life had improved greatly since the end of the war and even more rapidly since the more liberal agricultural policies of the late 1980s. In fact, in saying this Ly glossed over the very hard years of the late 1970s and pre–*doi moi* 1980s, after China halted its massive food aid in retaliation for Vietnam's embrace of the Soviet Union and its invasion of Cambodia. "During the war against America, we all dreamed when the war was over we would have a happy life," said Truong. "All the wartime propaganda told us that. But the opposite happened. After the war, the people went hungrier and hungrier, and that was very sad. I have to remind you that our peasants suffered from famine although it is they who produce the rice."

Ly concentrated on the present. He said the collectivized land has been redistributed among the village families, although formally it continues to belong to the government, and farmers are free to plant what they wish. "Our incomes are much better now, but everything we need we have to buy at market prices," he said. "There are no more subsidies." Looking about the house, it was hard to see anything that had been bought in a store. The couple laughed when asked why they were not taking advantage of the electrification, now that power was available in Xuan Dang. "It costs one million *dong* to have it installed," the teacher said. "That means our savings for a whole year, after we have paid for all the necessities we have to buy." The sum amounts to one hundred dollars.

Nguyen Kim Nguyen, one of the elected village leaders since he returned to farm in his native place after a fourteen-year army career in 1964, is better off. Not only is his one-story house built of brick and mortar, but he has also taken advantage of electrification. The unkind climate has made the house look far older than its date of construction, 1984, which is displayed over the entrance as is the custom. Three electric fans are deployed in his living room, two of them clearly never used, their plastic wrapping unopened, but displayed like proud possessions. But at noontime, with the sun beating down fiercely and the air hot and heavy, Nguyen and his family and friends were sweating from the exertion of beating the humid air around them with woven fans, which Nguyen's wife distributed. Electricity, the modern miracle that arrived only the year before, failed many weeks ago, Nguyen said, and no one knows when it will come on again. Not the first time, but no one complained.

Nguyen is Truong's brother, sixty-one years old and a veteran of the war against France. Two medals that he won then, framed on a wall, are the living room's principal decoration, along with family photos and garish calendar pages. The family altar, however, does not display photographs of grandparents and earlier ancestors, as is the custom in and around cities. In villages off the main roads, the majority of villages in northern Vietnam, no photographers were within reach in older days, when people rarely went far from their homes, Truong explained. Even today, few of the women have been farther away from Xuan Dang than the district town or, at most, Thai Nguyen, the provincial capital, and the men did most of their traveling in their military years. "Since *doi moi*, life has been better," said Nguyen. "Now we are comfortable. But until the 1980s people here were going hungry. There was simply not enough food to go around. There was the war first, and there were always the calamities of nature, either drought or flood."

Clearly, for the people of Vietnam's north and center, the great achievement of the economic reforms since the late 1980s has been to have put a virtual end to hunger. "That is the big change," said Truong. "But still not the nice food they would like. There isn't much meat." Freeing the farmers from the unnatural restrictions of producing collectively to centrally set targets, with rarely enough of the seed, fertilizer, and pesticides furnished to attain them, is providing the minimum necessary for most people no longer to go hungry. There are still regular pockets of hunger, particularly among the mountain tribes of the highlands, and extensive malnutrition exists throughout the country. But in village after village, people spoke of enough rice as the big new thing in their lives since *doi moi*. And often women looked toward their children and their eyes lit up when they spoke of this, and in their smiles one could read the sadness of the past, when parents could not fill their children's stomachs.

Although the days of hunger and the understandably big place that food occupies in their thought are the ground bass over which villagers tell of their lives, Nguyen's wife served a lunch of four courses, including chicken and meat, a holiday feast to welcome the visitor. The friendliness and hospitality of ordinary Vietnamese, in town and country, their readiness to share what they think with candor and what they own with generosity, goes well beyond the dutiful professions of "the war is over, no hard feelings" that present politics dictates; it comes straight from the heart. Nguyen's wife served her feast, as is the custom, only to the men, seated at the low table, under the family altar and the idle fans. The women continued to participate with great verve in the table talk, submissiveness not being a quality of Vietnamese women, but tradition was served.

Conversation turned to what the villagers expect from the government. The most important contribution they wish for — soon, they hope — is the building of a canal and dam system that would take them off the perennial knife's edge between flood and drought. Irrigation canals, Nguyen said, and a water reservoir. Xuan Dang's villagers must skimp on necessities to put aside fallback savings against time and tide. The government cannot afford a generous system of insurance; it can only offer forgiveness of land-use tax in case of a natural calamity. As elsewhere, villagers said that only with foreign assistance would Vietnam ever be able to afford the infrastructure that it lacks so badly.

However poor they are — and except for the more prosperous villages of the Mekong Delta, Xuan Dang is much more the national rule than an exception — the people of Xuan Dang, like those of many other villages, have shown at great cost that they do not live by rice alone. They have chipped in to rebuild the village shrine. The easing of ideological pressures on ordinary people — that is, those who leave politics to others — and the fortunate fact that some money has trickled into people's pockets has encouraged them to do what for so long had been unthinkable. The traditional sanctuaries of the guardian spirit of the village formed the core of local identity until such "superstition" became a sin against the new, "scientific" spirit. Communist dogmatism has eased, and although there was no official pronouncement permitting it, villagers have seized the opportunity of the perceptible lowering of a barrier to restore derelict buildings, often to put up new ones, and to commission local artisans to carve or hew new statues. They have dug deeply into their meager savings to satisfy a need that was frustrated for many years. Clearly a spiritual need was felt also by generations that had not experienced the cult that had always been central to Vietnamese life or the festivals that were the high points of the village year. Even worldly city people, who have spent their lifetimes in Hanoi or Saigon, identify themselves as coming from the village of their ancestors and try to travel there in the days following the lunar new year, the traditional village festival time.

The sanctuaries typify the syncretic character of Vietnamese folk religion. They combine — quite harmoniously, Buddhist scholars concede — Buddhism, Taoism, Confucianism, pagan practices, and ancestor worship. People visit them to give thanks for happy events or pray for favors in time of need. The average Vietnamese is little given to mystical religion. "The older people remembered the tradition and reintroduced it, and the young find a spiritual appeal in it," said Truong. "All the party officials participate." The Vietnamese see no contradiction in this; "I don't think ordinary peasants think much about that. And for intellectuals or government officials, the collapse of the Soviet Union created a spiritual vacuum. I think before that they believed in Marxism-Leninism. In the West people believe in one god. Here they believe in myths and many gods. Buddhism and other beliefs are mixed, and they are practiced much more strongly now. I am a Buddhist by origin, and basically I believe in Buddhism."

And a quarter century of membership in an atheist party, which took its condemnation of religion seriously and would never have tolerated that an army colonel declare himself a Buddhist? Truong laughed without embarrassment and wrote off official atheism as part of the former uncritical acceptance of the Soviet legacy. "I think the party has found a good answer to that: each country has to find its own way of development," he said, just as others used the same phrase to explain away the abandonment of the collective economy. "You can't just copy what others do. And the people have listened to that answer. Spiritual life used to be simple; today it has been enriched."

An informal procession formed when my hosts invited me to visit the rebuilt shrine. Led by the village children, but soon joined by many of the adults, we marched across the fields to the sanctuary, an open, shedlike structure of three concrete walls and a floor, topped by a tile roof. Empty and neglected since the

French war, it was renovated in 1992. Nguyen explained the meaning of the four statues — a pair consisting of a martial figure representing evil and a mandarin who stands for good, a Confucian saint offering his teaching, and the nameless and nondescript village deity. They were made by a craftsman from a nearby village, Nguyen said, and cost 1.5 million *dong*, or about one hundred and fifty dollars. The sight of the visitor lighting the traditional three joss sticks before each statue clearly enhanced his standing among the villagers. I hope the size of the modest monetary contribution, equally traditional, that he left did not cause it to decline by too much.

The ambiguities of Vietnam in this phase of transition from strict observance of a political dogma to whatever its future holds sometimes produce subtle ironies. In a village near the northern port city of Haiphong, an artisan had decorated the roof of the local shrine, dedicated to Tran Hung Dao, who freed Vietnam from the Mongol invasion, with a classical dragon motif in concrete. Complimented on his work, he said he had scoured many villages to find a dragon to his liking and taken great pain to make the restored temple as beautiful as he, a simple mason, could. He ran into his house to reemerge with a blank school notebook, which he presented with tears of emotion in his eyes to ask me to inscribe my contribution of a few thousand *dong* as the first entry in what he hoped would become a long register of generosity to the shrine. Did he intend irony, or was he unaware that his book of gifts to further religious observance was a gift to the brotherly Vietnamese people from the people of the Soviet Union?

Xuan Dang, despite its poverty, is a relaxed village, whose inhabitants seem to communicate easily with one another and whose men chat sociably while sucking on the traditional water pipe. "The radio talks a lot about the evil of tobacco, but it's not easy to give up an old habit," said Nguyen. Xuan Dang resembles the village of Truong's novel only in its poverty, not in its tensions. "What Truong wrote is generally a good picture of life in the countryside," said Ly. "But here the leadership is quite good. We elected a new leader last year. If he does his job well, he can stay in it. If not, we will vote him out. The head of the village and the party chief are the two bosses. In the past, the chairman of the cooperative was also very important, but now this has been greatly reduced. The village chairman and the party chief are equally important. But perhaps the party chief is more important, because it is the party that leads the country. Ours is a good man. The Comrade Party Chief must be an example for all the villagers." Ly is not a party member. He said there had been no recruiting among the teachers in his area. Vietnamese do not as easily volunteer for such abstract causes as party membership as they do for matters of substance, like repelling foreign intruders. But Ly said Xuan Dang was a village with revolutionary traditions.

"Since World War II, the most notable revolutionary characteristic of the village is the number of volunteers for the defense of the country," Ly said. "Even those who were too young volunteered. Two were killed in the French war, fifteen in the American war. Some families lost two sons, and so many were wounded. Two more were killed against the Chinese and one in Cambodia. There were many bombings around here by the Americans. The biggest was in September, 1967; a whole family was killed. You can still see the crater where their house stood, and there were many raids after that." Why target this village? "The army trained here," Ly replied.

"The people here are nice, and they have nice chiefs, so nobody has complaints," said Truong on the way to the shrine. "It is different in other villages." He said the return to individual cultivation had changed the forms of official corruption, but peasants were still exploited by many of their leaders. "The abuse of official power still exists," he explained.

In the past, all the cooperative's harvest of paddy was gathered in the cooperative storehouse. It was under the control of the chiefs, and they stole what they could. They took rice for themselves, and the farmers had no way of checking on it. The village chiefs took easily to corruption, and they split the spoils among themselves and the rank above. It was worse than in the former feudal times. Then the only official was the head of the commune. Under collectivization, the peasants had to pay for all those who dominated them. Even in the commune there was the party secretary, the commune chairman, the youth leader, the Women's Association leader. Then came the level of village officials. There were about fifteen such bureaucrats above a villager.

A commune is made up of two or three villages and counts a population of about five thousand.

"It is different now," Truong continued. "Now they abuse their power by the way they distribute the land. The good land goes to their friends. Then the farmers file petitions to a higher level of the bureaucracy, but often there is corruption at that level, too. Many cases have been exposed by newspapers. There have been fights, and some people have been killed. They always find loopholes for corruption, and the Vietnamese peasant is still not quite happy." The distribution of seed and seedlings, fertilizer, pesticides, and other necessities is still in the hands of village authorities, and Truong said officials continue to cheat on that by selling low-quality products at inflated prices and pocketing the difference.

Truong is an idealist assailed by skepticism of a type that has emerged in Communist or formerly Communist countries. They are more common in the former North Vietnam than in the south, which knows from dire experience the failings of both Communist and non-Communist economic systems and where people are far more skeptical than idealistic. Northerners like Truong, having seen the comparative riches of Saigon, harbor endearing illusions about the workings of the market. Similarly, in the Soviet Union and Eastern Europe in the early days of postcommunism, idealistic views of the healing power of economic liberalism, which would have rung melodiously to the ears of Ronald Reagan and Margaret Thatcher, were not uncommon. Truong welcomes the passing of collectivized farming but observes the functioning of the new system with growing perplexity. His reaction to the new reflects the solid Marxist grounding of a North Vietnamese of his generation. "Under the system of collective production, the relations between people were equal," he mused.

> Now, privileged landlords are reappearing. There are contradictions between rich and poor. Some hire the labor of others. The exploitation of man by man is reappearing, even if not on a big scale. I visited a village recently in Thai Binh Province. I met a landlord, a former army sergeant. In the village the authorities had auctioned off rights to exploit some marshland to breed fish and shrimp. He bought the marshland and some paddy fields, and every day he hires thirty laborers. He pays them decently, one hundred kilograms of paddy a month. That is worth about fifteen dollars. In Vietnam, one hundred kilograms of paddy feeds a family of four for a month. That is satisfactory in poor rural areas. His laborers are very happy and don't consider themselves exploited. Others praise him. The officials agree with this system.

Truong remains perplexed. He has observed negative effects that have become apparent even in this incipient stage of Vietnam's turn to a market economy. He regrets that earning money, now that the possibility exists, has become the sole goal for most, particularly the young. "In the old days, young people in villages were more interested in education than they are now," he said, recalling his youth, when full employment was guaranteed, a higher education assured a higher position in the bureaucracy, which was the only employer, and the ceiling on ambitions for wealth in a very egalitarian society was not much taller than a man's head. Greater opportunities are known to exist today, but to people of the countryside — the great majority of Vietnamese — they seem remote and restricted to the cities. "Today, young people don't want to complete a high-school education," Truong said. "They want to earn money. They want a cassette player, a television set, a secondhand motorcycle. I bought one myself with the earnings from the book. Before I only had a bicycle. Even if you learn more, there are very few jobs. So when young people realize that there is no point in going to the city because there is no work to be found, they have no interest in further study."

He said that early marriage, customary in the days before the Communist regime, was returning in the countryside. Young people marry because if they leave their parents' houses to found their own families, they are entitled to receive land under the redistribution scheme. "So they marry early, get a small plot, and begin farming," he said. "Every time I come to the village I notice how fast they get old. They work hard to make a living, they have children very young. It is very sad to see the village girls; they have no teen age anymore. Their life is very limited; they have no prospects. In the collective days our life was more spiritual. We had higher ideals."

The idealism of Truong, a tall and square-shouldered man with a soft voice and a broad face that lights up frequently with a wide, gentle smile, remains unwavering. He is moved by one goal; to use his pen to improve the hard lot of the people of the countryside. To tell the truth about the hardships of their life, he is prepared to confront the authorities with the reality that is prettified by the obligatory optimism in the self-description of Communist societies. The youngest son of a family of expropriated small landholders, he left his village when he joined the army in 1965 and served as a platoon leader in an antiaircraft artillery unit. After the fighting ended, the army sent him to Hanoi University, "so I could serve the cultural life of the military," and he wrote for military publications until his return to civilian life in 1991. Now he writes for a magazine published by the Writers' Union.

"I must take responsibility for reflecting the truth about the suffering of the majority, the peasants," he said.

Some party leaders didn't like my book. A month after it appeared, I was called by the head of the ideological section of the Central Committee of the party. He said it had caused him pain, but it reflected the truth. So he couldn't blame me. I was invited to talk to clubs after the book appeared. I'm sure some of the cultural police sat there to listen, but I always said what I thought, and nothing happened.

We who work in literature must play the role of bringing the problems of the peasants to the attention of the government. We must warn the central policy-makers about what is happening in the countryside. We have no power, no right to change it ourselves. But we have the power to tell the truth. My book is approved one hundred percent by the peasants. Even the farmers in the south appreciated it. I have been invited to many areas; they asked me to continue writing about the situation of the countryside. They want me to be their spokesman. Before, the peasants were afraid of the officials. They felt as peasants their status was low. They are not so afraid anymore. Some are angry about their unhappy state.

The people of Duc Thang, a hamlet a couple of hours' drive northeast of Saigon, in the southernmost fringe of the Central Highlands, have reason to be unhappier than Xuan Dang's villagers, but if they are angry they keep their wrath to themselves. They appear to tolerate their bottomless poverty as their fate. They have known little else as far back as their memory goes. Duc Thang is a cluster of houses on stilts in the woodlands at the edge of the rubber plantation area that was a main source of profit for the French, who introduced rubber to Vietnam. The combination of favorable soil and climate and dirt-cheap colonial labor made the plantations in Vietnam and the adjoining areas of Cambodia profitable indeed. The people of Duc Thang are members of the Chau Ro tribe of the minority mountain people, whom ethnic Vietnamese collectively called *moi,* or "savages." The term has fallen into disuse, but not the attitude that it bespeaks. The villagers' hold on their land is threatened, and not even a vague promise of electrification has been held out to them, and that, too, they seem to take for granted.

Like all the other houses in the hamlet of about five hundred inhabitants, mostly children, the thatch-roofed hut of Deu Ninh and his wife, Deu Khy, stands higher than a man's height above the ground. The lengths of split bamboo that make up its floor are securely, one hopes, tied together and sway underfoot like a boat as one treads on them. The house rests on sturdy logs deeply implanted in the ground. Split bamboo also forms the siding, and no partitions divide the single room. It contains all that Khy and Ninh own — a binful of rice at the entrance, which is reached by a ladder of steps carved into a single log, some pots, pans, and bowls around the fireplace at the opposite end, and a few clothes hanging from a line. Khy wears a handsomely fashioned silver necklace in the tradition of montagnard women. The couple own a buffalo, with which they and their children work their two thousand square meters of land. They deforested it with handmade tools when they settled there in 1975.

That was the year they were chased from their earlier homes in the rubber plantation as the victorious North Vietnamese took possession. "They told us this was not our land and paid us nothing," said Ninh, who was born there sixty-four years ago. He said the northerners, behaving like conquerors, settled northern people who had come with them in their village, an evident continuation of the land grabbing that has so regularly been the policy of the lowland Vietnamese under all regimes toward the mountain tribe minorities. For years the Chau Ro lived on their new site largely on vegetables growing wild and bananas. Now they raise a cash crop, sugarcane, which they sell to a nearby mill. Ninh was a plantation worker, beginning in the colonial days. "They paid us in rice and salt and a little money," he recalled. Later, under the Saigon regimes, the pay was better, and the war left the villagers largely untouched. American troops patrolled often through their area but were never based near them. They aroused no more animosity than the other armies the villagers have known.

Khy, who is fifty-six, bore eight children, of whom five survive, and the couple has twenty-five grandchildren. Many years ago, when she was much younger, said Khy, they converted to Roman Catholicism. Why? She said "people" told her that maybe a new religion would help to keep her babies from dying. Some of the family take the eight-mile walk to church in the main village of Phu Tuc every Saturday afternoon and return

Sunday after mass; Khy goes on Sunday, returning Monday. That is as far as they, their children, and their families ever travel. They have never been to the district seat, and Saigon seems to them to be in another world. Ninh said their life had been work, sleep, and church under all regimes, and he wouldn't say that he was happy. In fact, he added, he was not. What made him unhappy he wouldn't say. He said he hadn't given enough thought to the various regimes under which he had lived to express a preference. Perhaps, he said, their life was best when he worked for the French plantation owners. "I had a steady job," he said. "Since then, nothing has been certain." Most of the family have never learned to read or write. Their fifteen-year-old son is attending first grade. "I read a little," he said. "When it's easy." The family has no radio.

The outside world comes to them, the couple said, in the persons of lowland Vietnamese who are crowding onto their land, in the apparent hope of driving them out and taking over their cane fields. Six or seven Vietnamese families are already squatting at the edge of their village. Ninh said they had not attacked the Chau Ro personally but, to make life intolerable for them, had killed their chickens with rat poison and the fish in his pond with an electric wire.

Duc Thang is better off than most montagnard villages. Dr. Duong Huynh Hoa, the former health minister of the Provisional Revolutionary Government of South Vietnam, has made the village a modest project of her Center for Pediatrics, Development and Health in Saigon. A small dispensary has been built, and doctors and nurses take turns spending some time there, treating the ill and studying in particular the nutritional state of the children. "We eat rice, vegetables, and salt," said Khy, looking surprised at a question that she clearly regarded as capable of no other answer. "There is much chronic malnutrition," said Dr. Hoa. "There are all kinds of parasites, chronic diarrhea, anemia, respiratory illnesses. The government talk about health care for the mountain tribes is all propaganda. Sometimes there isn't even enough to eat." Not long ago, she said, an American war veteran, his wife, and his children spent a couple of weeks in the village to dig a new well, since the water from the old one was polluted. He represented a group called Vets with a Mission. "The lid is too heavy," said Ninh, suggesting that the big American had overestimated the physical strength of the local people. Dr. Hoa said that while the American may have considered his missionary service as a kind of atonement for American wartime actions, the Chau Ro bore no ill feelings toward Americans and considered the veteran's stay among them more as a continuation of the earlier American presence.

The economic liberalization has not affected mountain villages like Duc Thang. *Doi moi?* Ninh and Khy exchanged puzzled looks. "No one told us about it," he said.

In the villages of the Mekong Delta, south of Saigon, they know all about the new system and are prospering under it. In Giong Tron, a village near the provincial capital of Ben Tre, two hours' drive from Saigon, the complaints were those of farmers all over the world, and farmers anywhere rarely admit to receiving their fair share. With a little prodding, the fruit and coconut growers of Giong Tron can even be persuaded to admit satisfaction. "So far I'm satisfied, but I expect more," said Chau Quang Dien, a thirty-one-year-old farmer who exudes optimism. In his blue jeans and light blue T-shirt, with his relaxed, businesslike way of discussing his business, he could pass as a young entrepreneur in any of the booming Southeast Asian countries. Vietnam is still far from booming, not even in Saigon and the Mekong Delta, but it is there that Vietnam seems a part of its larger region, linked to the world beyond, instead of still somewhat an odd man out.

"Before *doi moi,* the farmers had no right to the land," said Dien. "But now we believe that what we put into the land we will get back from it. So we really try our best." Dien and his nine brothers and sisters were allotted the land that had belonged to their family before collectivization following the Communist victory. On his ten acres he grows coconuts and raises shrimp in a pond he has dug. What more does he expect from the government? "We hope for better," he replied. "The government could provide more capital to enlarge the scope of what can be done here. We could plant many more trees. We could raise cattle, there is enough land for that. The government could improve the roads. But people are pretty confident that more will be done and are ready to take advantage of this." More availability of agricultural credit would help, Dien said. He borrows now from the traders who buy his coconuts at the stiff rate of between 2.6 and 3 percent a month, which is an improvement on the usurious rate of 10 percent a month that he paid before business picked up under the liberalization program.

If Dien is enterprising, so is his wife, the mother of their two children. She is a primary-school teacher. After school hours, she buys tobacco from local growers and sells it on the market in Ben Tre. And during the summer school vacation she conducts private classes to prepare children for the next school year. "The Vietnamese people are industrious," said Dien, proud of his wife and himself, his neat house, and the motorcycle and two bicycles the family owns.

20

Home in Southeast Asia

"The collapse of the Soviet Union was ideologically and psychologically a devastating blow for us," said General Tran Cong Man, the unofficial Communist party spokesman. "The Soviet Union was our support, ideologically and psychologically, and also militarily and economically." The general was speaking in 1992, when he, a Communist of the old guard, was still far from having recovered from the shock to his sentimental revolutionary's heart and soul of the tragic fall of the motherland of the Great October Socialist Revolution. Nor was he exaggerating the magnitude of the material loss that the end of Soviet assistance in all vital fields represented for Vietnam. He was right; Moscow had been a faithful and immensely useful ally in Vietnam's wars and in its reconstruction after them.

And yet Vietnam today, standing largely on its own feet, is a healthier country, and its heightened confidence in its future seems justified. Economic liberalization and the steady growth that it has produced is certainly an achievement that continued reliance on Soviet assistance would have precluded. But even if this is the most visible result, it is not the only one. Vietnam today is a Southeast Asian country, a large and important one, that has begun to see itself as being at home where it lives and not as part of a bloc of nations held together largely by the fact that all paid lip service to a political creed in which few believed and followed the lead of the Soviet Union in a world divided into antagonistic blocs. In Southeast Asia, Vietnam was regarded as a foreign body and acted like one.

"We relied on the Soviet Union and Eastern Europe too much," said Le Van Bang, one of Hanoi's top diplomats, who later was named as the first head of the Vietnamese Liaison Office in Washington, the embassy in embryo that was the last stepping-stone before the establishment of full diplomatic relations in 1995. "We knew more about the Soviet Union than we knew about our neighbors." Today's Vietnam is learning about its neighbors and from them. It is gradually inserting itself into its region and gaining acceptance as an important partner and potential future rival among some of the world's fastest growing economies. It has a long way to go and many obstacles, domestic and foreign, to overcome, but it is no longer a feared or distrusted outsider. "Now that the cold war is over," General Man said, "we cannot rely on any one nation, but we must be friends with everyone." Deputy Foreign Minister Tran Quang Co put the same thought in the terms of a sophisticated diplomat of long experience: "It was very unfortunate for us that Vietnam was placed in the focus of superpower conflicts for many decades. And it is good for us not to be tied into the framework of bipolar confrontations, which have caused a continuous state of war in Vietnam. We would like to have the same fate as other Southeast Asian countries. What we want is independence, peace, and stability. Unhappily for Vietnam, there remains an enormous gap between Vietnam and ASEAN."

The minister spoke before the Association of Southeast Asian Nations in 1995 admitted Vietnam to membership. Its partners — Thailand, Malaysia, Singapore, Indonesia, the Philippines, and Brunei — are eminently anti-Communist countries that have not always been immune to being drawn into "bipolar confrontations" and are far from equal in the measure of economic success and social justice that each has achieved. But with supple diplomacy each has managed to avoid full absorption into the games that big powers play. Nor were their own internal conflicts, often caused by Communist insurgencies, anywhere near as lastingly and achingly divisive as Vietnam's convulsions. The result has been that the six earlier ASEAN nations have long participated, in varying measure, in the community of open societies of the most highly developed countries. Their citizens have traveled freely throughout the world and drawn on the excellence of the world's best schools and universities. Their scholars and diplomats, their businessmen and bankers, move with assurance among their colleagues anywhere in the world and speak perfect English, the entry ticket into international communication.

Vietnam, to its loss, has lived in the cocoon of the Communist world, where awareness of its arrears was covered over with much pretense of superiority until it all collapsed from the very arrears that it tried to hide. The individual relations of Vietnamese with their colleagues and contacts from beyond the Communist circle were burdened always with an awareness that they were likely to be obliged to account for them to their authorities and by the pretenses that they had to maintain about their own country. Their second languages tend to be Russian, or Hungarian, or the German of the defunct Democratic Republic, which makes meetings of the minds hard to put into words.

Now many of the pretenses have been dropped, and Vietnam has embarked on the road toward catching up. It is beginning to send significant numbers of scholars and students abroad or allow them to accept foreign scholarships. Its specialists are widening their international contacts across the ideological boundaries that continue to exist. The imposed limitations live on because of Hanoi's insistence on the forms of its official ideology, even after it has been drained of most of its content and only the old guard and the opportunists around them continue to pay it lip service. Learning English has become a national pursuit, for which people who can afford nothing but the essentials sacrifice some essentials to have their children learn English in the private schools that have sprung up in cities large and small.

Academics still observe caution in discussions, but they no longer hide the essence of their beliefs or disbeliefs. Le Dang Doanh, deputy director of the Central Institute for Economic Management in Hanoi, was discussing the patron saint of the system. "Marx was a man of merit in analyzing the capitalist economy," he said. "He was a serious economist. But as an ideologist, Marx is very different from Marx the economist. He didn't accept evolution, only revolution. He elaborated an idyllic society, without motivation. Too nice to be true. The existing conditions are far from allowing it. I'm far from declaring that Marx is dead, but I'm absolutely against accepting Marxism as the Holy Bible." And as a man of candor, he acknowledged the continuing limits on speaking one's mind. Asked whether he would publish such views, he replied, smiling, "It would be unpopular to write this." Clearly, the ice has cracked but not yet melted.

The immediate issue over which Vietnam broke with its past and took the decisive step into Southeast Asian normality was Cambodia. Vietnam's invasion and long occupation of its neighbor aroused far more alarm in Southeast Asia and elsewhere than had the horrors committed by the hideous regime of Pol Pot, which it overthrew. One day in January 1979 Thailand, the only ASEAN country bordering on Communist neighbors, found Vietnamese troops and armor in hot pursuit of the Khmers Rouges on its long border with Cambodia, with every intention of staying as long as the Khmers Rouges stayed. Thailand rallied not only its partners in Southeast Asia but also China and then its Western friends, led by the United States, to impassioned condemnation first, and subsequently to various forms of support for the Cambodian forces that entrenched themselves in border areas to resist the invaders. China and Thailand gave all possible military help to the Khmers Rouges, who for the first time in their murderous life found themselves elevated to be exemplars of international legitimacy. The other countries limited themselves, more or less, to diplomatic backing and hastened to forge an indecent forced marriage between the Khmers Rouges and the non-Communist resistance groups, whose leaders and followers had all lost many of their closest relatives and friends, as well as house and home, in the reign of terror of their new partners. The handshakes for the cameras were the most pained and hostile expressions of amity that I have ever witnessed. The Cambodians' ethnic hatred of every-

HOME IN SOUTHEAST ASIA

thing Vietnamese overcame all reserves; to be liberated by a people whom one considers the hereditary enemy creates uncomfortable and contradictory emotions. Unfortunately, Cambodians could not choose their liberator.

The United States gave what it called "nonlethal" assistance to the often-corrupt forces of the most right-wing of the resistance movements and found in the invasion an additional reason for refusing to establish normal relations with Vietnam. In 1978 the United States had appeared almost ready to do so. It reversed itself when the administration of President Jimmy Carter was seized by fear that this would hamper normalization of relations with China, then in the making. Vietnam became an international outcast. (When at about the same time Tanzania played a comparable role in helping to rid Uganda of Idi Amin, its tyrant, the international community showed far fewer scruples over the legality of that foreign intervention.)

Vietnam's occupation lasted as long as the Soviet Union remained ready to bear the costs of maintaining allies in China's backyard. This willingness diminished greatly with Mikhail S. Gorbachev's decision after coming to power in 1985 that reaching an accommodation with China would save Soviet Union resources, which he could more usefully apply to work for the benefit of that most neglected citizen, the Soviet consumer. In 1989 Vietnam withdrew its troops in a unilateral initiative, with maximum publicity, having somewhat earlier, without fanfare, pulled out the forty thousand or so soldiers that it had maintained in Laos since 1975, without ever acknowledging the fact.

But Vietnam remained determined to keep in power the client government, headed by Prime Minister Hun Sen, that it had put in place, guided, and assisted. Hun Sen, a defector to Vietnam from the Khmers Rouges during one of the lethal purges of regional potentates that punctuated the life of the Pol Pot regime, had been shaped into a somewhat credible, compliant leader by his Vietnamese tutors and supervisors. In 1990 Vietnam had the Cambodian rug pulled out from under its feet when the Soviet Union joined with the West and China in an understanding to remove the Cambodian issue as an irritant in their mutual relations. China could afford to appear conciliatory, in the certain knowledge that its allies the Khmers Rouges would never cooperate in making peace, no matter what accord they signed. For the other big powers, the Cambodian issue was marginal, as always no more than a sideshow.

Deserted by the Soviet Union and thus obliged to look for an accommodation with China, Vietnam signed the international agreement in Paris in October 1991, bringing a United Nations–supervised peace and free elections to Cambodia. In a sequence of exits and entries of star actors rich in symbolism, Ambassador Ngo Dien, Vietnam's arbiter of Cambodian affairs since the invasion, left one day in November; on the following day Prince Sihanouk returned, under United Nations auspices, to the capital he had left the day before the Vietnamese army conquered it in 1979. Within a day or two of the prince's departure, Ngo Dien had arrived to take up the post he occupied for the twelve years to come. Predictably, the Khmers Rouges quickly withdrew from participation in the peace process, and the international community contented itself with holding elections whose results were in effect a dead letter.

The Khmers Rouges and the Cambodian government and army controlled by Hun Sen and his associates continue their war. Outmaneuvered, King Sihanouk, who was returned to the throne he abdicated in 1955, remains in virtually permanent exile in China, where he is being treated for cancer. His son, Prince Ranariddh, who won the United Nations–organized elections, angers his father by serving as a window-dressing "first prime minister" while the loser, Hun Sen, effectively governs the country — inasmuch as fragile and embattled Cambodia can be said to be governed — as "second prime minister." He does so much in the arbitrarily dictatorial and corrupt way in which he ruled earlier, as Vietnam's man in Cambodia.

Vietnam, while clearly still possessing an intelligence network that keeps it abreast of Cambodian developments, is no longer able to maintain a compliant ruler in a country so profoundly anti-Vietnamese. As a continuing series of Khmer Rouge massacres of ethnic Vietnamese villagers proves, Vietnam is no longer capable even of protecting its own people in the country it occupied for so long. And the government in Phnom Penh shows no alacrity in protecting the unwelcome residents, nor eagerness to apprehend their killers.

However little change the Vietnamese withdrawal from Cambodia brought to that country, it has made all the difference to Vietnam. The rest of the world no longer has a Cambodian problem. Only Hanoi still worries about the perennially unstable neighbor on its western border and fears that someday its mortal enemy, the Khmers Rouges, will return to power. But despite this legitimate security concern, Hanoi's principal spokesmen say that never again will Vietnam unilaterally try to settle the Cambodian issue. They would like to believe that because of the 1991 international agreement and the United Nations commitment, the world at large has now made itself the guarantor of Cambodian stability. "We shall not stand alone," said Deputy Foreign Minister Co. "From 1979 on, everybody tried to isolate Vietnam because we opposed the Khmers Rouges. We suffered materially and politically for what we did. Now the main responsibility lies with the world community, the United Nations. We would not act unilaterally again. It is enough for Vietnam to have done this once in its history. Twice, we would not just lose our security but also our independence. There would be no more Vietnam. We shall be wiser and let other people do it." Vietnamese officials leave unanswered the crucial question of what Hanoi would do if, as is most likely, the big powers, having deluded themselves into a willful belief that they have resolved the woes of Cambodia, will not for a second time mount a two-billion-dollar international rescue operation.

The end of Vietnam's dependence on the Soviet Union removed the last vestige of direct outside dominance from Southeast Asia, leaving the problems of the region to be solved largely by its own forces, strengthened by outside support when it can be obtained. Already in 1975, with America's defeat in its intervention in Indochina, Southeast Asian issues were reemerging in a strictly Asian context. It was as though regional tensions that had been artificially defused by colonial intervention had remained in existence like a fly caught in amber, to reemerge intact when released from foreign embrace. Tension between Vietnam and Cambodia, subdued by French hegemony over both countries, reawoke even as early as the war of 1970–75. There were no uneasier alliances than those between the two American-supported regimes in Phnom Penh and Saigon and between the Communist forces of the Khmers Rouges and Vietnam. The peace of 1975 never took hold between the two victors, and the Vietnamese conquest of 1979 reawakened another rivalry suspended by France's seizure of a protectorate over Cambodia.

From the seventeenth century until the establishment of French domination over Cambodia, Thailand — then Siam — and the Nguyen rulers of southern Vietnam contended over who would exercise dominion over the enfeebled Khmer kingdom, often embroiling themselves in armed conflict. Thailand's almost hysterical overreaction to Vietnam's conquest of Cambodia in 1979 seemed an echo of that precolonial past. For Vietnam, of course, China's support of Pol Pot made him appear as the straw man behind whom the Middle Kingdom was renewing its permanent menace to Vietnam's independence, which had been lifted only during the period in which France deprived Vietnam of it. Until its demise, the Soviet Union was the potent counterweight that Vietnam could put on the scale against China. Now it must seek a balance elsewhere.

Co, the diplomat, believes that now, while China is preoccupied with the modernization of its country, is the time for Vietnam to strike a new regional balance of power. "It is not good for a middle-sized country like Vietnam to live beside a big power without other friendly countries," he said with surprising candor. "It would be good for us to have only one Southeast Asia." The "one Southeast Asia" that Hanoi envisions was greatly advanced when Vietnam became a full member of ASEAN in 1995, an organization that an earlier Vietnam had routinely denounced as a "lackey of the imperialists." From 1992 until 1995, Vietnam attended ASEAN's ministerial meetings as an "observer." Vietnam won its war against the "imperialists," but President Eisenhower's "row of dominoes," whose fall the American intervention was intended to prevent, has emerged the clear winner, setting the terms of Southeast Asia's new balance of power.

A price that Vietnam has paid for admission into the new Southeast Asia is the abandonment of Ho Chi Minh's design for dominance over Laos and Cambodia, a design that it had realized with the occupation of Cambodia and installation of a compliant regime. The Laotian Communist Pathet Lao movement had always been under Vietnamese tutelage. The Vietnamese Communists felt dominance was their due in reward for the leading role they played in expelling France and the United States from the three countries of Indochina. After their victory I heard Vietnamese officials in both of the smaller countries speak with the same condescension toward what they depicted as the limited capacity of Laotians and Cambodians to run their own affairs that I had heard from their American predecessors in the tutorial role. When I reminded them of this parallelism, I provoked moments of uneasy silence, followed by a change of subject.

Today, Vietnamese Communists describe their part in the Laotian and Cambodian wars as strictly a logistical necessity for their struggle in Vietnam, not a striving for domination. "One could not liberate Vietnam without liberating Laos and Cambodia," said General Man, noting the strategic importance of using the neighboring countries' territory as the main route for transporting men and equipment from North to South Vietnam. The general, who speaks in the vocabulary of one of Vietnam's last believing Marxists, said the leadership accepted the withdrawal from Laos and Cambodia as "historically inevitable." With somewhat melancholy resignation, he reflected, "With our older friends in Laos, it is as it was before. With the younger people we notice a certain reticence. This is natural; we cannot give them very effective economic assistance. In reality there are no more brotherly countries, not even ideologically. For the moment there is no country that is close to us. But we want to be on good terms with all the countries in the world, above all the developed countries, from the economic and also the social standpoint."

There is a rather pained realization that because of the intrinsic weakness of Laos and Cambodia, the lessening of Vietnamese influence has naturally created openings for Thailand, their other big neighbor. Thailand, which, beginning with the Japanese occupation in World War II, has greatly benefited from the continuing woes of Indochina, now plays a powerful role in the economies of both neighboring countries. It exports large quantities of Cambodian and Laotian timber, their most precious resource, which is smuggled into Thailand; it is the principal supplier of the goods of daily life to both, and its bankers have established strong footholds, particularly in Laos. Great quantities of Thai consumer goods are finding their contraband way into Vietnam from their two common neighbors. Over the centuries Vietnam and Thailand have been rivals for influence over Laos and Cambodia. "There is a long-standing problem," said General Man.

> Thailand has always coveted Cambodia and Laos. They were allies with Japan against France. In the American war, the Thai military were always on the American side. They didn't do much fighting in Vietnam, but they did in Laos. And there is no ocean separating our country and Thailand. After Cambodia they even thought we wanted to invade Thailand, so they drew closer to China and the Khmers Rouges. But now the Thais see the situation has changed. The Thais are showing a bit of hegemonism, above all in Laos and Cambodia. They are seeking big economic influence, and politically they are trying to lure them away from Vietnam. Yes, this is a problem for Vietnam.

Vietnam's former Russian allies, who have a wide network of old friendships, particularly among the Soviet-educated elites in many fields, detect a new mood among some of their friends. They attribute this to the collapse of the Soviet Union following upon the defeat of the United States. Russians are discovering a growing belief that the age of Asian superiority has dawned.

"There are some features of common Asian pride and solidarity on the rise here," a Russian said. "The Vietnamese feel that they belong to the dynamic Asian region, to the civilization of the twenty-first century. The intellectuals say that Europe is exhausted, the United States beset by domestic problems. They believe the center of gravity of economic and political power is shifting to Asia."

For the time being, however, Vietnamese are displaying a great eagerness for Western contacts. Some Vietnamese of the street have adopted an unfortunate attitude of ingratitude bordering on disdain toward the ordinary Russians who can still be found in the country, in which not long ago they were the most frequent foreigners. In Haiphong, which suffered intense American bombing and whose port was the principal point of entry for the massive flow of Soviet aid, I was received at lunchtime in a restaurant in the center of the city with solicitous courtesy and offered the choice of a seemingly limitless variety of dishes. There were no other customers until, in the middle of our meal, a modest pair of Russians, perhaps from a freighter crew, entered. The owner or manager told them, with detached coldness, that he had no more food to serve. The Russians left hungry. He had only one explanation when I questioned him about turning down customers. "They were Russian," he said, in an apparent belief that rejecting Russians was the best way to please an American. In Saigon I saw a Russian sailor doing a bit of black-marketing by offering for sale a satchelful of small jars of caviar to the owner of a gift shop on Nguyen Hue Boulevard, a main shopping street. The owner, in the tones of a fishwife, commanded the sailor to wait. She made him stand patiently while she fetched a bowl of water and immersed each jar to test whether its seal was tight. Then, haggling stridently over the price, she bought them, to sell the Russian delicacy later to Western customers at many times her cost.

"Before, they used to need us," said a Russian diplomat. "Now what they need most is Japanese capital. So now the Japanese ambassador sits on the dais, not the Russian." Of course, if there were an American ambassador, his place on the dais would be assured, the Russian continued. Even when the American embassy in Hanoi was opened in 1995, a chargé d'affaires, not a full-fledged ambassador, headed it. "The Vietnamese are very interested in an American presence in the region," the Russian said. "They want the United States to help to stabilize it. They are interested in an American military role to restrain China. They are interested in an American economic presence. They fear not only China but also Japan's ambitions. Without an American presence, the competition between China and Japan seems to them more dangerous for Vietnam."

For many years the United States responded to Vietnam's frank overtures for normalization of relations at a snail's speed, dictated by excessive consideration for the strong opposition of the small lobby that demands a "full accounting" for the fewer than two thousand Americans still listed as missing in action in Vietnam. If one considers the inaccessibility of the mountainous regions of the Ho Chi Minh Trail, where so many planes were shot down, the fact that many of the missing were air crews lost over the South China Sea, and the meager results of the elaborate searches since the establishment of the Joint Task Force–Full Accounting in 1992, at a cost to the American taxpayer of more than 165 million dollars by mid-1995, the Bush and Clinton administrations must be said to have exhausted all possible efforts. The families of the missing are entitled to a final word that their government has done all it could, and that no answers to the remaining painful questions can be found.

Normalization was accomplished gradually, over the enduring opposition. In 1993 the United States ended its effective veto on development loans to Vietnam by the World Bank and the International Monetary Fund. The following year it lifted the trade embargo that it had imposed on North Vietnam with the outbreak of open hostilities in 1964 and extended to the entire country at the Communist victory in 1975. Early in 1995 Washington gave its consent to the beginnings of a normal diplomatic relationship by agreeing to the opening in both capitals of liaison offices, and established full-fledged diplomatic relations in midyear.

"We understand the discussions of the wrongs and rights of the past that go on in your country," said Deputy Foreign Minister Co. "We have decided to live in the interest of coming generations. If you discuss indefinitely the wrongs and rights, your 'Vietnam syndrome,' it is not good for you or us. Both sides were victims of the war and suffered from it. The side that served as the battlefield suffered more, much more. But we choose not to live in the past." Self-serving as the argument may be, the United States surely had an interest in entering into a normal relationship with a country of seventy-three million people that simply cannot be ignored, if only to be able to offer normal consular protection to its hundreds of thousands of citizens of Vietnamese origin, many of whom visit the places of their birth and their relatives. They may need such protection, because Vietnam is one of the few countries that do not formally recognize that their people may change citizenship. Under Vietnamese law, once Vietnamese, always Vietnamese, and therefore subject to whatever a government not fussy about civil rights might do to someone whom it regards as its citizen.

With a new pragmatism astonishing in a nation that until not long ago saw the world in the most dogmatic terms and divided people categorically into "friends" and "enemies," Hanoi now counts on those who fled from its regime, "enemies" par excellence, to serve as a link between Vietnam and the United States. "The Vietnamese community in the United States will become active and could serve as a bridge between the countries," said Deputy Foreign Minister Le Mai, who is in charge of conducting Vietnamese-American relations. The minister expects Americans soon to become the largest group of foreign tourists visiting Vietnam. "After all, five million Americans were here during the war," he said. "More Americans will come to see that Vietnam is a country, a people, not only a war."

21

Not Yet the Happy End

Dining on the beach in Da Nang, not far from where the first marines landed in 1965, at the simple outdoor kitchens where men cook the fish or shrimp of the day's catch on charcoal fires and serve it at a handful of tables set in the sand, is a modest feast. The diner shares it with many begging children. It is not food or money the boys and girls beg for, although they accept all gifts happily. The handouts for which they wait, hustling and grappling with one another for the prize, are the diners' trash, the cans that have been emptied of soft drinks or beer. It takes a great heap of lightweight cans to make a hoard of scrap that is worth selling to a dealer, but the children wait for them patiently. They try from a gradually diminishing distance to judge whether a diner is taking his last sip, to be the first to pounce on the trophy. Nothing goes to waste in Vietnam, and the Vietnamese, young and old, don't take their poverty lying down.

Nor do they just settle for the minimum. Not all the tin cans are sold for mere scrap; some are meant for higher destinies. They wind up in sidewalk workshops, which consist of no more than a block of wood or a plank placed on stone supports. It is the workplace of a man seated on a low stool or on the ground. Wielding a hammer and a pair of shears, he pounds and clips the flattened cans and transforms them into model airplanes. Vietnamese children have simple toys; most have hardly any toys at all, yet I know few nations' children who play with such exuberance with so little.

The sidewalks of the cities are full of men and women who

sit or squat and toil. A Vietnamese sidewalk restaurant is entirely that, not a place where only the tables are on the sidewalk, with waiters scurrying in and out of the restaurant bearing trays with dishes. A Hanoi or Saigon sidewalk restaurant is kitchen and dining room all on the pavement, and cook and waiter are the same person, the owner-manager of the one-man or one-woman eatery. They serve many different dishes but mainly *pho,* the national soup of beef and rice noodles flavored with aromatic leaves, a full meal in one bowl. The customers wield their plastic chopsticks and tin spoons at low, small tables, carrying on their table talk unperturbed, as though they were not sitting in the middle of a bustling city sidewalk, with an unending to and fro of people rushing past them, whom they glimpse only from the waist down. And no one complains about blocked sidewalks. Inconveniences of daily life are taken for granted in Vietnam; they are the common lot.

Work of all kind is performed on the sidewalks. Men mend bicycles, others only their tires. Repairs on everything, from clothing and shoes to radios and typewriters, are performed on the street. Barbers seat their customers on wooden crates and clip as the wind carries away the clippings. Some of them have a sideline in removing wax from ears. There are scribes who type the many official applications and declarations that needlessly burden the ordinary citizen's life to provide employment for a pedantic bureaucracy. Men do metalwork over open fires, pounding red-hot iron and laughing at passersby whose faces show that they are frightened of the sparks. Some delicate operations are performed, like repairing watches or spectacles or refilling throwaway cigarette lighters. Vietnam is not yet a throwaway society, except for the worldwide affliction of plastic bags and bottles, which have turned Hanoi's lovely lakes into cesspools and clog the sewers to worsen the rainy-season flooding that many days every year snarls movement in the cities.

Many of Vietnam's artisans and craftsmen do without workshops. An umbrella or tattered awning is the closest thing they have to a roof over their heads, or any other overhead. Shops, too, need no more than a few crates or boxes to do business. The Vietnamese, far more than any of their neighbors, have learned not only to make do with little, but even to do very well with a minimum of everything except inventiveness. Saigon's pre-1975 antique blue-and-yellow Renault taxis were monuments to the art of making do, and the despair of spare-parts dealers. They were kept running years beyond their normal useful life with improvised bits and pieces of anything that came to hand, anything except Renault parts, which were far too expensive for drivers who often had to ask their passengers to pay their fare in advance so that they could put some gasoline into their tanks.

Modesty and economy of means in everything are national qualities. It is not just that Vietnamese make do with what they have — and that is little indeed — but that they do it so often with inventiveness, skill, and last but not least, grace. Foreigners have always wondered at the way in which Vietnamese women as passengers on noisy smoke-belching motorcycles, or in bicycle rickshaws that expose their fares to some of the world's most disorderly traffic and worst urban pollution, manage in their long-tailed pastel tunics to look fresh and flowerlike, as though they had just stepped out from a movie musical or, at least, a beauty parlor. Their wonderment would be even greater if they knew how small and crowded are most of the homes from which these flower maidens emerge, and how difficult is their access to running water and similar facilities.

These fleeting glimpses of everyday life depict a people that converts little into enough, and sometimes into much. They substantiate the air of hopefulness that has spread through Vietnam since the regime, deserted by its benefactor, has been compelled to stop treating its people like helpless children, incapable of organizing life for themselves and their families. A government that throughout the wars prevailed because it called on these same qualities of endurance, energy, and resourcefulness, and saw its antagonists fail because their foreign sponsors did not trust in these qualities and substituted their own men and means, stifled the use of these precious assets in times of relative peace. (Vietnamese soldiers did not stop dying on the battlefield until the bulk of the troops were withdrawn from Cambodia in 1989.) The Communist party's faith in an alien ideology rather than the native gifts of its own people held the country down, demoralized its population, and made Vietnam a backwater, while most of the rest of its region entered the international mainstream.

Vietnam remains far behind this mainstream, but its people believe that they have finally been authorized by their doctrinaire leaders to make up for lost time, and they are going about it with all they have. As they make the most of new opportunities, people ignore as much as possible the very existence of their government. Their spirit exemplifies a remarkable affirmation of endurance: despite the storms that have shaken the lives of all the present generations of Vietnamese, on either side of the former divide, society has largely withstood the assault on the age-old traditions that have shaped Vietnamese character and their common sense of nation. This was seduced neither by American promises — so clearly belied by the regimes America installed, supported, brought down, and replaced — nor by the Russian version of a German dogma, which produced so much poorer a harvest than it promised and had finally to be buried, leaving its high priests in power, to turn into its grave-diggers. What has survived is the reliability of the Vietnamese sense of community, the family first and foremost, and then the village, the city quarter, the group that shares a workplace. Despite the strong individuality of so many Vietnamese, they submit their individuality to the community more readily than is the rule in societies not Confucian. This may have helped to ensure the long survival of a Communist regime, without, however, making citizens believe that this is the best way of organizing a society.

Vietnamese families remain more cohesive in their sense of mutual obligations than most — except, sadly for their parents, many children born in emigration, particularly in the United States. This sense of family duty solidifies society through the unusually high importance attached to caring for both the aged and the young. The strong sense of family makes for a social stability that wealthier and freer countries, watching diminishing family links and social cohesion weaken their societies, might envy. Responsibility for elderly relatives is implicitly accepted, and three-generation families under one roof are commonplace. Obligations to the family are heightened rather than interrupted when Vietnamese emigrate. Living in wealthier countries only enhances the duty to support those who remained behind, much to the advantage to a country badly in need of foreign, convertible currencies, which allow it to buy on the world market.

Respect for elders goes beyond the family. A Foreign Ministry official assigned to be my guide and interpreter — an institution of Communist countries that is usually more a hindrance than a help — apologized profusely for keeping me waiting for an appointment. This is unusual; such "minders" all over the world tend to accuse rather than make excuses. I offered the customary trivialities to make light of the offense. But he said he could not forgive himself so easily; after all, he was younger than myself.

Education remains one of the goals to which parents aspire for their children, and for which they give up much else. For their part, the children and adolescents accept a responsibility for striving to excel. That they often succeed is proven by the unusually high educational achievements of many Vietnamese in their countries of immigration. It is sad that the present imposition of fees is reducing the number of those enrolled in schools, particularly in the countryside, but the concurrent spread of language and computer courses, as well as the enormous number of language, business, and computer textbooks, pirated from foreign publishers, which have replaced the collected speeches and writings of Ho Chi Minh and Lenin in the bookstores, show that traditional ambitions remain alive.

An absence of false pride or exaggerated sense of status helps Vietnamese, north and south, to adjust to the many transitions that their nation's agitated history has forced on them. Many a tour guide, driver, hotel worker, or seller of trinkets in the streets of Vietnamese cities has astonished me with his or her level of education and fluency in foreign languages. Often they have proved to be teachers, engineers, or other professionals, who saw no shame in turning to a lowly trade because it offers additional earnings and provides the money needed to improve their children's education. They are grateful that more relaxed policies afford them the opportunity to augment their small incomes.

The same applies to Vietnamese emigrants. It would be hard to admire General Nguyen Khanh's performance as head of the South Vietnamese regime in the 1960s or perhaps even the soup in his Paris restaurant, which he praised so highly. But it is difficult not to respect the unpretentious equanimity and humor with which he accepted his demotion from chief of his country to chef in his simple restaurant. The number of South Vietnamese ministers, ambassadors, or others of high station in their professions, who in their new countries, without misplaced pride, turned to opening small restaurants or coffee shops, is great and testifies to a pragmatic attitude that is, I believe, unmatched by refugees from other countries in the waves of exodus that the twentieth century has produced in such great number. Restaurants require minimal starting capital and provide work and meals for the entire extended family and friends. Another attraction is, of course, that working among the familiar, distinctive perfumes of Vietnamese food eases the pangs of loss of home. Another South Vietnamese general, a fellow plotter in the overthrow of Ngo Dinh Diem who took refuge in France after the defeat, showed me, without any of the sense of loss of face to which Asians are said to be so sensitive, his new calling card. The general was now offering appointments to be consulted as an "astrologue."

The Vietnamese feeling for family seems to extend to their attitude to others in general. I know of no other people who have borne so much adversity and yet contain their pain or anger so much within themselves. I do not believe Vietnamese to be stoics; it need not be emphasized that they feel these emotions quite as deeply as others. I have seen Vietnamese wives or mothers express their sorrow at the tombs of their husbands or sons fallen in war. Those are private occasions. But faced with others, the social sense that is instilled in Vietnamese does not allow them to burden the outsider with their griefs or hatreds. It is not mere form, not simple courtesy. On many occasions, after lengthy questioning of the families of boat people at the places of their first landing in other Asian countries about the circumstances of their arduous voyages, I have learned only from others that the family to which I had spoken was without a father or children who had perished at sea. The families did not believe that they had a right to sadden me with their loss. I believe this explains, at least in part, their unwillingness to speak of the hardships of war and the sentiments these engendered toward Americans or French. They turn aside expressions of sympathy for their suffering by making light of them, sometimes with a joke.

Dang Thai Son, the gifted pianist who won the 1980 Chopin Competition in Warsaw, told me shortly after his victory that he had received much of his early training after the Hanoi Conservatory had been evacuated because of American bombing to villages north of the capital. The faculty had brought only one piano, which gave the students little chance to practice. Frequent air raids further limited study time. But to reassure me that he bore no hard feelings to America as a result, Son said that the only other contact he had had with America had been more recent, with a superb Steinway piano, and that this more than the other shaped his attitude.

Vietnamese friendliness to outsiders clearly has deep roots. In his informative 1951 book on his travels in Indochina, *A Dragon Apparent,* the British author Norman Lewis cites this description, written in 1622 by a Jesuit, Father Borri:

> Whereas all the other Eastern Nations, looking upon the Europeans as a profane people, do naturally abhor them: In Cochin-China it falls out just contrary: for they strive who shall be nearest us, ask a thousand Questions, invite us to eat with them, and in short use all manner of Courtesie with much Familiarity and Respect. . . . This loving and easie Disposition is the Cause of much Concord among them,

they all treating one another as familiarly as if they were
Brothers, or of the same Family . . . and it would be look'd
upon as a most vile action, if one Man eating any thing, tho'
never so little, should not share it with all about him, giving
every one about him a bit.

Subsequent outsiders were not always treated with that
much brotherly love, nor did such "easie Disposition" always
prevail toward other Vietnamese; but then, much provocation
has been given since 1622.

Vietnam in transition is stable and calm. Its present leaders
say that this stability must be maintained at a political cost to
assure the right conditions for the acquisition of personal riches,
the enterprise that they have elevated to the supreme national
goal. To preserve stability, they have ruled out liberalization of
the political system, an easing of the high ideological barriers,
and freedom for Vietnamese to seek more effective ways to make
Vietnamese lives better, richer, and more fulfilling. They have
thus succeeded in ensuring their continued rule, but forbidding
free inquiry and unrestricted travel and regarding with suspicion
normal contacts with the outside world have reduced the economic progress that they strive for to a pace so slow that the gap
between Vietnam and the rest of Southeast Asia continues to
widen. They have worsened rather than improved the sine qua
non of economic and social development — the people's health
and education. And they continue to condemn their questing and
inventive people to the narrow path that they have themselves
traversed. Their fear of change makes them rule by fear.

It has worked so far, but will it always? Will the system
continue under the successors to the aged Politburo? It will, if
the archconservative, time-serving next generation of men, in
their sixties or early seventies today and as dogmatic in their
vision as the men who shaped their minds and furthered their
careers, move into the seats their elders vacate. But to many
Vietnamese the ruling party has become an anachronism, whose
presence and power is recognized but whose declarations are
ignored as irrelevant.

A distinguished scholar, whom I visited in his squalid

Hanoi one-room flat, laughed when I asked him how he or his friends squared the contrast between the hopeful enthusiasm with which Vietnamese are plunging into today's non-Communist economy and their leaders' constantly reaffirmed insistence on the Communist party's unique leading role in all phases of human activity. The elderly academic, a veteran of the war against France and a party member since the 1940s, replied with a family anecdote:

> It reminds me of my grandfather, a very strict mandarin. When I was a boy, he sent me letters, very severe letters. "If you don't obey your father and teachers, I don't recognize you as my grandson," he wrote. His strictness shocked me. But later I learned that he had mistresses in every town. This is just like the party speeches. People laugh at them. With my friends, whenever somebody mentions the differences between what we say and what we practice, all we can do is burst out laughing. The people in the countryside feel the same way. They are even more practical than pragmatists. They expect politicians to make speeches that they don't mean.

Are there enough well-educated technocrats willing to rationalize the inefficient system and challenge for the succession? And will the Vietnamese people hold still for whatever happens at the top? I doubt it. Vietnam, too, has a generation of students and young, educated men and women, who want at least as much freedom as exists in the neighboring countries of more or less open societies. Or, more tempting, the greater freedom that has come to the formerly Communist countries of Europe, which many know well from having studied or worked there. The Chinese student revolt on Tian An Men Square in 1989 frightened the Vietnamese leaders and caused them to reverse the loosening of intellectual blinders that had been part of *doi moi* in its early stages. But this retightening of the screws has added to the sense of disaffection of the most active generations and deepened their frustration.

"We Vietnamese are fed up with everything," said Bao

Ninh, the prize-winning forty-three-year-old novelist who wrote with unsparing realism of the war in which he fought against the United States and South Vietnam.

> With communism, with everything in our lives. Everything that has happened to us so far is nonsense. The politicians talk too much. In 1973 already we knew very well what the Khmers Rouges were up to, but our leaders called them comrades. That's why they let the Khmers Rouges enter Phnom Penh. Then the same with the Chinese, and there followed a bloody conflict on our border. Now they smile at each other. It shows that this nonsense has been going on over a long period. The younger generation is bored. This has to come to an end. If it doesn't, maybe this nation will perish. I haven't found a happy end for it yet.

INDEX